THE DRAMATIC WORKS OF CATHERINE THE GREAT

Performance in the Long Eighteenth Century: Studies in Theatre, Music, Dance

Series Editors:

Jane Milling, Dept of Drama, University of Exeter, UK
Kathryn Lowerre, School of Music, Michigan State University, USA

Focusing on performance culture during the long eighteenth century, this series offers studies of individuals, institutions, forms and trends in all types of cultural performance including theatre, opera, dance, musical performance, and diverse popular entertainments. It is a forum for interdisciplinary work, drawing the debates of historians, musicologists, literary scholars, dance, theatre and opera scholars into a creative symbiosis.

The editors welcome studies which are concerned with British, European, and early American cultural history. Studies that concern themselves with theoretical questions surrounding acts of performance during this period are also welcome.

The Dramatic Works of
Catherine the Great

Theatre and Politics in Eighteenth-Century Russia

LURANA DONNELS O'MALLEY

University of Hawai'i Manoa, USA

ASHGATE

Published by
Ashgate Publishing Limited
Gower House
Croft Road
Aldershot
Hants GU11 3HR
England

Ashgate Publishing Company
Suite 420
101 Cherry Street
Burlington
Vermont, 05401–4405
USA

Ashgate website: http://www.ashgate.com

British Library Cataloguing in Publication Data
O'Malley, Lurana Donnels, 1964–
  The Dramatic Works of Catherine the Great: Theatre and Politics in eighteenth-century Russia. – (Performance in the Long Eighteenth Century: Studies in Theatre, Music, Dance)
  1. Catherine, II, Empress of Russia, 1729–1796 – Dramatic works. 2. Politics in literature. 3. Politics and literature – Russia
  I. Title
  891.7'22

US Library of Congress Cataloging in Publication Data
O'Malley, Lurana Donnels, 1964-
  The Dramatic Works of Catherine the Great: Theatre and Politics in eighteenth-century Russia / Lurana Donnels O'Malley.
      p.   cm. – (Performance in the Long Eighteenth Century: Studies in Theatre, Music, Dance)
  Includes bibliographical references and index.
  1. Catherine II, Empress of Russia, 1729–1796 – Dramatic works. 2. Politics in literature. 3. Politics and literature – Russia. I. Title. II. Series.
  PG3311.C3Z78 2006
  891.72'2–dc22   2006003928

ISBN-13: 978-0-7546-5628-9
ISBN-10: 0-7546-5628-4

This book is printed on acid-free paper.

Printed and bound in Great Britain by MPG Books Ltd, Bodmin, Cornwall.

Contents

List of Figures

Acknowledgements

For assistance and support, I would like to acknowledge the following people: (at UHM) Ruth Dawson, Virginia Bennett, Marianna Podolskaya, Louise McReynolds, Pat Polansky, Sally Drake and the UHM Inter-Library Loan staff, Ted Kwok, Liudmila Finney, Marie-Christine Garneau, Svetlana Vovina, University Research Council, Dennis Carroll, Elizabeth Wichmann-Walczak, Dean Judith Hughes, Markus Wessendorf, Valerie Wayne, John Kearns, Frank Episale, Renee Arnold, RoseMarie MacDonald, Tana Marin, Lori Chun. Farther away, thanks to Helen Sullivan and IUC Slavic Reference, Marcus Levitt, Tatiana Artemieva and Mikhail Mikeshin, Giovanna Moracci, David Griffiths, Tony Cross, Hilde Hoogenboom, John Freedman, Julie O'Malley, John and Joan Donnels. For my first taste of Russian theatre, I thank Spencer Golub. And for all his support, I thank Oscar Brockett. Thanks also to all the students and friends who participated in readings of the plays. Grateful thanks to my husband Sean O'Malley for inspiration, always.

I thank the publishers and editors of the following journals and books for permission to include revised versions of previously published work: John Freedman and Routledge for portions of the introduction to my translation *Two Comedies by Catherine the Great*; Gabriela Lehmann-Carli, editor of *Proceedings of the VII International Conference of the Study Group on Eighteenth-Century Russia*; Tatiana Artemieva and Mikhail Mikeshin, editors of *Catherine II and Her Time: A Modern Outlook*, and the editors of *Theatre History Studies, Canadian-American Slavic Studies, Comparative Drama,* and *Essays in Theatre*. All are reprinted by permission of the editors. See bibliography under O'Malley for full citation information.

Research for this publication was supported in part by a grant from the International Research and Exchanges Board, with funds provided by the US Department of State (Title VIII) and the National Endowment for the Humanities. None of these organizations is responsible for the views expressed.

Dates and Transliteration

Spelling of most names and terms follows the Library of Congress system of transliteration, with the exception of my use of Western names for Catherine (instead of Ekaterina) and her immediate family (Elizabeth instead of Elizaveta, Peter instead of Petr, Paul instead of Pavel). Dates are given in the Old Style Russian calendar, which in the eighteenth century was eleven days behind the currently used Gregorian calendar.

Preface

This book combines a chronological and a genre study approach. By grouping
Catherine's published plays by genre (comedy, historical plays, operas) and
subdividing the category of comedies into early and later, I emphasize the varying
aesthetic strategies she employed to stage her political viewpoints. Each chapter
will also be organized chronologically as a way of charting development. I
interweave examinations of relevant historical events and issues into each chapter.

The purpose of the book is twofold. My first goal is to convince readers to
look more carefully at Catherine's work, looking for dramatic skill, well-sustained
characters, and humor. I will also demonstrate that even for an Empress with
virtually unlimited power, the stage was a valued means to educate her public and
to promote her political perspectives.

Lurana Donnels O'Malley

Chapter 1
Catherine's Life and Writings

You ask me why I write so many comedies. [...] *Primo*, because it amuses me; *secundo*, because I should like to revive the national theater, which has been somewhat neglected for lack of new plays; and *tertio*, because it is a good thing to give a bit of a drubbing to the visionaries, who are becoming quite arrogant. *The Deceiver* and *The Deceived One* was a prodigious success. [...] The cream of the jest was that at the opening, people called for the author, who [...] remained completely incognito.[1]

Although the playwright may have ostensibly remained anonymous to the audience at the Hermitage Theatre where both plays debuted, most of those present must have known that this was no ordinary writer and no ordinary spectacle. The plays were by none other than the Empress Ekaterina II—Catherine the Great. And although she assumed the mask of anonymity, Catherine's role-playing on this evening in 1786 was every bit as playfully deceptive as when, one night in 1763, she cross-dressed as a man and spent the evening flirtatiously courting a young woman at a court ball.[2]

In her role as monarch, Catherine the Great was a great cultivator of the arts, and her patronage of theatre during her reign contributed to its growth and stability. Given that the stage can be a potent means of shaping and reinforcing social values, the monarch-playwright is in a particularly powerful role. Catherine the Great as playwright deliberately exploited the stage's power to promote political ideas and ideology. Through her characters' perspectives and their dialog, through the constructions of her plots, through her use of imagery and symbolism, and through her adherence to classical models and her promotion of romantic ones, Catherine the Great the playwright advanced her own political agenda—an amalgam of Enlightenment philosophy, Russian cultural pride, and her belief in the value of authoritarian rule.

Catherine brought in the precepts of the Age of Reason in her plays' attacks on superstition, religious zealotry, and mysticism. Her *raisonneur* characters promote a balanced and rational approach to social and personal problems. In support of Russian cultural identity, her comedies satirize Gallomania and other forms of

---

[1] From a letter to Friedrich Melchior Grimm on 3 April 1785 (Grot, "Pis'ma imperatritsy" 328.) Translated from French by Pinkham in Troyat 259.
[2] Maroger 358–59.

foreign influence, and her operas in particular glorify the Russian historical past and folk traditions. Her own decision to compose the majority of her plays and operas in the Russian language was, at a time when Russian's prestige as a literary language was relatively new, a vote of confidence. Finally, Catherine's own unique position as a female, foreign-born monarch under constant threat of being deposed gave her a stalwart faith in the value of (enlightened) authoritarian rule. Her authority figures range from gentle parents to just rulers to generous noblemen. Her preferred format of comedy and comic opera ensures a sense of balance and resolution, brought about through the recognition of faults and flaws, and—very often—as a nexus of the social and the political, the celebration of a wisely chosen marriage.

Catherine's theatrical work is significant on many levels. Her playwriting must be seen in the larger context of her substantial patronage of theatre. Under her guidance and using her treasury, theatre buildings were built, training academies established, and a new repertory was created, performed, and published. The historical significance of her own playwriting is its testimony to the perceived power of theatre in this era. Although Catherine claimed to write simply for amusement, her plays communicated her views on social and cultural issues of the day to a primarily educated audience. The nobles who saw and understood her plays were the patriarchs and serfowners who, in turn, had the means (and the responsibility) to enlighten the rest of the empire.

The ideological basis for Catherine's use of theatre was her Enlightenment belief in the value of education for her entire populace. That populace was symbolized by the public theatre audience (even if the actual audience composition, made up mostly of nobles, was more homogeneous). Education through the medium of theatre was by nature indirect, but this very indirectness was in itself a test of the audience member's readiness for enlightenment. If they could get all the jokes, empathize with the right characters, and identify the moral lesson before the curtain line, then they were that much closer to refinement.

Catherine's first goal was for plays by herself and others to legitimize Russia's standing as a "European nation"[3] by demonstrating its artists' facility with dominant cultural models. But her second goal, one that distinguished Catherine from many of her peer-playwrights, was to emphasize Russia's cultural uniqueness. We see Catherine's desire to foster a Russian cultural identity in her use of folk motifs in her comic operas (which her composers often set to popular folk melodies), her dramatization of key events of early Russian history, and even in her choice of a Siberian shaman as title character. In building the world of her real Russian Empire, Catherine also constructed fictional stage worlds. These small realms reflected the flaws of her nation, while also revealing the philosophical hopes and social ideals of its Empress.

---

[3]   Her own words, in the first sentence of her *Great Instruction* (see Catherine II, *Nakaz* 1).

Life and Writings

Catherine the Great of Russia was born Sophia Augusta Fredericka von Anhalt-Zerbst on 21 April, 1729. The young Sophia, a minor German princess, was invited to Russia and groomed as a potential bride by the Empress Elizabeth Petrovna. In 1745, Sophia, now known as Ekaterina or Catherine, married the Grand Duke Peter, bearing him a son (Paul) in 1754. The Grand Duke acceded to the throne in 1761 as Peter III but in 1762 was deposed and later murdered by forces sympathetic to Catherine's interests. Catherine took the throne and proceeded to rule the Russian Empire as Catherine II from 1762–96, in a century in which Russia saw almost seventy years of rule by female monarchs.[4] She never married again, but took several lovers over the decades. Of these, Grigorii Orlov and Grigorii Potemkin occupied powerful positions within her government, although most of her "favorites" had little influence on her policies or decisions.

Catherine saw herself as the successor of Peter the Great (r.1682–1725), who had brought Western European (particularly French) values, customs, and esthetics to Russia. In Petrine Russia, the capital had been moved from Moscow to St. Petersburg, and European tastes were emulated in architecture, clothing, and theatre. In the early part of her reign, Catherine endeavored to bring the values and achievements of the Enlightenment to Russia. She corresponded with Voltaire and Diderot, promoted a relatively free exchange of secular social ideas, and initiated a large-scale reform of the Russian legal code. Her foreign policy greatly expanded Russia's territory: she secured part of Poland, annexed Crimea, and dominated Ukraine. Her official court anthropologists brought back information on cultural, linguistic, and social practices throughout her vast Empire. Catherine also patronized artists and writers, and sponsored the beginnings of the extensive collection of fine and decorative arts in St. Petersburg's Hermitage Museum. Censorship of drama in this era was "intermittent and unobtrusive."[5]

Catherine's vision for a more enlightened Russia was tested by the Pugachev Rebellion, a peasant uprising in 1773–74 that led the Empress to tighten the reins on her empire and to maintain the institution of serfdom. After the sobering events of the French Revolution in 1789, Catherine's policies became more guarded and conservative. Censorship became more restrictive, and she imprisoned the radical writers Novikov and Radishchev for their progressive views on social reform. Catherine died in 1796 of a stroke, and was succeeded by her son Paul (Paul I, r. 1796–1801).

In addition to being a ruler and a patron of the arts and letters, Catherine was a prolific author who wrote in many literary genres. Her first major achievement

---

[4]   Catherine I (1725–27), Anna (1730–40), Elizabeth (1741–61), and Catherine II (1762–96).

[5]   Wirtschafter 26.

Fig. 1.1 *Catherine II holding her 'Great Instruction'* [Nakaz], c. 1770.
Miniaturist artist unknown. Enamel on copper; bronze frame

was the creation of the *Great Instruction* [*Nakaz*, 1767–68], a lengthy work of legal philosophy and doctrine, based primarily on Montesquieu but altered by Catherine to fit the needs of the Russian state (see Fig. 1.1). Following her disappointment when the Legislative Commission dissolved without producing a full legal code, Catherine turned to another form of writing: the satirical periodical. In 1769, she initiated her own literary journal, *All Sorts* [*Vsiakaia vsiachina*], in which letters and essays appeared, signed by such characters as Perochinov (Pen-mender) and Pravdoliubov (Truth-lover). Catherine's neoclassical plays bear a resemblance to this and other satirical periodicals of the day in their use of hyperbolic and stereotypical characters to comment on social and artistic concerns.

All Sorts was the beginning of a brief but stimulating flurry of Russian satirical periodicals in the style of the eighteenth-century English periodical *The Spectator*, published by Addison and Steele. *The Spectator*'s hallmark was its playful yet pointed critique of social vices through witty epistolary debate. The first issue of Catherine's *All Sorts* invited other editors to enter the public literary sphere. Her challenge was soon met by the appearance of several other publications, including *The Drone*, edited by fellow publisher and intellectual Nikolai Novikov (1744–1818). Literary historian Marcus Levitt points to *All Sorts* and the numerous other satirical weeklies of the period as an example of a particularly eighteenth-century type of collective writing.[6] Although the exact extent of Catherine's authorship of any given letter is unknown because all letters were pseudonymic, her involvement in the periodical's collective creation is generally accepted. Catherine's sponsorship of the journal was secret; she was the publication's anonymous "babushka" or grandmother.[7] But many suspected her authorship, and Novikov himself may well have known the high rank of his partner in debate. Thus, the interchange of ideas between *All Sorts* and *The Drone* is today routinely considered to be a personal debate between Novikov and the Empress on questions of morality, literature, and politics.[8]

---

[6] From the introduction to a translation of *All Sorts* in Levitt, "Catherine the Great" 7.

[7] See Herzen for a refutation of the notion of Catherine's editorial role in this journal.

[8] Critical assessment of the relationship between Catherine and Novikov has varied greatly over the past two centuries, although both nineteenth-century and Soviet critics were united in their portrayal of Novikov as a progressive and anti-autocratic voice for change in an era of censorship and abuse. Harold Segel's 1967 essay clearly echoes this perspective: "From the first number of the journal, issued on April 5, 1769, it was clear that the lines of battle were being drawn. [...] *The Drone* struck out at the abuses of serfdom and other specific evils of contemporary Russian life. [...] The polemics ended in 1770 in a moral victory for Novikov. But Catherine's ire had been stirred, and when she saw herself unable to restrain Novikov by engaging polemics with him she turned to repression. The satirical journals [...] were gradually liquidated" (Segel, "Satirical Journals" 256). More recently, however, other scholars have taken a more balanced view of the literary quarrel; in his 1984 book on Novikov, W. Gareth Jones attributes the demise of *The Drone* to declining readership, and insists that the structure and style of the debate "were dictated to Novikov by the conventional demands of the European moral weekly" (25). Rather than seeing the

One significant aspect of their disagreement concerned satire's purpose, with Catherine strongly objecting to satirical portraits based too closely on real individuals rather than on generalized types. Novikov's *The Drone* argued for characters based on individual persons (*na litso*) so that specific and pointed critiques might be made: "I insist that criticism against the individual, but written not so that everything is revealed, can do more toward reforming a sinner."[9] Catherine's *All Sorts* argued that only general vices should be portrayed and examined (*satira na porok*), and only in a compassionate light: "Who sees only vices, possessing no love, is incapable of giving instruction to others."[10] Accordingly, the majority of Catherine's neoclassical comedies do indeed portray general vices; in Chapter 2, my consideration of her play *A Prominent Nobleman's Entrance Hall* will explore some exceptions to this principle, particularly in the satire of foreigners.

Among Catherine's other literary experiments were fairy tales she composed for her grandchildren, essays, letters, and a collection of proverbs. She also wrote non-fiction works, such as *Notes Concerning Russian History* and corresponded as an intellectual equal with the greatest thinkers of the century. Voltaire in particular was full of praise for Catherine on matters of both culture and power: "you make your court the most delightful in Europe, while your troops are the most formidable."[11] Although unpublished during her lifetime, the several versions of Catherine's *Memoirs* are an important example of women's autobiographical writing in the eighteenth century. Written in French at various stages of her life, the memoirs treat her childhood in Germany, her arrival in St. Petersburg, and her early years as wife of the Grand Duke Peter. Most versions end in 1759, before her husband's accession as Peter III. The memoirs were not published until 1859, in London.

Catherine somewhat disingenuously commented on the import of her own writing in a letter to her friend Doctor Johann Zimmermann:

---

interchange as a fierce political struggle, Jones finds that, "The general impression is of much literary rib-nudging, leg-pulling, and, at worst, mock indignation between understanding fellow editors" (38). In a 1983 article, Kenneth Craven argued that although by the mid-1780s, Catherine was deeply opposed to Novikov's involvement in Moscow's Masonic circles, in the earlier period of the satirical weeklies, their dialog was mutually supportive and stimulating.

[9]   Quoted in Segel, "Satirical Journals" 290. Translated from *The Drone*, number XXV, 13 October 1769. For more English excerpts of this debate, see Segel, "Satirical Journals."

[10]   Quoted in Segel, "Satirical Journals" 260. Translated from *Vsiakaia vsiachina*, May 1, 1769.

[11]   From a letter dated 12 March 1772. English translation in Lentin 132.

I consider all my writings to be trifles. It pleases me to experiment in various genres, but it seems to me that everything I've written is mediocre, and therefore I have never ascribed any importance to it, other than as a means of distraction.[12]

Despite this claim to modesty, the Empress's many literary endeavors were more than a distraction; the issues they addressed were central to her political and social philosophy. In an age when "Russian intellectuals relied almost exclusively on the written word to communicate with their publics and to influence the course of Russian society,"[13] each letter, play, or historical note could serve as an important tool for the education and enlightenment of her people.

Catherine and the Theatre

In comparison with Western Europe, Russia was relatively slow in the development of a national drama and professional stage, despite a thriving popular tradition of puppetry, storytelling, and festival performances. Under Peter the Great, there was a short-lived public theatre in Moscow run by German Johann Kunst from 1702–1706, and a private court theatre in St. Petersburg built for Peter's sister Natalia. Court entertainments flourished in the 1730s under Empress Anna, who invited Italian opera and *commedia dell'arte* performers to entertain private audiences. Under Empress Elizabeth (1741–61), who compelled her courtiers to attend all court performances, a French company also performed regularly. But it was not until 1756 that a permanent Russian state theatre was established. The troupe, led by Fedor Volkov, was made up of a group of actors brought in from Iaroslavl at Elizabeth's request. The troupe's director and leading playwright was Aleksandr Sumarokov, one of Russia's most important literary voices of the period. Although the court itself, being particularly fond of *opera buffa* presentations by the Italian Locatelli, continued to prefer performances by foreign companies, by the time Catherine took the throne, Russian plays and actors were visible and successful. While the court theatre audiences consisted only of the nobility, the public theatres catered to a more diverse audience, dominated by nobles, but also mixing in merchants and clergymen.

The great variety of plays and spectacles offered to theatregoers in Catherine's era is demonstrated by the following quotation from the *St. Petersburg Gazette*, October 1783:

the shows at the Stone [theatre] are set in the following manner: Tuesday, Russian comedies, Friday, Italian comic operas, both with ballets. The Wooden theatre: Sunday:

---

[12] Translated in Karlinsky 90; from Russian quotation in Brokgaus and Efron 11: 575. From a letter to Zimmermann on 29 January 1789. For original French, see Marcard 378.

[13] Marker xi.

Russian comedies, Wednesday, German comedies; Saturday, French comedies; alternate Mondays, one or the other, without ballet.[14]

The *Gazette* refers to two St. Petersburg theatre buildings, the Stone and the Wooden theatres. The Wooden Theatre (*dereviannyi teatr*) was built during the reign of Elizabeth, on the Tsarina's Meadow near the Summer Gardens. Originally the home of Locatelli's *opera buffa* company, it was then taken over by Karl Knipper in 1776–77 for the production of German plays and operas for his private company "Free Russian Theatre" [*Vol'nyi russkii teatr*], and was later renovated by Italian architect Giacomo Quarenghi.[15]   In 1771, Catherine ordered the construction of a public theatre in St. Petersburg. Originally known as the Stone (*kamennyi*) Theatre, it was designed by Rinaldi and seated approximately 2,000 spectators. The building (completed in 1783) became known as the Bolshoi Theatre, and was replaced in 1896 by the Rimskii-Korsakov Conservatory, which stands today on that site in Teatral'naia ploshchad' (Theatre Square).

Catherine also equipped her own palace with theatres. She first had an opera house built in the Winter Palace in 1763 (architects Felten and Vallen de La Mothe); it was converted to living quarters in the 1780s. Its replacement was the Hermitage Theatre, where the first production premiered in 1785. Quarenghi based its design on his studies of Palladio's neoclassical Teatro Olimpico, with its numerous columns and statues in a semi-circular auditorium (see Fig. 1.2). The theatre is situated at the east end of the Hermitage complex, across the Winter Canal from the current Hermitage Museum. The Hermitage Theatre was the site of numerous court performances, including presentations of Catherine's own plays and operas. Her plays were also sometimes presented at the public theatres in both St. Petersburg and Moscow. In addition to overseeing the creation of new theatre buildings, Catherine also formalized theatrical training in Russia by founding the Imperial Theatrical School for actors, singers, and dancers in 1779.[16]

Along with the blossoming of theatrical offerings came the birth of a Russian-language drama. Prior to the mid-eighteenth century, previous dramatic efforts included liturgical drama, school plays in Latin or Church Slavonic, and Biblical plays in Russian. With the creation of Volkov's professional troupe in 1756, Sumarokov was to become the first significant playwright writing in Russian, and indeed is one of the writers credited with formalizing a Russian literary language. Sumarokov's verse dramas were based on French originals. His plays treat

---

[14]   From the *St. Petersburg Gazette* in October 1783; quoted in Cracraft 229n. My translation from French.

[15]   The Wooden Theatre came under state control in 1783, and was renamed the Malyi Theatre. See Cracraft 229n and Borovsky 60.

[16]   See Wirtschafter for a detailed account of court, public, and serf theatres in St. Petersburg, Moscow, and the provinces.

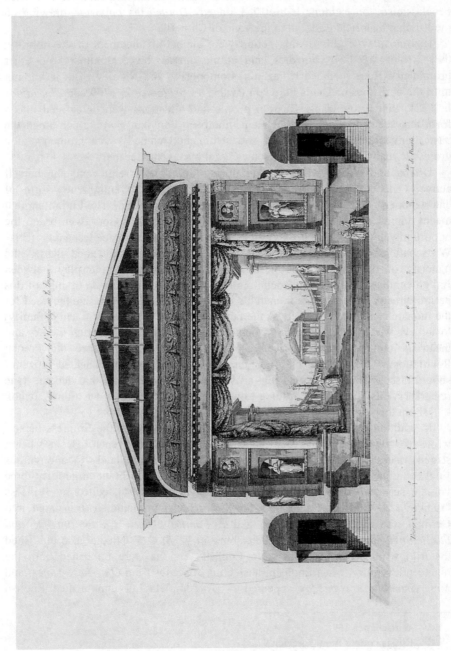

Fig. 1.2 Hermitage Court Theatre stage. Giacomo Quarenghi, *A Design of the Hermitage Theatre*

Russian subject matter while strictly adhering to the dramaturgical rules of French neoclassicism; an example is his 1771 tragedy *Dmitrii the Impostor*, drawing on the Russian historical past, but in the style of Corneille.

Russian playwrights of this period were almost all members of the nobility; they wrote tragedies, comedies, and comic operas; besides Sumarokov, other prominent writers included Kniazhnin, Lomonosov, and Nikolev. But it was not until the comedies of Denis Fonvizin (with *The Brigadier* in 1769 and *The Minor* in 1781) that recognizably Russian people and situations were integrated into a form that seemed original rather than imitative. Fonvizin's works combined the basic conventions of neoclassical and sentimental comedy with moments of a grotesque realism that would anticipate Gogol by several decades.

Drama and theatre were thriving during Catherine's reign, and she herself actively encouraged theatre as a social platform, as an enlightened form of entertainment, and as proof of Russia's cultural sophistication. The Enlightenment meant that as belief in human judgment replaced belief in a God-given order, the opportunity increased for a playwright to suggest paths to social change. Elise Wirtschafter asserts that theatre was a place for the Russian educated classes, the majority of audiences in public theatres, to examine the interplay between Enlightenment principles and social reality. Although few Russian dramas of this period directly challenge the monarch's authority, they did emphasize the need for the monarch (often symbolized by the familial patriarch) and her citizenry (family) to achieve what Wirtschafter calls "personal perfectibility."[17] Russian literary and theatrical cultures were relatively open spheres, at least before the French Revolution. Catherine actively encouraged the idea that an educated citizenry should discuss and debate, and that artists have a duty to foster that debate. One remark reveals Catherine's attitude toward theatre: "Theatre is a national school. [...] I am the senior teacher in this school."[18]

In addition to supporting the drama of other playwrights, the Empress herself wrote over two dozen plays and operas, in Russian and in French. Besides being staged, many of Catherine's plays were published immediately in anonymous single editions. Fifteen of the plays appeared anonymously in the large forty-three volume series *Russian Theatre* [*Rossiiskii featr*, 1786-94], edited by Princess Dashkova.[19] Four of Catherine's plays were also immediately translated into German (the anti-Masonic trilogy and *A Family Broken Up by Intrigue and Suspicions*), and published in St. Petersburg in 1786; C. F. Nicolai also published the trilogy in Berlin in 1788. No English versions were published until the nineteenth century, when English translations of scenes from *Oh, These Times!* and *Mrs. Grumbler's Nameday* appeared.[20] A complete but unpublished English

---

[17]   Wirtschafter 169.

[18]   Russian quote from Gurevich 97.

[19]   Volume and page numbers from the Dashkova edition are in the Appendix.

[20]   The former is in Wiener. The latter is in Bates, probably reprinted from Turner.

translation by Matthew Guthrie of Catherine's *The Beginning of Oleg's Reign* can be found in the British Museum.[21] Before my own two translations (1998), no complete translation of any of them had been available to an English-speaking readership.

The artistic value of Catherine's works for the stage has generally been underrated. For the most part, the plays display solid characterizations and skillful plotting, within a neoclassical esthetic. Catherine's alterations to her Western European models are often pointed and effective. For instance, the portrayal of comic foils like Mrs. Sanctimonious in *Oh, These Times!* is in the fine tradition of other medieval European Vices, seen in plays throughout Europe in the sixteenth and seventeenth centuries. Yet Catherine endows such characters with specifically Russian habits and attitudes, and uses their foibles as a means of education.

Too, her interweaving of subplots in *The Siberian Shaman* demonstrates mastery of the technique of parallelism. By comparing the Shaman to the deceitful Ustinia Mashkina, Catherine not only ties together the two main threads of her plot, but makes the point that deception and its companion, gullibility, are not merely an "exotic" import from Siberia, but can be easily found even in St. Petersburg. Although Catherine rarely wrote in verse (verse segments in her operas were usually by other writers), her colloquial dialog is lively, full of markers of emphasis, and replete with idioms and uniquely Russian expressions. The dialog makes sharp distinctions between the various characters' choices in diction and expression; for example in *Oh, These Times!*, Mrs. Marvel speaks in a scattered and fragmented manner in III.1 when frightened, while Mr. Notshallow uses only a very formal and reserved speech. In *The Siberian Shaman*, Amban-Lai's speech ranges from hypnotic to animalistic, and reveals his more mundane side in a scene with the butler.

Throughout her writing for the stage, Catherine employed techniques of metatheatricality, to call the spectators' attention to the artificiality of the stage. Although its most well-known manifestation is the play-within-a-play, metatheatricality can also be found whenever characters refer to theatre, plays, and playgoing. Metatheatrical moments are revealing; they crystallize assumptions about style and subject matter, reflecting and sharpening our understanding of the "outer" play.[22]

Whether or not they can be considered works of dramatic genius, her plays have a fascinating variety of genre, style, and subject matter. Catherine's dramatic output includes neoclassical comedies, adaptations of Shakespeare's plays, historical plays in the style of Shakespeare, comic opera *libretti*, dramas that

---

[21] Add. MSS 14390, folios 334–60; 363–88; 364–5; see A. G. Cross, "Royal Blue-Stocking" 97.

[22] O'Malley, "Plays-within-Realistic-Plays." See also on metatheatricality in Catherine's drama in Chapter 2 (*Mrs. Grumbler's Nameday*), in Chapter 3 (*The Siberian Shaman*), and Chapter 4 (*The Beginning of Oleg's Reign*).

include folk material and songs, plus several short proverb plays composed in French. Aleksandr Pypin's edition of her collected works also presents numerous unpublished play fragments, including partial adaptations of plays by Calderón and Sheridan.

In Catherine's many plays, the comic genre predominates; writing in the popular neoclassical mode enabled her to use foolish characters or ignorant characters both to please (through their ridiculous dialog and actions) and to teach. But although neoclassicism to some extent suggests a concern for universal human foibles, Catherine also addresses specifically Russian concerns and audiences. She tackles such contemporary national problems as ignorance, superstition, Gallomania, fear of progress, and anything she saw as mysticism—all from the perspective of an enlightened monarch who hoped to root out all traces of backwardness. Catherine's neoclassical comedies have stylistic devices and characters familiar from the seventeenth century in Europe: the use of confidants, stereotypical characters, telling names, and the inclusion of scathing references to current social customs. Typically, the plays feature ridiculous characters, such as the fanatically complaining Mrs. Grumbler, who reveal their foolishness and ignorance through a series of comic actions.

After an initial period of playwriting activity in the early 1770s (the five plays treated in Chapter 2), Catherine again turned to playwriting in the mid-1780s, writing a number of additional comedies such as *A Family Broken Up by Intrigue and Suspicions* (1787), and *The Misunderstanding* (1788). She also wrote three plays that are often called the anti-Masonic trilogy; these satires were her weapons against Masonic orders and mysticism. All three plays concern a family's gullible reaction to the arrival of an outside "mystic" who represents the forces of irrationalism. Another group of short proverb plays, written in French, were shared only with the elite audience of the Hermitage Court Theatre.

In the 1786, having read Eschenburg's German translations of Shakespeare's works, Catherine completed three plays "in imitation of Shakespeare." *The Beginning of Oleg's Reign* (1786) was one of two scripts modeled on English chronicle plays, but treating ninth-century pre-Christian Russian history. It bore the subtitle "without preservation of the usual theatrical rules." The play—classified as an opera due to its many songs and choruses—was produced lavishly in 1790 and 1794 with sumptuous costumes and scenery, and hundreds of supernumeraries. Its "Shakespearean" elements are primarily structural; the action moves freely from Moscow to Kiev to Tsargrad, and therefore takes place over a lengthy period of time. Her other scripts inspired by Shakespeare include *This 'tis to have Linen and Buckbaskets* (her adaptation of *The Merry Wives of Windsor*) and *From the Life of Riurik*. *Riurik* is, like *Oleg*, a historical spectacle treating events in the ancient Russian past, but not in operatic form. Although other contemporary playwrights such as Sumarokov were aware of Shakespeare's developing reputation as a dramatic genius, they adapted Shakespearean storylines and characters while remaining primarily within a neoclassical framework. By consciously rejecting the "usual" rules (i.e., the precepts of neoclassical dramaturgy), and by looking to Shakespeare as a model, Catherine was ahead of her time.

Catherine's five other opera *libretti* fall into the genre of comic operas. In Russia, comic operas were quite different from their counterparts in Western Europe. The Russian versions consisted of comic scenes featuring spoken dialog, with occasional songs interspersed among the words. Catherine herself probably rarely wrote in verse, and apparently did not have an ear for music, so her contribution to the operas is in plot, character, and dialog. Her comic operas, which incorporate Russian folk elements, include *Fevei*; *Boeslaevich, Novgorod Knight*; *The Brave and Bold Knight Akhrideich or Crown Prince Ivan*; *Woeful Knight Kosometovich*; and *Fedul and his Children*. These five operas contain peasant songs, and folk characters such as the Russian witch Baba Iaga, giving them a fairy tale quality. Indeed, *Fevei* was originally a story that Catherine composed for her grandchildren. Other operas have more political overtones: behind the parable of *Woeful Knight Kosometovich* lies a satire on the Swedish king Gustav III, with whom Catherine was at war at the time of its premiere in 1789.

Anonymity and Authorship

Of the many ways in which Catherine shaped her public persona, anonymity was a frequent strategy, particularly in the literary realm. Catherine concealed her literary identity behind a mask of an anonymous persona. By assuming this mask of anonymity, a common eighteenth-century device of artificiality, Catherine was able to assert her ideas and convictions about literature and society through public discourse, rather than official proclamation or imperial decree. This tactic may have enabled her to level the playing field, to ensure that ideas were judged on their strength rather than on her own status as Empress. Catherine consistently fashioned her anonymous identity as a male persona, as in her letters to Voltaire, in which she very often appropriated the male pronoun as her own.[23] In her social life as well, the Empress often used such strategies of gender concealment or disguise, seeming to enjoy the public display of a mixed gender identity. Transvestite balls were a favorite pastime in her court, a tradition from the era of Empress Elizabeth. In one autobiographical note, she recalls posing as a young male at such a ball, wearing "an officer's uniform and over that a pink domino." As she briefly wooed a young Princess, dancing with her and kissing her hand, the disguised Empress flattered her by claiming "What a happy man I am."[24] Famous

---

[23] "She [...] loved to play the part of 'Monsieur' in her correspondence." Anthony, *Catherine the Great* 229.

[24] Maroger 358–59.

portraits, such as the 1765 portrait by Vigilius Ericksen that commemorated her accession to the throne after the deposition of her husband Peter, depict her seated on a horse in full military uniform, further signifying the masculine by her astride position (see Fig. 1.3).[25]

Any critical objectivity that audiences and *literati* may have had was quite likely compromised by the extraordinary status of the playwright herself. Theatre historians seeking to determine the popularity of a play usually measure success by evidence of publication, production, and favorable critical reviews and commentary. Since Catherine, as Empress, controlled the means for plays to be presented in print and on stage, to some extent the theatrical scene as a whole reflected her tastes and sensibilities. That her own plays were given support and encouragement tells us very little about what contemporary audiences may have really thought of them, given the age-old tradition of flattering the monarch. For example, this entry on *Oh, These Times!* appears in the *Dramatic Dictionary* [*Dramaticheskoi slovar*, 1787]: "it played many times in the theatres of St. Petersburg and of Moscow, and pleased the Public with exquisite enjoyment [...] among the best of Russian plays."[26]

Still, the diary of Catherine's literary secretary A.V. Khrapovitskii provides clues that audiences did not always feel obligated to respond warmly to productions of Catherine's plays:

> 20 Jan. 1791: In the Hermitage, they presented again "Fedul" and the comedy "O vremia!" [*Oh, These Times!*] [...] "O vremia!" is a work of 1772 in the time of the plague; it was received coldly, but "Fedul" was applauded.[27]

Catherine's anonymity complicates the issue of reception. Initial publications of Catherine's work appeared both in single editions and in anthologized collections without mention of an author's name. Performances seem to have followed a similar practice of anonymity.

To what extent was Catherine's anonymity a transparent disguise, and to what extent were the plays judged on their own merits? In 1772, Novikov hinted at Catherine's authorship in a letter appearing in his periodical *The Painter* [*Zhivopisets*].[28] Other spectators clearly knew the author's identity. For instance, visiting Oxford don John Parkinson, who saw a production of Catherine's opera *The Beginning of Oleg's Reign* in 1792, called it "a sort of ballet composed four years ago by the Empress herself."[29] It is probable that members of the small

---

[25] Original painting is located in the Hermitage Museum, with a copy in the Peterhof Palace. Alexander, *Catherine the Great: Life and Legend* 178.

[26] Annenkov 99.

[27] Barsukov 355. All translations from Russian or French are my own, unless otherwise noted.

[28] See Chapter 2 on this letter and its relationship to *Oh, These Times!*

[29] Parkinson 57 [entry of Thursday 6 December 1792].

Fig. 1.3 Vigilius Ericksen's portrait of Catherine in military uniform, c. 1762

aristocratic circle of Catherine's court were well aware of her authorship, and treated her anonymity as a form of playful masquerade, a favorite eighteenth-century pastime.

Another factor that has influenced Catherine's claim to legitimacy as a significant Russian dramatist has been the controversy over the actual authorship of her plays and other writings. For many reasons, including her status as a non-native speaker and writer of Russian, and perhaps even her status as a woman author, many have assumed that Catherine's plays are not her own.

The level of Catherine's Russian language abilities is a matter of great debate. A native speaker of German, Catherine learned Russian as a young girl at Elizabeth's court. Even in her own era, her language skills were criticized, as this letter to *The Drone* (*Truten'*), commenting on Catherine's journal *All Sorts* [*Vsiakaia vsiachina*], reveals: "Madame Vsiakaia Vsiachina['s] entire fault consists in her not knowing how to express herself in Russian and her inability to fully understand how to write Russian."[30]

Assessments of Catherine's ability to write in Russian vary greatly, with Kazimierz Waliszewski on one hand disparagingly commenting that "she could never write with ease in any language" and Coleman on the other arguing that "her mastery of the Russian language was greater than is popularly supposed."[31] In Brown's opinion, "She never quite mastered Russian [...] especially Russian spelling, and the many works in that language had to be carefully gone over by her private secretaries (Grigorii Kozitskii and Aleksandr Khrapovitskii, both themselves writers) to correct her grammar and spelling."[32] Some scholars, such as V.N. Vsevolodskii-Gerngross, even doubt that her influence went much beyond providing a guiding idea for a play.[33]

Despite such reservations, the general scholarly consensus is that Catherine did indeed write the plays herself, with assistance from her literary advisors Ivan Elagin, Kozitskii, and Khrapovitskii. This controversy guided my archival research in 1996, where I examined Catherine's play manuscripts at the Russian State Archive of Ancient Acts in Moscow and the Russian National Library in St. Petersburg.[34] Because of Catherine's distinctive penmanship (a learned Cyrillic script), her pages are easily recognizable. The evidence from these manuscripts is a compelling confirmation of Catherine's authorship.

---

[30] Quoted in Berkov, *Satiricheskie zhurnaly* 58–59; English translation from McKenna 4.

[31] Waliszewski 93; Coleman 17.

[32] Brown 215. Kozitskii was the primary editor of *All Sorts*.

[33] Vsevolodskii-Gerngross, *Ot istokov* 252–54.

[34] Manuscripts in Moscow are in Ekaterina II Fond (f. 10, opis 1, dela 320–379) with additional materials in f.10, opis 2, dela 227–229. In RNL, materials are in Hermitage Fond (f. 885).

The manuscripts reveal Catherine as a writer who painstakingly returned to drafts to make revisions and corrections to scenes. Some plays are available in more than one copy, and often one is considerably less tidy, with many crossings-out and alterations. Sometimes there are also copies in Khrapovitskii's or Elagin's much neater handwriting, but the majority of the play manuscripts are in Catherine's hand. For example, in one copy of *The Siberian Shaman*, the manuscript shows that Catherine changed her original title to *The Siberian Shaman* from *The Tungusic Shaman*. Perhaps the Empress felt that the Tungus region was too specific for her purposes, that Siberia would be suitably exotic and yet recognizable.

I am not the first scholar to look at these documents. Pypin, as editor of her collected works, did exhaustive comparisons between the original published editions of the plays and the manuscripts of Catherine and her secretaries. He praises Catherine's abilities to write in colloquial Russian, and in general gives a strong defense for Catherine as primary author of her writings. His edition is a rare volume, however, and today his conclusions are often ignored. What struck me as I sat touching the fading pages in St. Petersburg was that, undergirding the doubts about Catherine's authorship, are questions not only about a monarch's priorities, but also about a woman's abilities.

A word must be said on the placement of these plays within an emerging new canon of women's dramatic writing, past and present. Tracy Davis describes the important tasks that lie before feminist theatre historians: revisionist history ("probably an indispensable first step of feminist scholarship"[35]) and feminist literary criticism. Revisionist history seeks not only to insert a woman's name where it has been missing, but also to question the categories by which authors are awarded acclaim, examining the context and the role of gender in determining historical reception. Feminist literary criticism questions and reveals the representation of women. Until recently, few feminists have written interpretations of Catherine's life and writings.[36]

Looking at Catherine from a feminist perspective enables one to analyze Catherine's various and intertwining roles as woman, as writer, as foreigner, and as Empress of Russia. While it is true that we should not impose today's feminist viewpoints on the past, we must not downplay the effect that her gender had on Catherine's life and work. Catherinian biographer John T. Alexander has argued persuasively that Catherine's notoriety and the popular myths of her voracious sexuality and infamous but fictional death as a result of copulation with a horse are in part attributable to a misogynist attempt to discredit Catherine's real achievements.

---

[35] Davis 63.
[36] One prominent exception is Ruth Dawson.

The biographical-psychological implications of the horse story appear aimed at undercutting Catherine's claims to greatness, by aggressively asserting that her primary motivation was unbridled sex.[37]

Catherine's status as a woman to some extent explains the continued doubts about her authorship, and the relative inattention that the literary world has given her plays over the last two centuries.

Russia maintained a highly rigid societal hierarchy in which only a very few women attained positions of power, so that class status greatly affected a woman's access to the pen. The elite women who did write in the eighteenth century had the freedom to experiment in various genres, such as autobiographical memoirs, poetry, and plays. This freedom is seen in the fact that the two most significant Russian women writers of this time, Catherine the Great and Ekaterina Dashkova, each wrote in many forms, ranging from the most personal and subjective (memoirs) to the most public and objective (plays). Historian Catriona Kelly explains that the reign of Catherine II

> marked a turning-point, as broadening educational opportunity for girls, increasing emphasis on reading as an acceptable, indeed requisite, private pursuit, and growing acquaintance with Western literature, including books written by women, fostered an atmosphere congenial to women who wished to take up the pen.[38]

Barbara Heldt, writing on Russian women's literature, asserts "that men and women inhabited a shared literary culture [...] but that women's writings provide an alternate perspective to literature by men."[39]

Although Catherine herself was certainly not a feminist in the modern sense, her writings and actions reveal her conviction that women should be entitled to participate in the intellectual revolution of the Age of Reason. She therefore had little sympathy with Russian women who remained tied to conventional modes of thinking, particularly to forms of ignorance or superstition. Accordingly, these views are reflected in Catherine's dramatic writings. Feminist readers can note the various portrayals, both negative and positive, of the female characters. Some characters, such as Mrs. Sanctimonious in *Oh, These Times!*, are clearly the focus of Catherine's satire. Yet the presence of young heroine characters enables the playwright to comment on gender-related double standards, particularly in education. For instance, in the ironic scene in *Oh, These Times!* between the servant Mavra and Khristina (I.12), we learn that Khristina's grandmother has deliberately kept her in ignorance, barely able to read or write. In *The Siberian Shaman*, the daughter Prelesta is debilitatingly shy, and is unable to voice her own concerns, because she can barely understand her lover Ivan Pernatov's speech.

37　Alexander, *Catherine the Great: Life and Legend* 333.
38　Kelly 2.
39　Heldt 4.

Feminist literary scholar Ruth Dawson notes that in the final scene Prelesta achieves a measure of autonomy only through assuming a third-person, fairy tale persona.[40] While these young women characters are common types in dramatic literature, we must notice that in portraying each of them Catherine raises important issues of women's education and self-confidence, concerns which were clearly important in her own life. In a similar way, seventeenth-century English playwright Aphra Behn (a woman writing for her living) brings issues of forced marriage and women's economic standing to the foreground of her plays.

Theatre as an art form is the performance of a state of in-betweenness: between the playwright and the text, between the character and the actor, between the audience and the production. Today's scholars of eighteenth-century studies are currently analyzing such liminal states, re-examining the accepted binary oppositions of public/private and man/woman.[41] Perhaps Catherine, notorious for defying attempts to place her in rigid categories of gender and behavior, felt that the stage was best suited for the expression of her new ways of thinking about a new Russia, and woman's place in it.

Catherine the Great herself was undecided about the value of her own writing, considering her writings to be "merely trifles." In a 1772 letter to Voltaire, she comments on a new Russian play she is going to send him in French translation. The play is *Oh, These Times!*

> Opinion here is that the anonymous author of these new Russian comedies, though he shows talent, has grave faults; he knows nothing about the theatre, and his plots are weak. However this is not the case with his characters, which are well-sustained and drawn from everyday life. There are flashes of wit, he makes you laugh, his morality is pure, and he knows his nation very well.[42]

---

[40] Dawson, "Catherine the Great: Playwright of the Anti-Occult."

[41] See Klein.

[42] Letter's date is c. 17/28 October 1772. Lentin 143–44. Original French from Reddaway 170–171.

Chapter 2
Early Comedies

Catherine the Great wrote her first five comedies sometime in the early 1770s, probably before April 1772. The first ten years of her reign had been replete with challenges, not the least of which was holding on to the throne. Before the end of 1772, she had written a major work of legislative theory (the *Great Instruction*), begun her first war (the Russo-Turkish War (1768–74)), ousted her first longstanding lover (Grigorii Orlov, from 1759–72), and brought her country through a plague crisis (1770–71). Although the *Great Instruction* was meant as a theoretical directive for the newly formed Legislative Commission, the work of that body was interrupted by the war, and that document's Enlightenment concepts remained largely unrealized. Catherine's other challenges in foreign policy included a troubled Sweden and a struggle for Poland. Domestically, she fended off conspiracies against her reign, took control of Orthodox church lands, supported agricultural reforms, and showed leadership with her own inoculation against smallpox in 1768.

Through all these crises, Catherine continued as a writer. After the closing of *All Sorts* in 1769, she began a version of her private memoirs in 1771. She also turned to the theatre, perhaps as a more direct means of gauging her audience's response than in the private realm of the periodical. Given that *All Sorts* explored contemporary manners through comic exaggeration and a wide array of character perspectives, it is not surprising that when Catherine the Great decided to begin her career as a playwright, her genre of choice was the neoclassical comedy.

Five Neoclassical Comedies

The rise of neoclassicism in Russia was simultaneous with the birth of a native drama. Whereas Italian and French writers followed the style of ancient Roman works, the Russians closely emulated the French, who by the mid-eighteenth century still dominated the literary stage. Although the early French neoclassical drama was faithful to classical precedent, writers such as Racine and Corneille began forging their own styles, to reflect contemporary religious values and esthetic tastes. By the late seventeenth century, the controversy of the Ancients versus the Moderns raged in France and England. In his 1672 essay, "Of Ancient and Modern Tragedy," Charles de Marguetel de Saint-Evremond (1610–1703) weighed in on the side of the Moderns, arguing that French innovations in tragic form were in fact superior and more suitable for the age.[1] Such support for the French dramatic models helped to further establish their prestige.

Not until one hundred years later, in his *Hamburg Dramaturgy* (1767–69), did Gotthold Lessing challenge French dominance with his idea that French playwrights had misinterpreted classical theory. For Lessing, English writers like Shakespeare were in fact closer to the aims of classical tradition. Lessing's ideas influenced the German *Sturm und Drang* movement of the 1770s and 1780s, at which point the battle was "at last decided in favor of the Moderns."[2]

While these battles raged, Russia's secular drama was being born. As happened centuries earlier in both Italy and France, two countries with the strongest commitment to classical models, two primary genres were emphasized in Russia: comedies and tragedies. The first secular Russian playwright, Aleksandr Sumarokov, began writing heroic tragedies in imitation of French style in 1747. Iakov Kniazhnin, Mikhail Lermontov, and many others soon joined him. Starting in 1750, Sumarokov also wrote comedies; by the 1760s other comic writers such as Denis Fonvizin and Vladimir Lukin had emerged. By the 1770s, although aware of Lessing's critique of French models, most Russian comedies and tragedies remained in conformity to neoclassical precepts, partially due to the strong influence of French language and culture in the Russian court. The rumblings of romantic change were not heard loudly in Russia until the early nineteenth century; Catherine the Great herself was one of the first champions of a Shakespearean approach in Russian dramatic literature (see Chapter 4).

Russian comedies not only followed the seventeenth-century French neo-classical style of Molière and Corneille, but also kept up with more recent trends in French sentimental comedy in the works of Marivaux and LaChausée. Although most Russians did not write *comédies larmoyantes* (tearful comedies), moral concerns were still of utmost importance in plot and character, and didactic lessons were a necessary ingredient. Russia also followed Voltaire's lead in integrating Enlightenment notions of reason into the plays' themes.

The typical neoclassical comedy is a tightly constructed piece with multiple acts (usually five) and black and white characters, each representing a necessary type for the creation of a lesson. The play takes place (following the Renaissance exhortation to imitate classical form) in a single setting, usually over the course of a single eventful day. Russian playwrights did not vary much from this model, but did adjust to include native themes, issues, and character types.

Catherine probably wrote her first series of neoclassical comedies sometime in 1771 or early 1772. The five plays, like her journal *All Sorts*, explore contemporary manners through a wide array of exaggerated character perspectives and actions: *Oh, These Times!* [O vremia!], *Mrs. Grumbler's Nameday* [Imianiny gospozhi Vorchalkinoi], *Mrs. Tattler and her Family* [Gospozha Vestnikova s

---

[1]   Saint-Evremond 271–6.
[2]   Carlson 171.

sem'eiu], *A Prominent Nobleman's Entrance Hall* [Peredniania znatnago boiarina], and *The Questioner* [Voprositel'].[3] The anonymous scripts were all published with the inscription "created in Iaroslavl."[4] The exact order in which Catherine wrote the five "Iaroslavl" comedies is not known, although *Oh, These Times!* is often presumed to be Catherine's first play because it seems to have been produced first.[5] It is also her most famous, with many mentions by her contemporaries, several later critical treatments, and two translations into French.[6]

These five plays of the 1770s (as well as two other completed but unpublished ones and one fragment) were edited and re-copied by Catherine's trusted literary advisor Ivan Perfilievich Elagin (1725–94), who had studied in the Noble Cadet Corps with Sumarokov and Kheraskov. Elagin was a playwright, poet, essayist, and translator, and an ally from Catherine's days as Grand Duchess. He had been exiled from St. Petersburg in 1758, the result of being caught up in a scandal displeasing to Empress Elizabeth; Catherine brought him back when she herself became Empress. From 1766–79, he replaced Sumarokov as Director of the Imperial Theatres. One of Elagin's dramaturgical innovations of the 1760s was "adaptation to our customs" (*sklonenie na nashi nravy*), in which foreign plays, particularly comedies, were transposed to Russian settings.[7]

---

[3]   All citations from Catherine's plays will be given in parentheses with page numbers from the appropriate volume in Pypin (see Appendix for corresponding volume numbers).

[4]   *Oh, These Times!*, *Mrs. Grumbler* and *Mrs. Tattler* were each published first in single undated editions, probably sometime between 1772 and 1774. *Prominent Nobleman* and *The Questioner* were not published until 1786, in Dashkova's *Russian Theatre* collection (*The Questioner* appeared under the incorrect title *The Invisible Bride* [Nevesta nevidimka], but with note about Iaroslavl). See Pypin 1: 246 for more on this publication confusion.

[5]   The premiere of *Oh, These Times!* is presumed to have been sometime before 12 April 1772—the publication date of a letter by Novikov that refers to the play as having been performed three times on the Imperial stage (Pypin 1: 43). El'nitskaia, for instance, is most likely using the letter as a reference when she gives the designation "before April 12" as a conjecture for the play's first performances. See El'nitskaia 456. El'nitskaia lists subsequent performances at both court and public theatres. *Mrs. Grumbler* was first done at the court theatre on 27 April 1772 (El'nitskaia 448). *Prominent Nobleman* was first done at the court theatre on 18 September 1772, according to its published frontispiece. *Mrs. Tattler* was not produced until 1780 at the public Free [*Vol'nyi*] Theatre in Petersburg (also known as the Wooden Theatre), and *The Questioner* may never have been produced (see entries in El'nitskaia).

[6]   *O temps! O moeurs!*, trans. LeClerc. In *Mélanges* 4:1–78 and *O temps! (O vremia!)*: trans. Legrelle. *Mrs. Grumbler* was also translated into French as *La Fête du Jour de Nom* in volume 23 of *Chefs-d'oeuvre du Théâtre polonais*. The text, however, was not attributed to Catherine but, for unknown reasons, to a Polish author, Oginsky.

[7]   Karlinsky 92. Pypin explains that for several of the plays, there are no extant manuscripts in Catherine's hand, only copies by Elagin. Giovanna Moracci argues for Elagin's position as a co-author of these comedies ("K izucheniu"). Elagin's copies possibly help to date two other unpublished comedies to this 1770s period: *The Unexpected*

Four of Catherine's comedies of 1772 (*Oh, These Times!*; *Mrs. Grumbler's Nameday*; *Mrs. Tattler and her Family*; and *The Questioner*) are of varying lengths but display a notably similar structure, which Catherine also later used in her 1785–86 five-act comedies (her anti-Masonic trilogy). A situation is established in which an obstacle stands in the way of a potential marriage of two lovers. The obstacle is usually related to one character's extreme behavior, and is often resolved through the intervention of a clever servant. Deviating somewhat from this structure is the one-act comedy *A Prominent Nobleman's Entrance Hall*, in which a string of supplicants gather to present their cases to the titular Nobleman. This short play does not follow a typical neoclassical form; there is not even a happy ending, as the petitioners leave disappointed and no marriage is promised.

Catherine's comic characters are not merely divided into "good" and "bad." A character can be delineated in many ways, emphasizing any number of relevant traits: morals, class, occupation, gender, age, beliefs—even dress or language. The intersections of these traits give the comedies a rich liveliness, as in *Oh, These Times!* with its aging female zealot, or in *Prominent Nobleman*, where we meet a pugilistic German Baron or an overly intellectual Frenchman.

This chapter will highlight three plays. First, in Catherine's first and most famous play *Oh, These Times!*, we see her develop the comic techniques that she will use in most of her subsequent work: sharply drawn humorous characters with strong vices, in contrast to clear-headed and rational characters; a plot hinging on the revelation of corruption or deception; and the engineering of a wedding. I explore the image of masks and identity disguises in the play. Finally, I compare the play to its German source, and conclude that Catherine's alterations strengthen the play and reveal her dramaturgical skill. I also treat in detail the various fools and foolishness present in another related comedy, *Mrs. Grumbler's Nameday*. Connected metatheatrically to *Oh, These Times!* through the character of Mrs. Grumbler who appears in both plays, this comedy illustrates the consequences of blindness and ignorance. After briefly summarizing *Mrs. Tattler and her Family* and *The Questioner*, I examine the unusually structured *Prominent Nobleman*. By presenting a string of eccentric characters, each with his or her own reason for approaching the influential but absent nobleman of the title, Catherine openly treatd such issues as Russian cultural identity, war, and the power of language.

Oh, the Morals: *Oh, These Times!*

Oh, These Times!, probably Catherine's first play, was written in 1772. The Russian title *O vremia!* derives from Cicero's famous Latin phrase "O tempora O

Adventure [Neozhidaemoe prikliuchenie] and the real *The Invisible Bride* [Nevesta nevidimka], published for the first time in Pypin volume 3.

mores," usually translated as "Oh the times, oh the morals."[8] Her best-known work, it is a satirical attack on many vices Catherine wished to root out from her society: religious hypocrisy, superstition, and slander. The main character, Mrs. Sanctimonious, is a superficially religious old woman who resembles Molière's Tartuffe. The play was first produced sometime before April 1772, and was revived every few years until 1791 in St. Petersburg; in 1782, the play was also produced in Moscow.[9] Catherine adapted *Oh, These Times!* from *The Prayer Sister* (Die Betschwester), a 1745 comedy by German playwright Christian Fürchtegott Gellert.[10] Although many aspects of the plot and some scenes are quite close to Gellert, Catherine makes notable improvements to many aspects of characterization, structure, and humor.

Voltaire seems to have received a copy from Catherine of two Russian comedies in February of 1773; one of these may have been the French translation of *Oh, These Times!* by LeClerc, doctor to the Grand Duke Paul. Voltaire's comments are favorable, despite the fact that Catherine seems to have given him no indication that she was their author. He comments, "the dialog is always true to life and natural. This in my opinion, is one of the most important qualities in the art of comedy."[11]

The plot of *Oh, These Times!* concerns marriage negotiations that Mr. Notshallow is conducting on behalf of his friend Mr. Milksop, who would like to marry a young Muscovite girl named Khristina. Her grandmother, Mrs. Sanctimonious, a religious hypocrite and a miser, continually thwarts their efforts; Sanctimonious is not eager to part with Khristina's dowry. The servant girl Mavra recounts both Sanctimonious's externally devout behavior, and her stinginess and cruelty to those around her. Meanwhile, Milksop begins to have doubts about Khristina, who is completely silent in his presence. Mavra assures him that her upbringing is to blame, for Sanctimonious deliberately kept her in ignorance and isolation.

We next meet two other comical old women, companions to Sanctimonious: Mrs. Tattler and Mrs. Marvel, who are respectively overly gossipy and overly superstitious. Their interactions and ridiculous tales form the backbone of the play's humor. The marriage is almost called off when the two men smirk at the old ladies' belief that a grasshopper's chirping portends disaster. With a little well-placed bribery, Mavra smoothes things out for the wedding to take place, as Sanctimonious jokes that she will expect interest on the dowry.

---

[8] Classicist John Kearns has suggested to me that a more appropriate translation of the vocative case here would be "You Times, You Customs."

[9] El'nitskaia 456.

[10] For original German text, see Gellert, *Die Betschwester* 145–220. For an English translation, see Gellert, *Christian Fürchtegott Gellert's The Prayer Sister*. Gellert's play was translated into Russian by Mikhail Matinskii in 1774 as *Bogomolka*, two years after Catherine's adaptation appeared. Chebyshev 394.

[11] Letter's date is 13 February 1773. Lentin 147–48.

In *Oh, These Times!*, the variety of perspectives reveals much about Catherine's own priorities, as her views are embodied in several of her characters: in the male character of Mr. Notshallow who provides Enlightenment standards; in the educated servant girl Mavra who is the play's most likable and sensible character; lastly, in Catherine's negative portrayal of Sanctimonious and her two cronies. In the characterization of Sanctimonious, Catherine presents a portrait of the anti-Empress; the old lady is superficially devout, superstitious, ignorant, stingy, old-fashioned and downright cruel in her behavior towards her servants—everything which Catherine, as self-styled enlightened monarch, abhorred and resisted. By using the dramatic genre, Catherine could tangibly and playfully demonstrate the conflicting behaviors and philosophies that prevailed in her era, while structuring plot and manipulating audience sympathy to favor her own perspective on matters such as education, religious hypocrisy, superstition, and serfdom. Kevin McKenna, writing on Catherine's inclusion of a variety of perspectives in her satirical periodical *All Sorts*, comments that, "Catherine constructed a polyphony of personae."[12] Her use of the multi-vocal genre of drama was consistent with her larger political philosophy: although a dedicated autocrat, in the early part of her reign Catherine encouraged free thought and debate as hallmarks of her country's intellectual enlightenment. By disguising her true position as monarch through the creation of various characters, she was better able to foster the free exchange of ideas, and to enter into that exchange herself. As a playwright, Catherine participated in the particularly eighteenth-century game of masks, disguising her own views by splitting her ideas into various characters. Too, her own persona as a playwright was also a character created by Catherine, adding another voice to the rich multi-vocal variety that characterized Russian comedy and satire in the eighteenth century.

As a female monarch, Catherine both possessed and lacked power. Because Russia's emerging literary world, based as it was on European models, was primarily a male-dominated arena, Catherine's fictional maleness may have helped her to enter that sphere more easily. Shielded by this cloak of masculine anonymity, Catherine made two published statements about her play *Oh, These Times!*: one was a letter addressed to Nikolai Novikov, the second was a claim of the play's relation to the era of plague, printed on the title page of the play's first edition.

The letter to Novikov was but one part of an ongoing correspondence between the two, published via the medium of their own satirical journals *All Sorts* and *The Drone*. Novikov's *The Drone* ceased publication in April of 1770, as did *All Sorts* a few weeks later. By 1772, Catherine had tried her hand at a different literary medium by writing her first play, *Oh, These Times!* That same year, Novikov created a new periodical, *The Painter* [*Zhivopisets*]. In its first issue, dated 12 April 1772, a letter appeared, addressed "To the unknown Mr. Creator of the

---

12 McKenna 7.

comedy *Oh, These Times!*" Although both are masked by anonymity, Novikov's letter and Catherine's reply (published seven weeks later) formed yet another public dialog between them, reminiscent of their earlier discourse.[13] In commenting on the play's content, Novikov consciously manipulates the convention of anonymity. The noun form which Novikov applies to the play's author is *sochinitel'* (creator)—in the Russian masculine gender. Likewise, Catherine signs her letter of response "*vash okhotnyi sluga, Sochinitel' komedii O Vremia*" (your willing servant, Creator of the comedy Oh, These Times), using a masculine adjective and noun formation. The fiction preserved by each letter is that the author of the play is unknown. Yet Novikov teasingly toys with the hidden identity of the playwright by invoking Catherine's name:

> But, sir, why hide your name, a name universally deserving of gratitude; I do not find reason for this. Is it perhaps that having insulted vice so cruelly and having set vicious people against oneself, you are afraid of backbiting? No, such weakness can never have a place in your heart. And can such noble courage be afraid of oppression in this time, when to the good fortune of Russia and to the *prosperity* of the human race, the *wise* CATHERINE has dominion over us: HER pleasure, shown in the presentation of your comedy, is certified in her patronage of writers like yourself.[14]

Shrewdly, Novikov flatters Catherine as an enlightened monarch, as a burgeoning playwright, and as a patron of writers. Novikov himself was enjoying Catherine's support of his satirical and historical publishing efforts, and his words imply a congenial relationship between the wise Catherine and this unknown playwright.

Yet as his letter continues, Novikov introduces a note of discontent, by questioning the writer's fears of defamation and coercion: "What remains for you to be afraid of? But there must be particular reasons which compel you to hide your name; if this is so, then I will not try to penetrate them." This quick juxtaposition of imperial patronage with a feigned paranoia shows that Novikov has not abandoned the techniques of playful epistolary satire.

Just as in the letter she wrote to Voltaire six months later, Catherine's letter of response to Novikov shows how she creates the persona of a humble beginner. The anonymous author tells *The Painter* that "his" motives are personal.

> I write for my own amusement: and if my small works gain success, and bring pleasure to thinking people, then I would be very rewarded. If I were to hear that on the contrary there is not any entertainment in them, hating idleness, I would not restrain myself from writing, yet I would not give them out anymore.[15]

---

13 S.V. Kalacheva considers the play *Oh, These Times!* to be a continuation of the debate between *All Sorts* and *The Drone*.

14 Pypin 1: 45–46.

15 "Otvet zhivopistsu Imperatritsy Ekateriny II," in Longinov, *Novikov* Appendix 1: 03.

The writer she creates is a modest novice, whose humility is perhaps more a literary and social convention than a genuine expression of feeling.   The playwright's satirical targets were determined through personal acquaintance and experience.

> [...] regarding that creation I didn't take the frames of mind located in it from anywhere except from my own family. Consequently, without leaving my own house, I have found in it alone, for the creation of an amusing show, extensive enough ground for a skillful pen, which I do not consider my own to be.

Her use of the image of a house is interesting; one objection raised by those who doubt Catherine's authorship is that she could not have possibly known about everyday life in a middle-class household.   Soviet critic Vsevolodskii-Gerngross, for example, objects that, "There is evident in the comedies a knowledge of the daily existence of the lower nobility, with which Catherine was unacquainted."[16] Yet, in this letter, Catherine fictionally places herself in the center of such a household; in this incarnation, the Empress is not the all-powerful ruler of a nation, but rather a spectator from within a single family, able to observe and characterize the minutiae of that milieu. Catherine's letter to *The Painter* enabled her to adopt the new persona of playwright-observer, while continuing her earlier dialog with Novikov, and thus with Russian literary society as a whole.

Catherine's second key statement about *Oh, These Times!* is the description that appears on the title page of the first publication of the play in 1772: "Comedy in three acts created in Iaroslavl in the time of the plague."[17]   This is a strange designation concerning the time of the play's composition, as "comedy" and "plague" seem hardly fitting companions.[18]   Although there was a plague in Iaroslavl in this period, Catherine herself had not visited there since her tour in 1767.[19]   Therefore, the published phrase "created in Iaroslavl in the time of the plague" is yet another example of Catherine's manipulation of her own persona. But what is the connection between the fictional Iaroslavl comedies and the events of the 1770–72 plague, which was itself very real?

The story of the plague itself illuminates Catherine's attitude toward superstition, a major theme of the play *Oh, These Times!* This disease was yet another trial for Catherine's relatively new reign; moving northward from Kiev, the epidemic had spread to Moscow by late 1770, claiming hundreds of lives every

---

[16]   Vsevolodskii-Gerngross, *Ot istokov* 253.

[17]   1772 is the presumed date of publication (e.g., M. N. Longinov, "Dramaticheskii sochineniia"). The play was originally published as *O vremia! Komediia v trex deistviiakh. Sochinena v Iaroslavle vo vremia chumy* (St. Petersburg: n.p., n.d.).

[18]   The four other plays considered later in this chapter were published with the notation that they were composed in Iaroslavl, but do not mention the plague.

[19]   See Alexander, *Bubonic Plague* for a discussion of the plague's impact on Iaroslavl, where there was a significant rise in the 1771 death rate.

day. During the course of the city's plague, between 75,000 and 100,000 died. In September of 1771, the Archbishop Amvrosii removed a sacred icon from the Varsavskii Gate in order to prevent the panic-stricken Muscovites from gathering together to pray to the icon and to kiss it. According to Catherine's own account, a rioting public tracked down the Archbishop at the Donskoi monastery and murdered him in revenge: "These Impostors found Means to collect the major Part of the People to one of the City Gates, where there is an image of the Virgin Mary, and worked on their Credulity, by false appearance of Religion, to gratify their own lucrative Intentions."[20] Three hundred were arrested in the riot provoked by the removal of the icon.

Catherine was a St. Petersburg monarch, who visited Moscow, the former capital, on only a few occasions in her lifetime. Her relationship with the city was uneasy; as her biographer John Alexander puts it, "her initial dislike [for Moscow] gradually festered into deep disgust."[21] To Catherine, Moscow signified everything that needed changing in her Enlightenment Russia; its people were, to her, uneducated, overly religious, old-fashioned, and full of rumor and superstition. The brutal behavior of the mob during the plague riot reinforced these conceptions. It is interesting that, in the end, Catherine publicly attributed the unrest to "false appearance of Religion." In these words we can find the link between the devastating events of the plague, and Catherine's light comedy *Oh, These Times!*, which is set in Moscow. The vices of religious hypocrisy and superstition are the major themes of the play, and may provide the link between the plague and the so-called Iaroslavl comedies. Her letter to Novikov's journal specifically alludes to the state of isolation afforded the playwright: "I wrote my comedy living in solitude during the raging plague."[22] It is as if the anonymous author, while battling physiological disease in Iaroslavl, took the opportunity to look critically at Moscow and its spiritual disease.

In both her letter to *The Painter* and the title page statement about the Iaroslavl plague, Catherine created and manipulated her own persona as the playwright of *Oh, These Times!* In the play itself, Catherine molds the various *dramatis personae* to support her views. The major sympathetic characters are shown in a positive light because they espouse Catherine's progressive ideas; the play's comic villains are shown to be foolish and execrable precisely because they oppose the Empress's views on such matters as education and superstition.

First, the Empress's views are embodied in the figure of the male confidant, Notshallow (Nepustov, derived from *ne pustoi*, means "not shallow"). Confidants were commonplace in neoclassical drama, having evolved in part as an attempt to

---

[20] Alexander, *Catherine the Great: Life and Legend* 156. Alexander's source for Catherine's letter of 27 September 1771 to the St. Petersburg newspaper is the London *Daily Advertiser* of 5 November 1771, which printed an English version.

[21] Alexander, *Catherine the Great: Life and Legend* 44.

[22] Longinov, *Novikov i Moskovskie Martinisty*. Appendix 1: 03.

lend realism to the former practice of soliloquy; the hero would now speak to a friendly confidant rather than to the air (and the audience). Perhaps the most famous eighteenth-century Russian confidant is Pravdin from Fonvizin's *The Minor*, who transforms by play's end from a wise and passive listener-confidant to a government officer who is the undoing of the cruel Mrs. Prostakov. Notshallow's role in *Oh, These Times!* is to secure the marriage contract between Milksop and Khristina, assuring for Milksop's guardian that there will be a sufficient dowry. As Milksop himself constantly brings up the notion that he is rich enough without this dowry, that all that matters is Khristina's affection, Notshallow must inject a note of practicality and business-like common sense into the proceedings. This rationality serves to set him in opposition to Sanctimonious. When she bemoans the fact that her deceased husband's favorite piece of pottery has mysteriously fallen from a shelf, Notshallow is there with a reasonable explanation: "Why be frightened by such a thing, madam? Perhaps a cat or a mouse caused the pottery to fall from the shelf" (15). Catherine also uses Notshallow as a mouthpiece to speak against the superstitious practices of prophecy and fortune-telling, and for conservative, yet thoughtful values:

> I too respect old-fashioned sincerity. The ancient loyalty of friendship is commendable, truly commendable, and so is the strict adherence to having given one's word, so that not keeping it is shameful! In this matter she and I are of one mind. It's a pity, a real pity, that in these times no one is ashamed of anything [...] . (8)

For Notshallow, such old-fashioned virtues as sincerity are the eternal qualities of a noble person. True to his Enlightenment role models, he does not rely on the dictates of religious piety; he cites practical rather than religious reasons for proper social behavior. Unlike Sanctimonious, he is motivated neither by exterior religious practices, nor by hard-headed clinging to old customs for their own sake. When Sanctimonious demonstrates her impatience with one of her servants, Notshallow comments, "You offer prayers out of duty, madam, just as I do; but mercy and love towards one's neighbor are also duties ordered by law" (11). In this conception, Notshallow seems to make a distinction between religious duty and a more secular moral law (i.e., Catherine's governmental wisdom) that inspires and encourages fine behavior; he implies that genuine compassion is worth any number of hypocritical prayers.

Notshallow's character is in sharp contrast to that of the three superstitious ladies; he calls their talk "shallow nonsense." Unlike the family he is visiting, Notshallow is not a Muscovite, but rather belongs to the more elite and (in Catherine's eyes) more civilized circle of Petersburg society. Yet he also differs greatly from his young friend Milksop, whose love for Khristina is also a kind of shallow nonsense. Fed up with Milksop's indecisiveness, Notshallow finally advises him that there are some things more important than love: "To enter into such an engagement, above all you need to be compatible; if you find this compatibility between you, then I advise you to marry her" (20). Although Notshallow functions as a confidant, the playwright has painted his character with a lightly humorous touch that is rare for such "straight men." For one thing, Notshallow has an impatient streak, which might be played comically. Because Catherine has given him the added urgency of needing to leave immediately, we hear him again and again insist that Sanctimonious must attend to the business at hand; a typical line is "We must return to St. Petersburg right away" (31). Catherine also makes use of the somewhat dry nature of Notshallow to good comic effect in II.3, when Milksop reports how Sanctimonious superstitiously believed that a grasshopper had presaged the death of her spouse. Because Catherine does not choose to dramatize this scene, but rather has Milksop narrate events that occurred offstage, we have this view of Notshallow from the young man's perspective:

> Hearing all this nonsense, I could not hold back, and laughed loudly. Mr. Notshallow, for all his usual sternness, couldn't control himself. He cracked too, and we both laughed aloud. (26–7)

Notshallow's sense of humor sneaks in occasionally. When Milksop complains that Khristina seems unable to speak a word to him, Notshallow archly comments: "But that's wonderful! We've found the one silent girl in the city of Moscow!" (20). Clearly, Catherine has created a dryly humorous but somewhat dull man. Rather than seeing the Empress herself in his manner, we see her in his philosophy.

C.L. Drage comments that Notshallow and Mavra each function in *Oh, These Times!* as "Voltairean *raisonneur*, except that they are the spokesmen not of a philosophy but of the empress herself."[23] Yet Catherine does not give the play's final moralizing speech to Notshallow, bastion of eighteenth-century rationalism, but rather to Mavra. Despite her lower class status, Mavra also embodies the Enlightenment virtue of reason, but in a much more warm and accessible way than Notshallow does. By assigning such a key role to a woman character, Catherine echoes her own dual status as female intellectual.

Mavra is an unusual combination of traits. She is certainly in some ways a confidante; yet Arthur Coleman prefers to classify her as a "pert maid."[24] Although each of these types is familiar from the neoclassical gallery of characters, Catherine has given Mavra many specific characteristics that take her beyond either of these types. Like Notshallow, Mavra represents the contemporary generation, being considerably younger than the three old women, but also wiser than the two young lovers, who are in need of advice and education. Unlike Notshallow, who is a member of the upper class, Mavra is clearly in an inferior position as a servant in Sanctimonious's household. Catherine's use of a servant

---

[23] Drage 239.
[24] Coleman 63.

character was a deliberate change from Gellert's play, in which the young girl confidante (Lorchen) is a sweet but colorless sentimentalist heroine, a governess and companion rather than a servant. Unlike Lorchen, Mavra is under constant threat of abuse from Sanctimonious. This domineering lady of the house once threw a prayer book at Mavra's head—an ironic comment on Sanctimonious's true use for religion.

In other ways, Mavra is exceptional for someone of her class status. She is clearly educated, perhaps as a result of having formerly been employed in the house of a worldly French family—it is she who has taught Khristina how to read and write "*ukradkoiu*" (in secret). Like Catherine, Mavra is also clearly an avid reader, to the dismay of her employer:

> She is angry with me often enough without such a reason. She calls me a heathen because I sometimes read *Monthly Works* and sometimes a novel about Monsieur Cleveland. (7)

The reference to *Monthly Works* connects Mavra and the play to the world of the fashionable satirical periodicals, in which Catherine herself participated.[25] The latter refers to a rambling adventure novel by Abbé Prevost: *Le Philosophe anglais ou Histoire de M. Cleveland* (1731–39), which was translated into Russian in 1760.[26] This rather surprising sophistication on the part of a servant character may violate neoclassical rules of decorum and verisimilitude, but it underscores the Enlightenment theme of the "self-made man." Mavra's literacy and self-education is implicitly linked to the wisdom which she displays throughout the play.

To Sanctimonious and the other ladies, however, Mavra is nothing more than a functionary who will brew coffee or announce visitors. These elderly ladies are blind to Mavra's true ability to manipulate the day's events. Mavra's success is derived from her keen understanding of her victims' weaknesses. For example, she preys on Tattler's greed by arranging for Milksop to bribe her with a ring, and frightens Marvel out of Sanctimonious's room by telling her that the lady of the house died thirty years ago in the very spot in which she is sitting. Yet because Mavra's maneuverings are aimed at the three ridiculous ladies, she is not presented as a mean-spirited character but rather as a sound and sensible force, with whom spectators can identify on the grounds of her intellect rather than her class.

Catherine uses several structural means to encourage this audience identification. Mavra gives the play's only asides. Predictably, she comments to the audience at the expense of one of the three old ladies, Tattler, who is complaining about the poor conditions of the streets. Mavra suggests that the old

---

[25] The specific periodical is probably *Monthly Works* [*Ezhemesiachnye sochineniia*], an early journal published in St. Petersburg by the Academy of Sciences from 1755 to 1764, edited by G. F. Müller. See Marker 96. In the Gellert play, Lorchen makes specific reference to *The Spectator* (Gellert, *Die Betschwester* 147).

[26] Chebyshev 399n.

woman is ignoring her own culpability: "But what we won't say is that her horses are not shod, her wheels have no linchpins, and her harness is no good!" (16). Mavra even gives an aside at the expense of Notshallow. When he tells Milksop that what matters most in a marriage is compatibility (*soglasie nravov*), Mavra comments, "They are spouting such nonsense!" (20). By metaphorically winking to the audience about the foolishness of these two male characters, Mavra draws on audience empathy and identification.

Catherine further strengthens Mavra's position by giving her two speeches "alone" on the stage. In II.2, after having given advice to Khristina in the previous scene, she comments in a brief four-line soliloquy on the ways of love, saying "Love, you enter into the human heart before one knows what love is!" (26). That brief speech, which demonstrates both Mavra's deep affection for Khristina and her involvement in the play's events, is in sharp contrast to the play's closing speech. Its rigid structure and moralizing tone lift it out of the play into a metatheatrical realm, where we hear Catherine the Empress through the mouthpiece of Mavra.

> MAVRA *(alone)*. Here's how our century passes by! We condemn, we judge, we mock, and speak with spite of everyone and everything. But what we don't see is that we ourselves are deserving of laughter and condemnation. When our biases displace common sense, then our own vices are hidden from us, and only the mistakes of another are visible. In the eye of a neighbor, we can see a speck of sawdust, but in our own eye we don't see the plank. (41–2)

Mavra is then both the chief representative of the play's moral and philosophical substance as well as—like Catherine may have seen herself—a clever and self-assured woman who intervenes when necessary into foolishness and injustice.

Although Mavra and Notshallow may be sympathetic to the Empress's philosophy and ideals, their dialog is not the main source of her commentary. Rather than have these two spokespeople spout moralizing maxims directly, more often Catherine chooses the strategy of dramatic satire, by showing the behaviors she most wishes to discourage. This didactic strategy is hardly unusual; dramatists in medieval Europe used the comic Vice character to get belly-laughs, while distancing the spectator from him through dramatic irony. The three ladies, Sanctimonious, Marvel, and Tattler, are "the embodiment of three vices: hypocrisy, superstition and passion for news and gossip."[27] Their telling names are none too subtle. Molokososov (Milksop) derives from the word for milk (*moloko*). Khanzhakina (Sanctimonious) is derived from *khanzhestvo*, meaning sanctimoniousness and hypocrisy; Chudikhina (Marvel)—from *chudnoi*, meaning unusual, amazing, astonishing, or *chudnyi* (magical); Vestnikova (Tattler)—from *vest'* meaning news, and *vestnik* meaning messenger. The practice of telling

---

[27] Solntsev 120.

names, common for Russian dramatists in this period, exaggerated the characters, draws attention to the play's artifice as a comedy, and distills the character to mask-like essences rather than fleshing them out as human beings. Catherine's inclusion of telling names echoes the use of similar names in such weekly satirical periodicals as Catherine's own *All Sorts*.

The addition of Sanctimonious's two cronies is one of Catherine's primary changes to Gellert's original. Although each character has her own essential fault, as evinced in her telling name, the three also share many characteristics, functioning as a comic chorus of bad habits. Sanctimonious has many undesirable qualities: she is hypocritically pious, she is cruel to her servants, she is greedy, she is a gossip-monger, she is stingy, she is superstitious, she is afraid of literacy, she has a quick temper, and she is quick to judge others. Each vice has its mirroring virtues. The inference is that a truly worthy person is genuine, kind, generous, reserved, altruistic, sensible, educated, stable, and non-judgmental. But these virtues are hardly the stuff of drama, and Catherine has wisely chosen to reinforce her Enlightenment values through these negative comic characters. Through the actions and dialog of these three old women, the audience learns "lessons" about education, religion, and superstition.

Mavra's discussion of Khristina's upbringing reveals the ignorant and stifling atmosphere of the Sanctimonious household. Khristina is deprived not only of company, but also of literacy: "her grandmother feared that if the girl learned reading and writing, she would begin to write love letters" (21). Marvel further articulates the fear of women's education:

> Why should a girl learn reading and writing; why does she need to? The fewer things a girl knows, the fewer lies she'll tell. My mother forced me to swear that until I was fifty years old, I would not take pen in hand. What's more, they say that these days in Petersburg even a girl can study anything ... (37–38)

From Catherine's perspective, such logic, although laughable, was a perverse repudiation of one of her most deeply held values: education. Her own difficult adolescence, spent in the inhospitable company of her immature husband Peter at a strange and unfamiliar court, was a triumph of spirit. Besides applying herself to the challenges of learning about the Russian language, customs, and religion, Catherine also began a massive campaign of self-education by reading key philosophical, political, and historical materials, ranging from Montesquieu to Diderot. Catherine clearly felt that her gender was no impediment to her own enlightenment. It is little wonder, then, that Catherine made the education of women a priority in her reign. She made plans for a system of free co-education in Russia, officially approving Ivan Betskii's 1764 treatise entitled "General Plan for the Education of Young People of Both Sexes."[28] In 1764 she founded the

---

[28] Madariaga, *Catherine the Great: A Short History* 105; also Klabik-Lozovsky.

Smol'nyi Institute, a boarding school created for the secular education of girls—of which Marvel complains, "in Petersburg even a girl can study anything." In the context of the play, the backwardness of Sanctimonious in regard to Khristina's upbringing might have been amusing to the play's elite and middle-class spectators at the court and public theatres, but for the playwright Catherine, the implications for society were quite serious.

In addition to ignorance and illiteracy, another major target was religious hypocrisy. Molière's words about his comedy *Tartuffe* in his 1664 petition to Louis XIV could well have been Catherine's own:

> The duty of comedy being to correct men's errors in the course of amusing them, I thought there was nothing I could do to greater advantage, in the exercise of my profession, than attack the vices of the age by depicting them in ridiculous guise and hypocrisy being, beyond question, one of the most prevalent and pernicious among them, the idea occurred to me, Sire, that I should render no small service to all good men among your subjects if I wrote a play attacking hypocrites [...] .[29]

The underlying comic principle of Catherine's play is that Sanctimonious lacks the charity that is the inner core of the Christian faith, concentrating instead on exterior rites and observances. This hollow religion masks her many vices: cruelty to her servants, miserly greed in her dealings with her debtors, and harsh treatment of her granddaughter Khristina.

> She observes each holy day strictly; she goes to mass every day; she always lights a candle before a festival; she doesn't eat meat at fasting time. She goes about in a wool dress—and don't dream that that's out of stinginess—and she despises all those who do not follow her rules. (8)

Oh, These Times!, like Molière's play, is not directed at those believers who practice religion in good faith, but rather at religious hypocrisy. Yet neither play enthusiastically endorses spirituality. Catherine does not provide her audience with a genuinely devout character to counteract Sanctimonious, but rather chooses to counter-balance Sanctimonious's extreme superficial devotion with Notshallow's decidedly secular logic, speaking of the necessity for sincerity and loyalty in friendship. Even more so than in *Tartuffe*, religion itself cannot escape untainted by the play's merciless portrayal of pious duplicity. Perhaps Catherine allowed herself this freedom because, unlike Molière, she had no King to please and no Cardinal to fear.

Another related target was superstition. Catherine's memoirs reveal her early fascination with folk beliefs, as well as the Empress Elizabeth's propensity to trust

---

[29] English translation from Molière, *The Misanthrope and Other Plays* 104. For original French version, see Molière *Oeuvres Complètes* 2: 5.

in magic remedies and superstition.[30] Such early encounters with mysticism were later contradicted by her formative reading of rationalist writings from the foremost thinkers of the European Enlightenment. As she struggled to balance the secular demands of such political philosophy with her country's deep-rooted Orthodox faith, she could never aim criticism directly at religion. Her targets were the parareligious, the "pagan," the un-Orthodox. For instance, although she initially encouraged and supported Novikov's Moscow printing efforts, his predominant interest in occult and Masonic materials led her to close the press and to imprison him in 1792. *Oh, These Times!*, written twenty years earlier, was an attempt to use dramatic satire (rather than imprisonment) to accomplish her goals.

Catherine's stance on mysticism and superstition was unwavering; we find her using drama to attack these same vices thirteen years later in her anti-Masonic trilogy. In those three comedies, she equates freemasonry, alchemy, and shamanism with superstition and thus attacks both a gullible older generation as well as a younger set anxious to believe in new and magical phenomena. Like *Oh, These Times!*, the plays of the anti-Masonic trilogy hinge on marriages that are nearly prevented by foolishness. But the emphasis in these later plays has shifted to a focus on deliberate con artists who manipulate fears, away from the characters' own naiveté.

In Marvel, Catherine creates a vivid portrait of a woman gripped by such "senseless" fears and convictions. These fears render her unable to function, as when she cannot come into the main room because she has heard a cricket, or when Mavra chases her from the room by preying on her weaknesses. Sanctimonious is also prone to see bad omens in everything. More than her false piety, Sanctimonious's superstition is the engine that drives the plot, or rather, brings it to a sudden halt when Notshallow and Milksop laugh at her belief that a grasshopper is a foreboding sign of imminent death. Their *faux pas* is the primary complicating incident of the play, which Mavra and Notshallow set right through a combination of bribery and flattery. Even in the play's final moments, when at long last Sanctimonious is about to approve Khristina's marriage to Milksop, an omen gets in the way:

> but there's just one thing that scares me .... Today is of course a Monday, and what's more, it's also the first day of the month. I never begin anything on either of these days. It's a bad omen! There are many examples of such signs, and my dear departed husband is the proof of it. One day, ten years before his death—may he rest in peace—he foretold that he would die on a Monday. And that's just what happened! (39)

Superstition in *Oh, These Times!* stands in the way of dramatic progress, just as in Catherine's eyes it stood in the way of societal progress in her country and century.

---

[30] Maroger 373; Erickson 136.

One particular issue was one of the thorniest of Catherine's reign: the institution of serfdom. Catherine herself maintained an ambiguous relationship toward the long-standing institution of Russian serfdom.[31] In the enlightened theoretical pronouncements of her *Great Instruction* (1767–68), she espoused notions of human equality. Yet the reality of keeping power and authority over a vast empire meant that the unjust system was out of even her reach—her legislative commission met and adjourned with no change to serfdom in Russia. Decades later, she would recall her shock at the attitudes of her nobility towards the serfs:

> You hardly dare say that they are just the same people as we and even when I myself say this I risk having stones hurled at me [...] even Count Alexander Sergeevich Stroganov [...] with indignation and passion defended the cause of slavery, which ought to have betrayed the entire structure of his soul [...] . I think there were not even twenty persons who would have thought about this subject humanely and as human beings.[32]

Immediately after writing the *Great Instruction*, a work modeled after the philosophical treatises of Montesquieu, Catherine turned to two distinct yet similar literary genres as outlets for her Enlightenment philosophy. *All Sorts* provided a site for the interplay of many voices; essays and letters, some written by Catherine herself, espoused the varying perspectives of her Empire's citizens, with reasonable comments in normative styles, and unenlightened views seen through the lens of satire. If even the Empress herself felt she risked stoning in speaking directly about issues such as serfdom, she could hope for moral reform by means of correcting general vices.

Satiric comedy on stage has similar advantages to the satirical periodical, and it is interesting to note that Catherine first began writing comedies in 1772, only a few years after the *Great Instruction*'s "failure" to reform Russian society. By creating characters who, through the conventions of the genre and through their own exaggerated and grotesque speech and action, are easily perceived by the audience to be foolish, Catherine is able to reform thinking without ever herself directly stating her belief "that they are just the same people as we."

In *Oh, These Times!*, Catherine penned several references to the serfs on Sanctimonious's estate, and her treatment of them. Sanctimonious describes how a young man who works for her interrupted her prayers to ask permission to marry. She has him beaten: "to write his marriage contract on his back!" (10). By implicitly contrasting Sanctimonious's ridiculous concern for losing track of the number of her prayers with her quick willingness to have the young man beaten, Catherine raises the issue of humanity and draws audience sympathy toward the hapless serf.

---

[31] See Kamenskii 50.

[32] Quoted in Alexander, *Catherine the Great: Life and Legend* 119 from Catherine II, *Zapiski imperatritsy* 175.

In another passage, Sanctimonious complains about the greediness of the peasant women: "if you give them something, they only harp 'give me more, give me more'." She goes on to complain that, "the government should establish a process whereby it, rather than we, would provide for our servants' marriages" (11). The play's male *raisonneur* Mr. Notshallow responds that, "the people who serve us [...] should be in our hands" (12). It is important to note here that neither he nor anyone else questions serfdom as an institution. Rather, it is up to the individual landowner to be just and wise and fair—a trickle-down sentiment of Enlightenment that Catherine hoped would eventually reform her entire society. In short, Catherine uses the vehicle of a dramatic presentation to persuade. It is to her advantage to overstate the barbarity of Sanctimonious and her friends. It is for this reason, I would argue, that she extends her play much farther into the realm of the grotesque than does Gellert: the stakes are much bigger. Although Catherine's well-known preference in her satirical journal *All Sorts* was for a comedy against general vices, by creating specific dramatic characters she was able to go much farther in demonstrating the ill-effects of foolish and vulgar behavior.

As its title predicts, *Oh, These Times!* alludes often to time, and to the times in which the characters live. For Mavra, time is measured by the daily schedule of each of Sanctimonious's devout rites, while for Notshallow, the ravings of Sanctimonious and her friends are a waste of time, as there is no time to be lost. For the three women, Tattler in particular, the olden times are something to cling to; Marvel fears the changing times: "Since the entire world turned upside down and the devil brought alien sciences to us, everyone became wicked, and the times became senseless" (36). Yet for Catherine, the times were finally becoming sensible, precisely through the aid of such "alien sciences"—the new thinking of the Enlightenment. The comic structure of Catherine's first play is itself inherently optimistic, as Khristina and Milksop's union is secured. The underlying message is of hope in time of the plague, of the triumph of good sense in a time of ignorance and disorder. The times are relative, as multi-faceted as Catherine herself. By presenting a polyphony of personae through her characterizations—not only of the play's central figures but also of herself as the anonymous author of the comedy *Oh, These Times!*—Catherine showed that, as she had told Voltaire, she indeed knew her nation very well.

The Prayer Sister

Catherine's indebtedness to Gellert's play *The Prayer Sister* [Die Betschwester] was not acknowledged until 1905, when D. Prohaska first examined and compared the two works. It is unsurprising that Gellert would have served as a model for Catherine's first dramatic efforts, as Gellert's works were quite popular reading for young German ladies. While Gellert's play primarily focuses on the single vice of religious hypocrisy, Catherine uses her play to address several prevalent customs and social problems in Russia. Russian drama in the 1770s displayed a growing

Russification of characters, settings, and subject matter. Although many of the first Russian neoclassical tragedies were set in the classical era, writers of Russian comedies were quick to adapt plays to fit their own context. This adaptation meant setting plays in Russian cities, giving characters Russian names, and instilling a sense of Russian cultural practices. Some of the particularly Russian touches in *Oh, These Times!* are passing references to societal predilections, such as Tattler's drunken coachman, or to Russian items and customs (the stovebench, the icon-lamps, ice-hills at the carnival-like *maslenitsa* celebration, Gallomania). In my comparison of these two plays, I will focus on several structural elements: Catherine's changes to Gellert's characters, her superior handling of plot structure, and her incorporation of specifically Russian concerns.

The plot of Gellert's *The Prayer Sister* concerns marriage negotiations which Mr. Simon is conducting on behalf of his friend Mr. Ferdinand, who would like to marry a young lady named Christianchen. Her mother, Frau Richardinn, is a religious hypocrite and miser who strives to prevent the marriage. In a series of complications, Christianchen's governess Lorchen catches Ferdinand's eye, and they are almost married instead. By play's end, however, Lorchen's unselfish devotion to her mistress has won out, and Ferdinand and Christianchen are happily engaged.

The opening scenes of the two plays are remarkably similar. Catherine's dialog follows Gellert's very closely for the first six scenes of the play, which set up Sanctimonious's stinginess and sanctimony, and expose the basic situation. In Catherine's eighth scene, however, a new character appears (Tattler) and from this point on the two plays begin to diverge.

Whereas Gellert concentrated his vice into one character, Frau Richardinn, Catherine multiplied it by three, creating an impression not of a single idiosyncratic character, but rather of an entire stratum of society, a generation of the foolish and superstitious. Mavra is a much more vivacious and clever foil to Sanctimonious than is Gellert's governess Lorchen; in comparing the two plays in 1905, Prohaska called Lorchen the ideal of German society of the time: the sensitive, sensible and pathetic heroine.[33] Prohaska points out and I agree that Catherine preferred to create a rational servant character with common sense, while keeping the detail of Mavra's education as a contrast to Khristina's ignorance.

Catherine's character names are scarcely related to Gellert's originals. The only similarity is the heroine Christianchen and her Russian counterpart Khristina. Otherwise, Catherine opts strictly for telling names. Gellert's characters remain much more in the realm of verisimilitude with ordinary names such as Ferdinand, Simon, Lorchen, and Frau Richardinn.

The crux of the plot in both plays is the sudden obstacle to the marriage of the young lovers, an obstacle revealed midway through each play's second act. In

---

[33] Prohaska 568.

both plays, an offstage event precipitates this change in the suitor's fortunes. In both, the suitor comes in to report that because of a small slip-up on his part, the engagement is off.

In Gellert's version, Simon reports in II.4 that while he was drinking some coffee that Frau Richardinn poured for him, "she told me a story of a sign that occurred while she was in child bed with Christi. It was impossible to suppress my laughter. [...] While coughing from laughter, [I] threw the cup which landed on the floor" (25). Because of the broken cup, Simon lets out a curse, which greatly angers Frau Richardinn, leading her to break off the courtship. In Catherine's version, the emphasis is on the superstitious story itself, and on the insignificance of this story in comparison to Sanctimonious's explosion of rage. Milksop starts off by declaring "All my hope has vanished! [...] Because of a damned grasshopper!" (26). In itself, this statement is a much better beginning to the scene, setting up a bit of suspense as well as comic incongruity. He tells a much more detailed story than Gellert's Simon does. Where Simon mentions generally that Richardinn was telling "a story of a sign," Catherine's hero Milksop spells out the trifle. The speech gives specificity to the superstitious belief being mocked. It also paints a comic portrait of the three old ladies setting in on the hapless Milksop, accusing the men of being atheists and heathens for not believing a quite fantastical story.

Sanctimonious was explaining that not quite a year before the demise of her spouse, for three days, a grasshopper chattered without ceasing in her wall, and—her rooster laid an egg. Her inevitable conclusion was that her spouse would die, and so, without losing a moment, she ordered him to prepare for death. Hearing all this nonsense, I couldn't hold back, and laughed loudly. Mr. Notshallow, for all his usual sternness, couldn't control himself. He cracked too, and we both laughed aloud. All three old women suddenly got angry. They all began to cross themselves, to spit and puff. They began to cry and scold us in chorus, calling us scoffers and heathens and atheists who don't believe in anything. Sanctimonious and her friend Marvel fell on Mr. Notshallow; Tattler overran me ferociously. Well, the nicest thing she called me was a "stuck-up fool." I wanted to demonstrate to her—in a civil way—that superstition is a vice, that moral law forbids believing in such absurd fables: but she was in a rage and tried to prove that the grasshopper prophesied the death of Mr. Sanctimonious, that it truly happened, and anyone would believe it except for a fool like me. At the same time, Marvel, in a rabid state of rage, was setting in on Mr. Notshallow from the other side. Then your gracious lady, stirred up and panting from wrath, rushed first to one, then to the other, helping these two bad-tempered old women. She supported their "proofs," with words improper for a widow. Finally out of all this commotion, she told us in no uncertain terms that we (that is, both matchmaker and suitor) were unbelievers, lawbreakers, heathens, and were ordered to leave her house. She said that she would never give her granddaughter to such a good-for-nothing young man, and in future we would not be allowed in her home. (26–7)

To modern tastes, neither Gellert nor Catherine realizes the full potential of this scene. In their tasteful neoclassical avoidance of violence, they each place off-stage a scene of great farce. Be that as it may, Catherine's version is much more vivid. Again, the addition of the other two ladies multiplies the humor of the scene. In Gellert, because the crime of cursing seems to be the most reprehensible to Richardinn, the whole conflict is on a much more reasonable, realistic level. Because it is inappropriate to curse in front of a lady, Simon is at fault, and Richardinn's anger does not seem completely unfounded. On the other hand, Milksop is here clearly meant to be a normative figure, representing the audience member who also surely would have laughed at such an outlandish tale of a grasshopper and rooster. Catherine thus steers her audience's sympathy away from Sanctimonious, and emphasizes the ridiculous aspects of the three ladies' quasi-religious beliefs, without ever calling Christianity itself into question.

In Gellert, the result of this falling out is that Simon immediately declares his love for Lorchen, heading the plot in another unexpected direction. The plot will remain centered on Simon's choice between Lorchen and Christianchen, and Richardinn will recede to the background. In Catherine, the event serves to crystallize the rest of the play's action: Mavra must devise a way to get Milksop back in Sanctimonious's good graces, which she will do through appealing to Tattler's greed. Catherine thus maintains Sanctimonious's role as the chief obstacle in the play.

In each play, events in the final scene transpire rapidly, and the plot's loose ends are knit up quickly. In III.11 of *The Prayer Sister*, Lorchen suddenly reveals that she will no longer go through with the plan to marry Simon, that he and Christianchen are meant for each other. Ferdinand quickly swoops in to say that Lorchen will be for him the daughter he never had, and that he will support her. Lorchen has the closing line: "Permit me to accompany you to your bride. The good child is in for a shock."[34]

In III. 6 of *Oh, These Times!*, Tattler (swayed by the flattery and ring Milksop gave her) takes over the action, overpowering even Sanctimonious by insisting that Khristina and Milksop should marry. This penultimate scene has several comic moments, completely absent from the more somber Gellert script. One instance is Tattler's assertion that she herself could fall in love with the handsome young Milksop. Another comic exchange comes when Tattler announces the dowry for Khristina without having consulted Sanctimonious. The stingiest character is outwitted, and will end up losing the most. But Sanctimonious has one final bit of advice: that Milksop should lend out the dowry, so that he can collect interest on it. Even as the play's plot draws to a close with the marriage plans, Sanctimonious is still focused on money, and still manipulative. Like Molière's characters, she has not changed.

---

[34] Gellert, *Christian Fürchtegott Gellert's The Prayer Sister*. Trans. Johanna Setzer, 45.

Whereas in Gellert, the play ends with dialog, Catherine allows Mavra to end the play alone on stage, in a soliloquy that invokes the biblical notion of judging neighbors while not seeing one's own sin: "In the eye of a neighbor, we can see a speck of sawdust, but in our own eye we don't see the plank" (42). Catherine achieves a great deal in this final passage: she brings back the audience's liaison, Mavra, for final comment on these times, while pointing out the need to examine one's own deficiencies. Catherine also brings in a religious reference (Matthew 7:3) without specifically discussing religion.[35] This latter strategy reflects the play's opposition of outwardly-pious, ritualistic religious behavior (which is reprehensible) to good and just living, which for Mavra and Catherine are inextricably tied in with "common sense." In this final passage, religion is associated with reason and self-examination, rather than with external rites. By including this final pronouncement, Catherine elevates the comedy to a commentary on the age, and on her philosophy. Gellert's characters merely exit.

I have compared the apples of Gellert's sentimental comedy and the oranges of Catherine's humorous or laughing satire. Despite the fact that Molière's *Tartuffe* may have inspired both writers, stylistically the plays are quite different. Gellert wrote for an audience who came not to laugh but to appreciate the fine sensibilities of the characters, and to be repulsed by the indiscretions of his Prayer Sister. Catherine employed the tools of satire, to write a laughing comedy that mocked the very vices she wished to eradicate from Russian society.

Fools in the Mirror: *Mrs. Grumbler's Nameday*

"If your face is lopsided, don't blame the mirror."[36] Nikolai Gogol used this proverb to begin his comedy about the power of rumor and intrigue, *The Inspector General* [Revizor, 1836]. Catherine used comedy to hold a mirror up to her people, to expose and therefore correct the problems of her society. In *Mrs. Grumbler's Nameday*, wise persons are those who can truly see themselves. Whereas *Oh, These Times!* and *Mrs. Tattler and her Family* focus respectively on hypocrisy and rumor-mongering, *Mrs. Grumbler* goes even deeper to examine what Catherine saw as the roots of her nation's social problems: blind foolishness and ignorance. *Mrs. Grumbler* was first produced in Catherine's court theatre on 27 April 1772 and later appeared on the public stages in both St. Petersburg and Moscow.[37]

---

[35] The phrase was also a common Russian proverb, noted in the mid-eighteenth century. Paczolay 134.

[36] Gogol 91.

[37] See Annenkov 38. The play was first published in St. Petersburg, probably in 1774 (see Pypin 1: 115 for information on editions).

It was perhaps the Empress herself who wrote the following lines in the first sheet of *All Sorts*, regarding potential readers:

For after today they—it may come to pass—will not only see themselves from without as in a mirror, but also glimpse their inner virtues sketched out on paper. Oh, how gratified must your pride be on this day, when this new means has been devised to mock the faults of others and to admire yourself.[38]

In this passage, the journal's writing is compared to a mirror that helps the readers to see themselves "from without"—a beneficial function. But the mirror, as in Gogol, should also not be blamed. And the reader may still be able to angle the mirror so that his or her own faults are unseen, or reflected onto others.

Because its author was passionately committed to the Enlightenment philosophy of secular rationalism, *Mrs. Grumbler* is, at its heart, a rumination on wisdom. The comic characters are decidedly un-wise, in various ways: they are gossips or debtors or cowards or fops or Francophiles or fools. The wise characters are those who take a measured and practical approach to life. The title character Mrs. Grumbler (Gospozha Vorchalkina) is particularly foolish and extremely susceptible to rumors and gossip. Like the three old women in *Oh, These Times!*, Grumbler continually refers to the contrast between the present day and the era when she was a girl. By portraying Grumbler as a comic character, Catherine reveals the backwardness of this backward-looking approach. Wisdom in the play is not to be found by those who look back to the past or believe rumors; in Catherine's mirror, wise characters live in the present, and can truly see themselves.

The plot of the play hinges, as it does in four of Catherine's five early comedies, on the marriage of a young girl.[39] In this case, Talarikin is courting Khristina, but her mother Mrs. Grumbler refuses to agree to the engagement because Khristina's older sister Olimpiiada should be married first. Two rascals (Spesov and Gerkulov) convince Grumbler that the government will be banning marriage for ten years; their motive is to persuade her to betroth her daughters to them. Other characters include a muddle-headed schemer named Nekopeikov, who continuously reads his plans for improvements; Firliufiushkov, a foppish Francophile with debts he does not intend to pay; Gremukhin, a timid suitor; Dremov, Talarikin's uncle and the play's *raisonneur*; and two practical servants, Praskov'ia and Antip.

Over the course of the play, Catherine examines foolishness in many guises, from an obsession with the past and parental customs, to self-obsession, to the harmfulness of intrigue, to physical abuse. Her primary dramaturgical strategy is

---

[38] Levitt, "Selections from *Odds and Ends*" 11. For original Russian, see Pypin 5: 279. The title *Vsiakaia vsiachina* has been translated in many ways, such as *All Sorts*; Levitt uses *Odds and Ends* in his translation and commentary.

[39] *Prominent Nobleman* is the exception.

the use of exaggerated characters, although metatheatrical scenes also set the stage for her fools.

As in *Oh, These Times!*, the play satirizes older characters (in this case, Grumbler) who insist on the virtues of the past. Cultural theorists Iurii Lotman and Boris Uspenskii argue that Russian culture in the eighteenth century self-consciously defined itself in relation to the past: "The history of Russian culture [...] provides convincing evidence of the culture's clear-cut division into stages that replace one another dynamically. Every new period [...] is oriented toward a decisive break with what preceded it."[40]   Such cultural conflict characterized the eighteenth century in Russia; when Peter the Great ushered in a new era of Westernization, noblemen were forced to shave their beards, and the new city of St. Petersburg was constructed in a European style.   Catherine aligned herself with Peter's progressive approach, and added her own amalgamation of Enlightenment political and social philosophies.   Her reforms touched every aspect of Russian life: education, medicine, law, and literature.   When the play was written in 1772, Catherine had spent the first ten years of her reign actively pursuing changes in Russia's governmental and cultural landscape.   Enthusiastic about bringing progressive Western ideas to Russia, Catherine saw the success of her reign as dependent on breaking away from older ideas and patterns of thought.   Although Catherine made a deliberate effort to preserve and renew Russian cultural pride, like Peter the Great she saw change from the past as a positive and healthy step.

The play argues that the old times so revered by Grumbler were not necessarily the best of times.   Grumbler herself is blind to the possible benefits of reform and change, and clings to older customs even while admitting their negative consequences:

> GRUMBLER.   That's all well, sir: but the trouble is that Olimpushka is my oldest.   I don't want to hurt her feelings, my dear, by giving away the younger sister first.   I know that in the present century they don't follow this example. However, I cling to the old ways, and don't like to spoil the order.   I myself was the fifth daughter of my mother and was forced to wait until all my older sisters got married; what can you do about it?   Seniority demands such order.
> DREMOV.   I'm sure that must have been very boring for you?
> GRUMBLER.   And how to relieve it!   I cried often ... 'they are not marrying me off, they are doing nothing, indeed ....' (71)

Although her personal experience has proven the cruelty and injustice of the practice, she remains inflexible, married to the old ways.

Later, a similar issue arises, again concerning Grumbler's conviction that her daughter Khristina should suffer the same conditions as her mother.   Aghast to find Khristina and Talarikin together, she lectures them on the impropriety of their behavior, contrasting it with her own experience: "My dear departed parents gave

---

[40]   Lotman and Uspenskii 31.

me away in marriage to my dear departed husband, and I never saw him, much less spoke with him, from the moment I was born until I got to the church" (83). She offers no evidence that this arrangement was pleasant; her logic is again that the practice is appropriate because that is how it was done in her day.

Grumbler's affection for her own past and upbringing is even shown to be potentially dangerous. When the news comes that Khristina has fallen ill, Grumbler is immediately skeptical about the usefulness of doctors:

> GRUMBLER. Here again! what fabrications you have nowadays. As if one can keep off death when it comes. No, my dear fellow, it is not obedient to physicians. When the hour of the will of God comes, then all the doctors cannot help. It's better to give oneself up to his will, and never undergo medical treatment: I myself haven't used medicines since birth, and I indeed am living.
>
> DREMOV. Physicians and doctors cannot always save one from death, perhaps because they are human. It's always unnecessary to take medicines unnecessarily; however it is necessary not to forget the just proverb: rely on God, but don't make a mistake yourself ... in some cases physicians and doctors are essential. (85)

Grumbler's logic, that she herself never used a doctor, epitomizes the conservative, fearful approach that most aggravated Catherine. The view that the past is always better was anathema to an Empress who sought progressive reforms in law, education, and medicine.[41] On several occasions, she had struggled to educate an ignorant populace about modern medical advances. In 1768, Catherine supported a smallpox vaccination campaign, and even volunteered to be immunized herself. In 1770–72, the plague epidemic led to incidents of mass hysteria and superstitious suspicions. What she may have seen as her own virtues—practicality, courage, logic—were demonstrated in her dealings with these medical crises. Such virtues are absent in the characterization of Grumbler.

In presenting such stubborn behavior, Catherine mirrors the divided nature of Russian society in her historical moment. It is no wonder then that Grumbler's conservatism, repeatedly emphasized as a principal example of her essential foolishness, forms the backbone of the play. Grumbler's obsession with the past is even related to the play's title. The nameday celebration is an annual event, a tradition; her character clearly has respect for established customs. Yet the yearly celebration of a nameday carries the connotation of age, which in turn reminds Grumbler of her status as one of the older generation. While on the surface her complaints about "the times" may seem to be merely character detail, her resistance to change symbolizes the opposition to Catherine's political reforms in the early part of her reign.

---

[41] Where her own health was concerned, however, the Empress often preferred more old-fashioned remedies, and manifested a distrust for physicians (See Alexander, *Catherine the Great: Life and Legend* 144).

Generational conflict in the play is related to the notion of parental impact, often presented in a negative light. Grumbler, for example, is a parent whose decisions (and caprices) affect her children's lives. In the play's first act, Catherine introduces the audience to each of the major characters. The Francophile Firliufiushkov is the first character to refer to his father's actions to justify his own:

> Never, *mon coeur,* never. I didn't pay, am not paying and never intend to pay. [...] *D'ailleurs* in our family paying debts is never the custom. In this I follow the laudable example of my father. He never paid anyone; and died like that. (57)

In the next scene, Firliufiushkov shares the stage with Nekopeikov, who also lacks wisdom in many ways, but particularly flaunts his ignorance in a discussion of books.

> But here, sir, is how it is! I, speaking just between us, was ruined [in trading], for this reason: that I never liked either writing or notes; and I never kept books at all. And why have them? Even our fathers lived and traded without them. My father didn't have them either in his time, and he died with honor, it's true it was in prison [...] . (59)[42]

The sins of the fathers recur in the actions of the sons. Both men are blind to their fathers' mistakes. Catherine here creates another echo of her theme: the foolishness of slavish devotion and respect for the past, regardless of consequence.

Parental influence reappears in other ways. Spesov's defining characteristic is his repeated and prideful invocation of his status as a nobleman. Throughout the play, he emphasizes the nobility of his father and grandfather: "remember me, and who my father was" (77). On a more positive note, Dremov defends his own grandfather as a nobleman who earned his title through service. As the play concludes, Gremukhin reveals his plan to travel to visit his sickly father; his filial devotion, in contrast to that of the more comic characters, is a positive virtue.

The play never reveals the cause of the death of Grumbler's husband, so there is no way to assess his impact on the lives of the two daughters. Unlike *Oh, These Times!*, in which Khristina's foolishness and ignorance are blamed on how she was raised by Sanctimonious, in this play there is no direct correlation to be made between upbringing and character. Because the play presents two contrasting sisters, one shallow and flippant, the other solid and sensible, neither heredity nor environment can be impugned. Whereas Khristina in *Oh, These Times!* was a

---

[42] Arthur Coleman finds Catherine's characterization of Nekopeikov's ignorance to be inconsistent with his pedantry: "He certainly belongs to the class of those shallow professional wiseacres who frequented the salons of *les précieuses* and pretended to read every book that came out. Thus Catherine's attempt to make of him a Russian of the type which did not believe in learning results only in distortion" (62). Nekopeikov, however, seems to be referring to book-keeping rather than literature.

product of her circumstances, Khristina in *Mrs. Grumbler* is able to be wise in the midst of fools. Although many other of Catherine's comedies espouse the importance of a nurturing environment in the creation of a solid citizen, *Mrs. Grumbler* moves beyond the idea of upbringing and education as determinants of character, to one of the more radical ideas of Enlightenment thought: that people are responsible for their own wisdom. Catherine's two servant characters, Praskov'ia and Antip, are two of the play's wisest persons, a dozen years before Beaumarchais's *The Marriage of Figaro* (1784).

Errors, however, are much more entertaining onstage than wisdom. *Mrs. Grumbler* features a large and varied assortment of rascals and idiots; their common trait is self-obsession without self-knowledge. The play criticizes those characters unable to see their own faults, and often uses comic irony to reveal their blindness. Gerkulov, one of the play's biggest scoundrels, complains about the faults of Dremov, Firliufiushkov, and Talarikin, respectively:

> To tell the truth, I don't like them either. They like to show off their intelligence a lot. They are opposed to everything, they scorn everyone, one of them is a chatterbox, the other is a gambler, the third is a fool; but they do not cast a glance at themselves. In a word, these people are not our sort .... (66)

Gerkulov does exactly what he claims to dislike; he opposes and scorns everything and everyone. When a fool calls someone a fool, he grows even more foolish in the eyes of the audience. Gerkulov's comment ("they do not cast a glance at themselves") is aimed at the others, but applies perfectly to his inability to recognize his own foolishness. From Catherine's perspective, such fools are both laughable and dangerous because they do not see themselves.

Another example of such lack of sight is Olimpiiada's commentary on Firliufiushkov: "how wise he is!," she declares (92). At this point in the play the audience has learned so much about his lack of wisdom that her judgment makes her laughable. She also derides Spesov's snobbishness: "Akh! And how funny Spesov and the others are, giving themselves airs ... I can't recall them without laughing ... ha! ha! ha!" (92). By giving this line of dialog to a character who has done nothing since Act I but preen and put on airs, Catherine displays Olimpiiada's own blindness, and encourages the audience to laugh at this character who is laughing at others.

In *Inspector General*, the most famous of all nineteenth-century Russian comedies, Gogol would put a different twist on the matter by having his Mayor turn to the audience and say, "What are *you* laughing at? You are laughing at yourselves!"[43] Although Catherine does not address her audience directly, her implication is similar: to avoid being laughed at, be aware of your own shortcomings. The down-to-earth servant character Praskov'ia finally enlightens

---

[43] Gogol 157.

Nekopeikov, who throughout the play is unaware that his hare-brained schemes are boring and ridiculous to others:

> Will you play the fool long? Do you really not see that everyone abhors you, everyone is bored by you, runs from you, no one listens to your writing? And indeed who can listen to such nonsense without falling asleep? And if some order you to read, that's only in order to make a fool of you. (105)[44]

There is also another idea imbedded in the play's characterization of its fools: the fools are those who criticize others. Here Catherine as monarch may have been subtly suggesting a code of discretion and silence for her courtly and public audiences.

Gossip breaks the code of silence, and can have serious consequences. Like *Oh, These Times!*, this play examines the harmfulness of rumors and intrigue. Gullibility is Grumbler's central weakness, and it enables the principal plotline (the false tale of the ten-year prohibition on marriage). Thus, believing or spreading gossip is not only shown as an idle pastime, but as a direct inhibitor of wisdom. Because Grumbler believes the lies of Spesov and Gerkulov, her behavior becomes extreme and rash—the opposite of wise:

> GREMUKHIN. These gentlemen (*indicates Spesov and Dremov*) want to convince us that the rumor in the air is true, that soon there will be a prohibition to marry and the prohibition will last for an entire ten years. What would happen, if no one were to marry for ten years?
> GRUMBLER. Akh! what disorder this will be! What, do they really want to destroy the human race? Oh! Oh! would God stand for this!
> DREMOV. Lies! Impossible nonsense! Stupid and impossible ravings! (72)

Dremov performs the role of *raisonneur*, quickly assessing the validity of the rumor and denouncing its credibility. In response, Grumbler attacks him as someone who believes nothing. Although Catherine rarely addresses the issue of religious belief in her plays directly, the contrast between Grumbler's appeal to God and Dremov's logical approach implies the author's preference for a more secular life philosophy. Dremov is also quick to identify the rumor's instigator as a fool, reinforcing the idea that the wise person neither spreads nor believes rumors.

> GRUMBLER. It's so, my dear fellow, it's so. You don't believe in anything. You'll start fighting about everything.

---

[44] Berkov argues that Nekopeikov is based on the Scottish-trained law professor S. E. Desnitskii, who presented Catherine with his own plan for legislative reform in Russia. According to Berkov, Catherine saw Desnitskii's proposal as a criticism of her own *Great Instruction* and set about caricaturing him in the comedy (*Istoriia russkoi* 146–47).

DREMOV. At least about this; some fool thought up this rumor.

GERKULOV. No, sir, not a fool; everyone, everyone is saying it.

SPESOV. Even I heard it.

NEKOPEIKOV. And I heard about it from them.

GRUMBLER. So, how can I not believe it? Everyone's saying so. Oi! Oi! Oi! What times! What astonishing things are happening today! Why did we poor ones live to see this! (72)

Again, Grumbler appeals to a sense of a bygone era in which everything was better; her hysteria about the present is fed by her over-attachment to the past.

This rumor of the ten-year prohibition is the crux of the play; spreading and believing in rumors are among the comedy's principal vices. Praskov'ia, a servant with more innate wisdom than most of those around her, describes the effects of gossip: "Every rumor is like a snowball, the further it rolls, the more it increases: and finally, having disintegrated, it disappears, as if nothing ever happened" (104). P. K. Shchebal'skii notes how frequently cryptic and disturbing rumors appear in the plots of the five Iaroslavl plays.[45] Catherine's repeated indictment of rumor-mongers throughout her early comedies is not surprising, given the political circumstances in that year. The years just before the composition of the play were fraught with other tensions for Catherine's administration. The plague epidemic that swept southern Russia from 1770–72 made it to Moscow in August of 1771. The Russo-Turkish War of 1768–74 had begun to put a strain on Russian citizens, who experienced raises in the poll-tax and in the conscription levy. Isabel de Madariaga comments that "it is against this background of increasing social tension that the great plague riots of autumn 1771 in Moscow must be seen."[46]

The appearance of several pretenders to the throne was also a troublesome problem for Catherine. Rumors about their claims and supporters were rampant during her early reign. Although the Pugachev Rebellion did not occur until 1774, there had been a series of other pretenders (claiming to be Peter III) between 1764 and 1772.[47] One in particular, F. I. Bogomolov, had appeared in March 1772, but was arrested later that year. Shchebal'skii notes that Catherine must have seen the problem of false rumors as quite serious. Writing in 1910, he asserted that the readiness to believe such negative rumors was prevalent in Catherine's time: "this trait characterized Russian society throughout the eighteenth century and is not completely exterminated still today."[48] Comedy became a means to address a heavy matter in a light manner.

Catherine clearly indicts those characters who are backward-looking, narcissistic, or gullible. But one moment in the play is more ambiguous: the scene in which Gerkulov beats Firliufiushkov with a cane after finding out that he refuses

---

[45] Shchebal'skii, "'O vremia!'" 133.

[46] Madariaga, *Russia in the Age* 13.

[47] Madariaga, *Russia in the Age* 240.

[48] Shchebal'skii, "'O vremia!'" 133–34.

to pay his debt. It is unclear whether either of the characters is meant to draw on the audience's sympathy. The encounter, which takes place toward the end of Act IV, combines two storylines: not only is Firliufiushkov in debt to Gerkulov, but they are also rivals for the hand of Khristina. By writing a scene in which the two men come into conflict over these issues, Catherine connects the play's typical neoclassical plot concern (marrying off a young girl) to its satirical targets: society's fools.

> GERKULOV. [...] I don't want to let you out of my sight—either the money, or this cane ... *(holds the cane)*
> FIRLIUFIUSHKOV. You'll really start a duel for such a trifle? Let me go.
> GERKULOV. You'll see how I'll begin to pay your debt myself! *(beats him with the cane and keeps talking)* Don't deceive honest people; hold to the word you give; don't allow people to treat you as an idler; here ... they beat rogues, they beat deceivers, they beat idlers, swindlers ....
> FIRLIUFIUSHKOV. *(The whole time he cries Oi! Oi! Oi! and finally falls, but Gerkulov, having beaten him as much as he wanted and having broken his cane, exits. Firliufiushkov, lying on the ground)* Oi! Oi! Help! Help! They are beating me to death, they are killing me. *(Antip and Praskov'ia come running to his cry.)* (96)

The scene can certainly be played completely farcically: the repetition of Firliufiushkov's cries throughout his beating can be comic, as can the breaking of the cane. But the ferocity of Gerkulov's lines, combined with the fact that he himself is a rogue and a swindler, might also create a sense of injustice and harshness.

What did Catherine have in mind by including an onstage beating? Neoclassical plays, comic or tragic, typically do not present violence in view of the audience. Catherine may have been thinking instead of the comic duels in such Shakespearean plays as *Twelfth Night*, which she might have read in German translation by Wieland.[49] The beating of servants is mentioned frequently in many of Catherine's comedies (as when Sanctimonious has her servant beaten for interrupting her prayers); this cruelty, however, is always only alluded to or carried out as an offstage event. Early in *Mrs. Grumbler*, the servant Antip argues that beating is not useful as a corrective strategy: "As if you could change human behavior with blows!" (54).

---

[49] Christoph Martin Wieland's translation of twenty-two Shakespearean plays were published between 1762 and 1766, and thus Catherine may have read them or become acquainted with their contents. Wieland, however, did not translate *Love's Labors Lost* or *The Merry Wives of Windsor*, two other comedies with humorous fighting scenes. Catherine would not have been able to read these in German until the publication of Eschenburg's complete German translation in 1775–82; in 1786, Catherine wrote her own version of *Merry Wives*, entitled *This 'tis to Have Linen and Buck-Baskets*.

In this scene, however, a nobleman beats another nobleman, something that was apparently shocking to audiences in Catherine's day. In her response to Novikov's letter addressed to the unknown author of *Oh, These Times!*, Catherine humbly accepts thanks for Novikov's praise of her first comedy. Although Novikov's letter had not mentioned *Mrs. Grumbler*, Catherine's reply addresses concerns about the beating scene:

> And thus leaving this, allow me to include several notes on the comedy created not long ago by me, called *Mrs. Grumbler's Nameday*. It has come to me that several critics regard it as indecent, that *Mr. Firlifiushkov* (sic) is punished with a cane for unashamedly not keeping his word. They say, "how is it that a nobleman was beaten with a cane for a dishonorable deed?" I will not begin to cite here whether such actions have happened somewhere or not: below I want to excuse the behavior of *Mr. Gerkulov*. He really is cruel in ordinary society. Yet I can easily justify myself, by referring to the Code. In it, the gentlemen critics will find what people are subjected to for not keeping one's word and for idleness.[50]

Catherine's rhetorical strategy, as the anonymous author of new comedies, is to defend her choices on the grounds of both realistic action (such actions have happened before) and legality (the Code).[51]

Catherine justifies the scene's inclusion by focusing on the fact that the man being beaten is a fool. His behavior has broken the rules of gentlemanly decency, just as the cane is broken on his back. Already portrayed as a hyperbolically ignorant and pretentious character, Firliufiushkov is in little danger of drawing sympathy. The subtle implication for the play's court audience, however, is that the nobility should control its behavior or risk public humiliation and harm. By referring to a legal code in the letter, Catherine invokes authority for her dramaturgical choice.

Whether Catherine intended the beating of Firliufiushkov to be laughable or reprehensible, it is an example of extreme behavior (violence) prompted by a violation of societal norms (debts). Each is a fool in his own way, and each is punished. Firliufiushkov leaves the play, disgraced, in Act IV. In V.8, Grumbler forbids both men, along with Spesov, to set foot in her house. Although she remains a comic character until the end, as soon as she rids her house of the three clowns, she makes the wise decision of allowing Khristina to marry Talarikin, thus finally resolving the play's marriage plot.

Catherine satirizes her society's fools in many ways throughout the comedy— by depicting their foolish actions, by giving them ridiculous and un-self-conscious dialog, by contrasting their behavior with sensible servants and siblings. One final indirect method of critiquing her fools is the technique of metatheatre, or theatre that comments on itself.

---

[50] Quoted in Longinov, *Novikov* Appendix 1: 03 (sic).

[51] Probably a reference to the 1649 *Ulozhenie*, or Muscovite Law Code.

Although the exact order of composition of Catherine's first five comedies is not known, there are several connections between *Oh, These Times!* and *Mrs. Grumbler*. For instance, Catherine discusses *Mrs. Grumbler* in her above-mentioned letter to Novikov thanking him for his praise of *Oh, These Times!* There are also several metatheatrical allusions in *Mrs. Grumbler* to characters in *Oh, These Times!* In the final act, for example, as preparations for Khristina's dowry are finally underway, Olimpiiada comments to her mother about Sanctimonious, the principal comic lead in *Oh, These Times!*, and Tattler, her gossiping side-kick:

> Madam matushka, seek advice about this from your friends. Not long ago, Mrs. Sanctimonious gave away her granddaughter's hand. Talk with her and with Mrs. Tattler; they'll advise you what to give. But I'd wish at least that my sister would have a dowry no less than that of Mrs. Sanctimonious's granddaughter. (112)

By referring directly to characters and events in *Oh, These Times!* as part of her world, Olimpiiada implies a connection between the two plays, and indeed links Grumbler to the vices of her cohorts in the other play.

Elsewhere in *Mrs. Grumbler*, however, Catherine employs a more sophisticated use of metatheatrical commentary, by having her characters argue about drama in general, using *Oh, These Times!* as an example. Whereas before Olimpiiada had referred to the women in *Oh, These Times!* as "real" acquaintances, in this instance some of the onstage characters in *Mrs. Grumbler* (the "outer" play) refer to the characters in *Oh, These Times!* Other "outer" characters argue that those "inner" characters are fictional yet drawn from reality. The ambiguity here is the point: by alluding to several levels of reality at once, Catherine playfully theatricalizes the issue of fiction versus life.

On Grumbler's first entrance in I.7, she immediately begins to grumble about a new comedy in which two of her relatives are mocked and ridiculed. In their discussion of this comedy, the various characters reveal their disparate perspectives on one of the key literary debates of this era: the *na litso* controversy regarding the proper use of satire. In this play, Talarikin adopts Catherine's perspective, defending the use of comedy to portray general vice:

> If you're talking about the new comedy, then I can tell you about it. I was there when they performed it. We laughed a lot, because of the amusing characters represented in it. But I don't know whether someone was alluded to in it. The comedy's creator wanted to portray three vices on the stage, and did so in the form of three women. One was miserly, the other was an eccentric gossip, and the third was superstitious. (62)

To Talarikin, the laughter was at the expense of the characters' flaws, which were representative of overall societal problems. According to Catherine's own dramatic theory, the depiction of such flaws is the function of comedy, which "presents a person with more faults than is usual."[52]

Besides articulating Catherine's viewpoint, Talarikin's description of the comedy is a metatheatrical reference to *Oh, These Times!* His comment creates a metatheatrical moment: a character in *Mrs. Grumbler* (the outer play) is referring to characters in *Oh, These Times!* (the inner play). The author of the inner play was Catherine the Great; she is not, however, mentioned by name in the outer play, but is referred to as *sochinitel'* (the male-designated noun meaning creator). The author of the outer play was also Catherine the Great, but both the production and subsequent publication were anonymous. Since Catherine wrote both plays, the audience would have experienced enjoyment on several levels. If it was widely known that Catherine was their author, this teasing mention of the *sochinitel'* would have emphasized Catherine's influence without stating it directly. In addition, there is the playful and ironic fun of having characters in a fictional play argue about the difference between real life and fiction. Overall, Catherine's use of this metatheatrical discussion of her first play—to have one of the play's sensible characters defend her position and refer to one of her other works in doing so—reinforces her own argument about satire on general vices.

Firliufiushkov presents the other side of the coin. As a Russian version of a *petit-maître*, he is obsessed with the changeable and superficial aspects of society life. Thus, he is quick to point out his own in-the-know status by recognizing the same real-life persons that Grumbler does. When she complains that the comedy portrayed two of her relatives, Firliufiushkov agrees that they were characterized "very vividly, *parbleu!* Very vividly. I saw the comedy and they are portrayed to the letter. How funny it was!" (62). Because the more comical characters, Grumbler and Firliufiushkov, are the ones who think they recognize their friends, their gossip is a reflection on their own maliciousness and rumor-mongering, rather than on the comedy itself.

Dremov's commentary points out how the reactions to the comedy reinforce the outer play's main theme: the foolishness of those who cannot see themselves.

But, how does one take it into one's head to present on the stage a ridiculous fool, who then will recognize himself in this mirror? I think that first he should admit that he is similar to the model.... However, I would bet that although there are fools in the world, out of self-love no one will see it as referring to himself, but will recognize someone else. (63)

---

[52] Drizen, "Imperatritsa Ekaterina II" 154. Drizen quotes from Catherine's own unpublished notes, written in Russian and French. They can be found in the collection of Catherine's writing in the Russian State Archive of Early Acts [Rossisskii gosudarstvennyi arkhiv drevnikh aktov (RGADA, formerly TsGADA)] in Moscow (fond 10, opis 1, dela 320–21; opis 2, dela 227).

This self-love is the vice at the play's core, the central problem that must be remedied.

Although Dremov is the play's *raisonneur*, his remarks on censorship do not necessarily reflect the Empress's own viewpoint.   When Grumbler and Firliufiushkov insist that they know the real people upon whom the comedy's characters are modeled, Dremov comments that, "It seems to me that if there are speeches that disturb someone, then they shouldn't be allowed to be performed" (62).   Literary censorship in Russia in the 1770s was not yet as systematic or pervasive as in later decades.   Catherine's own *Great Instruction* promoted freedom of expression for writers, and the principal censors were the Russian Academy of Sciences and the Church, each overseeing its own presses. Catherine herself was the "prime censor."[53]   In 1783, private presses were permitted and placed under police censorship. Gary Marker argues that Catherine's censorship of printed material was mild throughout the 1770s, despite the fact that "absolutism was, after all, still in effect, and no one questioned the empress's right to ban a book."[54] Isabel de Madariaga calls the time of the composition of *Mrs. Grumbler* in 1772 an "exceptionally free period" in which "writers of various kinds were allowed to express daring thoughts."[55]

Theatre censorship was similarly liberal in 1772.   The government administered Court and public theatres in St. Petersburg and Moscow. After the 1783 creation of the Administration of Imperial Theatres, the police supervised subject matter. In general, the 1770s seems to have been a period relatively free of governmental intervention.

> The theatre was a tool [Catherine] herself used very extensively, and it is therefore reasonable to assume that she appreciated its value in influencing public opinion. Consequently, as in the literary sphere, she could be expected to foster its development by granting it a relatively high degree of freedom, provided she could supervise its use.[56]

Catherine herself became more restrictive in the 1790s as she changed "from an enlightened to a frightened despot."[57] More severe forms of theatre censorship became common practice in the nineteenth century, greatly limiting the freedom of writers and theatre companies.

Dremov's comment that the offensive sections should not be performed is, however, difficult to reconcile with the climate of freedom in 1772. On the one hand, if his remarks mean that a work should be censored if anyone takes offense,

---

[53] See Ruud.

[54] Marker 214.

[55] Madariaga, *Russia in the Age* 334.

[56] Papmehl 105.   Welsh points out several examples of Catherine's personal prevention of a script's performance but his evidence is inconclusive (29).

[57] Welsh 29.

it is hard to see how the playwright Catherine could approve of this drastic curtailment of authorial license. Perhaps the speech is aimed more at would-be authors in the audience, a gentle reminder from the Sovereign that deliberate and pointed libel is intolerable according to Catherine's own preference for *na porok* satire. In general, Dremov's remark supports the Enlightenment ideal of authority-derived wisdom that permeates the play: wise writers will not need to be censored, as their work will offend no one.

Talarikin echoes Catherine's own sentiments about the purpose of satire and comedy as corrective forces:

> Why talk about this? A comedy presents foolish manners, and mocks those who deserve laughter, but by no means personally harms anyone. Thus, if I were to notice myself represented in it, and were to learn through it that there is something funny about me, then I would try to correct and conquer my vices. I would not be angry; on the contrary, I would consider myself obliged to the author. (63)

Talarikin's comments are particularly appropriate for Firliufiushkov. Metatheatricality brings humor when Firliufiushkov predicts his own appearance as a comic character: "I see how they'll force me onto the stage as well.... But if that happens, then *morbleu! ma foi! (stamps his foot)* everyone will catch it ... I ... I *(starts for his sword)*, I'll make a formal petition!" (62). Catherine's use of metatheatrical technique again reinforces the theme of fools who do not see themselves. Firliufiushkov is blind to what the audience sees: that he has already been made into a comic character. The comic irony is heightened by his pretentiousness and braggadocio, as the audience laughs at a character who fears being made into a character in a play.

By play's end, most of the play's principal fools have been banished. One remains: the schemer Nekopeikov. Although Grumbler is ready to banish him as well, Praskov'ia argues for leniency:

> Don't drive him out completely, madam; when your fool Stepanida dies, then he will come in handy, and in place of her stories, he can read his schemes.[58] Indeed one can't live without a fool in the house. (113)

Praskov'ia also has the play's concluding speech, and her voice sounds uncannily like Catherine's: "The fools and their vices are driven away and punished, but the virtue is rewarded—that pleases me" (114). In her own notes on dramaturgical theory, Catherine wrote that "Comedy must be amusing, but not injurious, have mockeries but not insults; it allows salt, but not gall and vinegar."[59] Whether her

---

[58] Stepanida, Grumbler's fool, never appears onstage, but her offstage antics are compared several times to the ridiculous actions of the other characters (for example scene I.8).

[59] Quoted in Drizen, "Imperatritsa Ekaterina II" 154.

medium was her satirical periodical or the stage, her desire was unchanging in the early part of her reign. Although Grumbler planned to keep one or two of hers, Catherine worked to rid her house of fools, so that she could have the last laugh.

Mrs. Tattler and her Family

The short one-act comedy *Mrs. Tattler and her Family* continues the comic world of both *Oh, These Times!* and *Mrs. Grumbler*. Here, the central character Mrs. Tattler (familiar from *Oh, These Times!* as one of Sanctimonious's cronies) has her own problem: a hopelessly childish unmarried daughter (known simply as Doch' (meaning Daughter)). Tattler, however, fails to acknowledge her own daughter's shortcomings, preferring to heap criticisms on her daughter-in-law (Snokha).[60] Catherine creates a parallel between Tattler's inability to recognize the daughter-in-law's quality and the main crux of the plot: a suitor's confusion between the daughter and daughter-in-law.

Halfway through the sixteen-scene play, when the suitor Tratov is left alone with Snokha, we realize (although the characters do not) that he has made a mistake, assuming that she is the unmarried daughter. Scene twelve contains the climactic moment, when Tratov takes Snokha's hand and she, horrified, explains that she is already married. In the play's remaining scenes, Tattler angrily blames everyone for this calamity.

Catherine deftly employs different shades of comic irony throughout the short piece. The audience delights in knowing that Tratov's hopes for Snokha's hand are misdirected; he is portrayed as such a sincere and earnest young man, however, that his situation is also pitiable. In contrast, Catherine uses comic irony to great humorous effect in scene eleven, as the ridiculous Daughter prepares for a suitor that the audience knows is not meant for her. When the serving girl Mar'ia and Snokha counsel Daughter to extend her hand willingly to her suitor, she replies:

> DAUGHTER. Good, good, I know now. But ... if he begins to ask me for my foot instead of my hand, should I extend it?
> MAR'IA. What nonsense! What is it about?
> DAUGHTER. Indeed the hand and the foot are equal: you told me that the glove and the shoe are made from the same leather.
> MAR'IA. How long will you be so muddle-headed? (201)

When Mar'ia lays the blame on Tattler's unceasing pummeling of her daughter's head for making her "half-brained," Daughter insipidly replies "Half-brained! ... Hee! hee! hee! However I have a suitor; and you have none.... Hee! hee! hee!" (202).

60　Since Daughter-in-Law is an unwieldy name in English, I will keep the Russian name Snokha.

Besides her mistreatment of her daughter, Tattler has an array of other vices that are revealed in the play's first scenes. She is jealous of Snokha, forcing her to bend to capricious whims. She is cruel to the servant Prokofii. She gullibly believes rumors proffered by the merchant woman Terent'eva. She is condescending to her husband, whose comic characteristic is his strong propensity to sleep.

As we see in several other early comedies by Catherine, a strong-minded female keeps an entire household under her thumb, to its detriment. Although Tattler is not a widow like Sanctimonious, her husband is an ineffectual sleepwalker, who isn't even listening as Tratov's mistake is revealed. He and his daughter are simpletons; they leave the play without realizing the impact of the events that have unfolded: "Papa, lookie, I have a new little dollie" (206). Their ignorance is as culpable as Tattler's fierce tyranny.

Although its plot turns on a suitor's proposal, the play is unique in lacking a typical comic resolution: there is no one for Tratov to marry. The suitor leaves unfulfilled, and there is little indication that Snokha's situation will change, surrounded as she is by tyranny and sleepwalking. There is no one for Daughter to marry either, so in that sense the antagonist (Tattler) is foiled.

Mrs. Tattler and her Family has less direct political commentary than other comedies Catherine wrote in 1772, but it may have more direct autobiographical content. The constant refrain of Tattler, like Sanctimonious and Grumbler in the other plays, is that times are not as they once were. But this familiar theme of clinging to old-fashioned behavior is made more complex by the sub-theme of the elder's jealousy. In this play, Mrs. Tattler's daughter-in-law Snokha represents the threat of youth; her marriage to the Son and her motherhood are an affront to the elderly woman, who controls Snokha's actions and appearance. Many aspects of Catherine's life as the wife of Grand Duke Peter were similarly controlled by her own mother-in-law figure, the Empress Elizabeth (actually Peter's aunt). At the birth of Catherine's son Paul in 1754, Elizabeth even took the child into her own custody immediately. Also, Catherine took her first extra-marital lover, Sergei Saltykov (possibly the father of Paul), at age twenty-three, perhaps explaining the presence in the play of the suitor Tratov who bears such devotion to the married Snokha. This close autobiographical connection may explain the play's unusually unresolved ending—Snokha, with only the help of a clever serving girl, could hardly be expected to change her situation as Catherine did, when she seized the throne with the help of another lover, the guardsman Grigorii Orlov.

The Questioner

Written in 1772, *The Questioner* was not published until 1786 in Dashkova's *Russian Theatre*. Essentially a one-joke comedy, it centers on the annoying central character, Vestoliub (News-Lover), who is a man of a thousand questions. Like the other comedies, it still features a young woman (once again named Khristina) whose marriage is in danger of being thwarted, in this case by her father's preference for the wealthy Vestoliub, the Questioner of the title. The play also features a clever servant (once again a Mavra), who helps to defeat Vestoliub's suit by alleging his affections for Marem'iana, Khristina's aunt. Simple as the short play is, there are some amusing moments, such as the father's statement of metatheatrical disbelief: "This is the kind of thing they talk about in comedies, but nowhere else" (242). Almost every line of Vestoliub's dialog ends in a question mark; a highlight of the play is scene six, in which Mavra torments Vestoliub by answering his questions with more questions, prompting him to protest, "What, my dear, don't you have strange questions today?" (237). Marem'iana is also a source of humor, by gullibly believing that she is the object of Vestoliub's affection and failing to recognize her own age.

The Questioner Vestoliub proves the fool in the end; through over-confidence, he loses Khristina. Although it has only sixteen scenes, the play resolves with three potential marriages: Khristina will wed her man of choice, Kraftin; Vestoliub must either wed Marem'iana or pay the enormous fee of ten thousand rubles; finally, Mavra indicates that she will wed Egor, who collaborated with her throughout the play in helping Khristina and Kraftin and thwarting Vestoliub.

The play's single parent, Vzdornoi, is not very culpable, nor is he very wise; he is matter-of-factly concerned with finding a wealthy match for his daughter. Vestoliub and Marem'iana represent the play's principal vice (lack of self-awareness), but they are hardly the cruel antagonists found in other plays. Nor does the play raise any particularly Russian social or political concerns—one could argue that the play's point is that it's harmful to ask too many questions, but it is unlikely that this was Catherine's veiled message to her subjects.

To find the play's moral center, we must turn to the two servants, Mavra and Egor, who effect the union of the two families they serve as they pursue their own union. When the two are explaining their system of coded information-sharing, Egor jokes that, "Indeed, madam, not even a creator of a comedy makes such complex inventions as an agile servant when he truly wants to serve his master" (230). Once again, Catherine assumes a mask of modesty to gently poke fun at her own writing; at the same time, she also compares herself to the servants, who are the play's most intelligent and personable characters. The conclusion, with their betrothal, hits a happier note than the conclusion of *Mrs. Tattler and her Family*.

Babblers and Dabblers: *A Prominent Nobleman's Entrance Hall*

"In any society, language, culture, and the nation make up a three-legged stool, ready to topple if just one leg is removed."[61] Although this formulation by Albert

---

61   Schütz 339.

Schütz was intended to describe the tightly-knit relationship of language, culture, and nation in my own current home—the former kingdom of Hawai'i—it can be easily applied to the emerging Russian cultural identity in the eighteenth century. With *A Prominent Nobleman's Entrance Hall*, Catherine made a comedy out of the serious issue of how language defined Russia's identity in the eighteenth century.

In the short play, nine men and women descend upon the foyer of the nobleman Khrisanf's house, but only encounter his servants and assistants. Most of the characters are Russians, but three of the "locusts" (as the servant Mikhaila calls the petitioners) are foreign: a German, a Frenchman, and a Turk. In *Prominent Nobleman*, language is equated primarily with cultural identity, which is in turn equated with power. Catherine, who had herself grown up speaking German and French, wrote a play in which command of Russian is key to the access of power. The foreigners, who comically use and abuse Russian, are the least able to plead their cases to Khrisanf. These three foreigners are presented as dabblers: hacks with no real contributions to make, only greedy favors to ask of the powerful but invisible Prominent Nobleman (who may be seen as a Catherine figure). The three men are also babblers: possessing varying skills at speaking the dominant language of the play, they nevertheless chatter incessantly at Khrisanf's representative, Faktotov. Their towering babel creates a cacophonous nonsense that undermines their status and points to the emptiness of their quests.

This one-act comedy was first presented in the court theatre on 18 September, 1772, but was not published until 1786 (in Dashkova's *Russian Theatre*). The nine babblers and dabblers of *Prominent Nobleman* have various needs. The Russian women Pretantena, Meremida, and Vypivaikova want, respectively, a widow's compensation, entry into a nunnery, and permission to live in an almshouse (despite her fortune). As for the Russian men, Urtelov is a gossip who wants to ingratiate himself with the Nobleman; Perilov is in love with a married woman; Tefkin wants to discuss his court cases. As a result, the play has no character to fulfill the typical neoclassical role of the confidant or reasonable man; the only normative Russian characters are the servants and Faktotov, yet they are mere middlemen, not wise voices of enlightened sentiment.

The play's structure is also unique in the absence of its titular nobleman. David Welsh asserts in his study of Russian comedy that Khrisanf the boyar is absent because his presence as a high-ranking character would have violated the neoclassical ideal for comedy as a middle-class genre (88). Khrisanf's disinterest in the petitioners comically reinforces their powerlessness, but his ultimate and total absence also creates an aura of both power and mystery—nearly two hundred years before Godot.

In this play, Catherine portrays three distinctly non-Russian characters, whose nationalities are significant to the context of the Russo-Turkish War, which had begun in late 1768 and did not end until mid-1774. There is no doubt therefore that the war would have been pressing on the minds of the author and her audience when the play was performed in 1772. How does the babble of these three foreign characters reinforce the Empress's goal of a proud Russian cultural identity?

During the earlier Seven Years' War (1756–63), Russia had fought against Prussia, with France and Austria as Russian allies. But when Peter III acceded to the throne in 1762, he made peace with Prussia, and Catherine signed a Prussian alliance in 1764. This cooperation was in part due to the countries' joint interest in the partition of Poland. Prussia had also consented to the "Turkish clause," meaning it agreed to provide support on the occasion of an Ottoman attack. Although Prussia did not actively participate in the Turkish war, Frederick II did in fact pay annual subsidies to Russia over the course of the Turkish conflict. Thus in the play, the German character is appropriately hostile to the Frenchman, and aggressive toward the Turk.

Baron fon Donnershlag is described in the list of dramatis personae as a German military man.[62] His telling name, Donnershlag, literally means "thunderclap" and his personality certainly reflects the idea of something loud, unexpected, and possibly harmful.[63] He punctuates his conversation with German exclamations, the majority of which are vulgar or insulting. These German-language curses and mutterings function almost as asides, to be understood by the German speakers in the audience (in 1772 in a court audience there would have been many German speakers among the nobility, including Catherine herself).

The Baron does not arrive until scene three, and immediately curses in German: "*Hols der Henker!*" ("Hangman take it!," roughly meaning "Oh, hell!")—a curse at the presence of the other visitors (165).[64] From his initial rude outburst, Donnershlag then goes on to greet his fellow petitioners and to inquire about the length of their wait. Upon hearing that it has been over an hour, he is paradoxically both polite and coarse in the same moment:

BARON. *Was Teufel* [What the devil], he is still asleep! And have you been here long?
PERILOV. About an hour already and a little more.
BARON. Even the ladies wait so long! *hol mich der Kukuck* [Oh, hell] it's not civil. For us on German soil, that is not customary! *Ich schwere Ihnen* [I swear to you] for ladies everywhere you will open the door. (165)[65]

The Baron's next target is Oranbar, the Frenchman. Donnershlag is incensed that Perilov questions Oranbar about the war.

---

[62]   This is the Russian spelling of the German name von Donnerschlag.

[63]   Berkov offers the possibility that Donnershlag is based on Prince Henry of Prussia, who visited St. Petersburg in 1770 and 1772 to negotiate an end to the Turkish war (*Istoriia russkoi* 151). See Soloviev on the Prince's stiffness and lack of "diplomatic finesse" (161).

[64]   Translations from German courtesy of my colleague Kirstin Pauka.

[65]   Thanks to Liudmila Finney for her Russian translation advice for this play.

BARON. How to wage a war? Who! Orenbar (sic) wants to speak of war? He? *daß
dich der schwere Noth*! [Thou be caught by misery!] He doesn't understand a thing:
I think he wouldn't dare fight with a pen-knife.

ORANBAR. *Monsieur le Baron*, I don't know how to fight because I don't wish to
fight. (166)

As seen in the above exchange, the Baron's tone is frequently pugilistic and
antagonistic; a German-born playwright created this negative portrayal. The issue
of Catherine's Russian vs. her German identities is one that must continue to be
examined. Ruth Dawson, a literary historian with a specialization in the field of
German women writers, while not denying Catherine's status as a Russian writer,
also groups Catherine with other female German playwrights of this period,
categorizing her this way on the basis of the culture of her youth:

> She was born in Germany (bearing in mind the fragmented patchwork implied by that
> name in the 18th century) of course and lived there into her teens; she could write and
> speak German. Like many other of the numerous princesses produced in the assorted
> German principalities, she married out and adopted another language and culture. My
> argument is that within the specifically German terms of women in the high aristocracy,
> Catherine's situation was not unusual.[66]

On the other hand, we must remember Catherine's various "conversions" to
Russian culture (religion, language, clothing, and so on), and indeed her role in the
very creation and promulgation of a Russian culture, literature, art, history,
language, and Empire. In *Prominent Nobleman*, Catherine as satirist does not
address the complexities of her own identity, but clearly aligns herself with the title
character, who can be inferred to be wise, helpful, Russian, but intolerant of fools
and beggars.

The German Baron is certainly portrayed as one such fool. In general, he is
annoyed with the Frenchman for his prolixity and intellectual ramblings. Here
Catherine contrasts the practical military man with the intellectual but ineffectual
counterpart, Oranbar. The Baron's anger builds to such a pitch that he strikes the
Frenchman on the shoulder. The Baron curses at him again in German at the end
of the scene: *daß dich der tausend Teufel holl!* [The thousand devils shalt get
thou!] he cries, again seizing the Frenchman by the shoulder (168).

In scene 4, when the German encounters Mr. Faktotov, his first words are
revealing: "I am a foreigner," he cries out (169). He then emphasizes his rank and
family connections, in order to impress Faktotov and thereby win an audience with
the elusive Khrisanf. "I am a baron, the Baron fon Donnershlag, I have sixteen
grandfathers and sixteen grandmothers in the familial register, and all are
prominent in the nobility, so I want to be first—" (170). Note that in speaking with
Faktotov, the Baron holds back both his rudeness and his German words until well

---

[66] Dawson, "Catherine as German Woman Writer."

into the fifth scene. Here, when the Baron discovers that Khrisanf has left the premises, he again asserts his nobility and his military savvy: "I am of a prominent and old nobility, *Gott soll mich strafen, es ist erbärmlich!* [God punish me, it is wretched]. I have nothing; I want to demonstrate to everyone I know how to fight face to face; I ask first for some money for my project—" (175). The Baron aligns himself with Khrisanf linguistically as well as aristocratically: his choice of words "I am of a prominent and old nobility" [Ia znatnoi, i staroi dvorianstvo] calls to mind the title of the play (*Peredniaia znatnago boiarina*).

The French seem to have instigated or at least encouraged the Russo-Turkish War. From 1758–70, French Foreign Minister Duc de Choiseul promoted "an active anti-Russian strategy,"[67] in part a reaction to the defeats and lowering of status France suffered during the Seven Years' War (in spite of the fact that the French and Russians fought as allies). According to Alexander, the Turks were "[e]gged on by lavish French bribes and calls to challenge Russian arrogance."[68] The play reflects this attitude of French sympathy towards Turkey; for example, the French character Oranbar repeatedly insists that the Turk should not be beaten.

After the conclusion of the Seven Years' War, other matters had also put a strain on Russia's relations with French. Catherine had been highly offended by a book, *Voyage en Sibérie, fait par ordre du roi en 1761* by Abbé Jean Chappe d'Auteroche, published in Paris in 1768; in it, Chappe d'Auteroche denigrated many aspects of Russian culture and life. The incensed Catherine zealously defended Russia by writing her *Antidote* as a reply to Chappe d'Auteroche in 1770, two years before the composition of the play.

"The whole world is stupid .... I alone know everything," says the Frenchman Oranbar (175). Several scholars agree that Catherine's characterization of the Frenchman is based on her encounter with a real-life Frenchman, the French legal advisor Mercier de La Rivière.[69] La Rivière arrived in St. Petersburg in 1768 to advise Catherine on her work with the Legislative Commission. Her letters express her disdain for what John Alexander calls his "arrogant loquacity."[70]

The real-life Frenchman had much to recommend him to Catherine, who looked often to French thought for guidance. In June of 1767, he had published *De l'ordre naturel et essentiel des sociétés politiques,* a natural law theory of economics. On 30 July 1767, Catherine convened the Legislative Commission, and by September she had invited La Rivière to Russia, on the advice of Diderot. He was nicknamed "Solon La Rivière," ironically alluding to the great Athenian lawgiver. According to Catherine, he was an unbearable snob. The memoirs of Count Ségur, the French ambassador to Russia from 1785–89, tell a comical

---

[67] Scott 11.

[68] Alexander, *Catherine the Great: Life and Legend* 129. Scott, however, asserts that the war "owed less to French promptings than is sometimes supposed" (21).

[69] Gukovskii 79; Berkov, *Istoriia russkoi* 150; Shchebal'skii "Dramaticheskiia" 149.

[70] Alexander, *Catherine the Great: Life and Legend* 114.

anecdote about La Rivière's arrival in St. Petersburg. According to Catherine herself (as reported by the Count), upon his arrival in St. Petersburg in January 1768, the economist immediately set about arranging his rooms into various departments and offices: "Upon the doors of the numerous apartments he had written in large characters: *department of the interior, department of commerce, department of justice, department of finance, tax-office, etc.*"[71] In a 28 January 1768 letter to Count Nikita Panin, Catherine writes disparagingly of La Rivière and his manner:

> Ivan Fedorovich Glebov says that de-la-Rivier has hardly reduced his arrogance: he is only a chatterer, thinks much of himself, and he resembles a doctor.[72]

Although Catherine had summoned him as an advisor, it soon became clear that he felt he was in Russia "to govern the Empire of the Tsars."[73] She dismissed him within a few weeks, and had her revenge five years later in the form of a one-act play.

There are many general traits about Oranbar that are reminiscent of the pompous La Rivière. Meremida lambastes Oranbar for being too wordy and pedantic: "how my ears droop! He speaks like a book" (165). Beyond this overall characterization, which might have only hinted at La Rivière, Catherine deliberately includes two specific references to her real-life model. One definite allusion to La Rivière comes straight from Oranbar's mouth. The Frenchman enters with most of the other petitioners in scene 2. In scene 2, and in most of scene 3, Oranbar is timid in his speech; most of his lines are short and fragmented and many of them end in ellipses, indicating either that he has been interrupted or that his voice trails off uncertainly. Suddenly, in the middle of the third scene, after enduring curses, threats, and a blow from the German, Oranbar finds his voice, and speaks the following:

> ORANBAR. No, *Monsieur*; if you wish, you can find out right away. I came here for this reason: I was in my country, and thought that everybody here walked like this … *(he demonstrates walking on all fours)*. I'm a kind man, with a good heart, I know a lot, I read a lot; so I came here, in order to put all of you on two legs, and for this purpose I wrote *l'évidence* and brought it here: it is strongly *demonstratio* that it's better to walk on two legs, not on four. Then it's more beautiful, the face is visible: but if one walks on four legs, he has to pull his neck, his throat and chin will … This is *évidence, Messieurs, évidence!* […]
> TEFKIN. How great he is to us, coming here, and doing us this honor. Of course this man has gone out of his mind!

---

71 Ségur, *Memoirs* 3:32.
72 Catherine II, "Spisok s pis'ma."
73 Larivière 100.

URTELOV. I think so too. Although he says he knows a lot, it's clear that this is not true. How can one get it into one's head that people walk on all fours! I think he's the one who needs to be admonished. (167)

This image, of the Frenchman come to enlighten the Russian people by teaching them how not to walk on all fours, is a deliberately provocative metaphor. But Catherine cleary felt provoked by La Rivière. In a scathing letter to Voltaire, she commented on "M. La Rivière, who six years ago supposed that we walk on four paws, and who very politely took the trouble to come from Martinique to set us on our hind feet."[74] This letter makes it clear that Oranbar and La Rivière are one and the same, and that Oranbar is, in Catherine's mind, not merely a hyperbolic hypothetical character.

The dialog mentioned above still would only have identified La Rivière to a select group of court insiders. To broaden the possible audience for her satirical commentary, Catherine includes in the play a pointed reference to La Rivière's published legal theory. A key aspect of La Rivière's 1767 treatise was its reference to the Physiocrats and their theory of *évidence*, which can be defined as "a certitude so clear and so manifest by itself that spirit cannot reject it."[75] Over the course of Catherine's short play, Oranbar says the word "evidence" (in French) ten times, as when he tells the others "*L'évidence, l'évidence, Messieurs, est une belle chose; cela est convainquant*" (165).[76] By constantly interjecting the same word, often twice in a sentence as above, Oranbar reveals an obsessive, excessive personality; by harping on the word *évidence*, Oranbar also reveals his ties to La Rivière, in an explicit reference which many in her audience would have recognized.

If Catherine truly based Oranbar on La Rivière, a specific and recognizable personage from within her court circle, her dramaturgical license calls into question the esthetic philosophy most often associated with Catherine the Great: that general satire (*na porok*) is superior to pointed satire (*na litso*). However, in the case of the character of Oranbar, and also in the later comic opera *The Woeful Knight Kosometovich* (1778–89), Catherine is more direct in her satire.[77] The latter work is generally felt to be a spoof of the Swedish king Gustav III; Catherine composed it while in the midst of the Russo-Swedish War and it premiered before peace had been achieved (see Chapter 5). A direct portrait of a rival ruler produced during the course of a war is hardly an example of a general vice looked

---

[74] Reddaway 203. Letter is from 22 octobre/2 november 1774. French original: "M. La Rivière même, qui nous supposait, il y a six ans, marcher à quatre pattes, et qui très poliment s'était donné la peine de venir de la Martinique pour nous dresser sur nos pieds de derrière."

[75] Quoted in Franklin 108n, from Quesnay entry in Diderot, *Encyclopédie*, Vol. 13.

[76] Evidence, Messieurs, is a beautiful thing; that is convincing.

[77] I will argue in Chapter 3 that the short proverb play "The Voyages of M. Bontems" also has a reference to La Rivière.

at in a "compassionate light." *The Woeful Knight* was one of Catherine's last dramatic works, written just before the French Revolution, an event often seen to define a harsher period in Catherine's reign and writing. *Prominent Nobleman*, however, was one of her first plays, written only three years after the *na litso* debate—why would she defy her own principles to create a portrait of a specific and well-known figure?

I would argue that in both cases, Catherine is satirizing a foreign personage, rather than a recognizable Russian figure.[78] At the heart of the *na litso* debate was Catherine's fear of a damaging critique of her inner circle, or perhaps even herself. In *Prominent Nobleman*, however, Catherine takes on La Rivière (who by this time had departed Russia anyway) as an insidious outside influence, personifying her perception of the self-important and meddling Frenchman. The context of the Russo-Turkish War also explains Catherine's willingness to satirize, just as the Russo-Swedish War provided the impetus for the creation of *Woeful Knight*.

Her characterization of Oranbar is of course not completely based on La Rivière. As David J. Welsh notes, "Gallomania was so widespread in Russia that there is hardly a comedy between 1765 and 1823 which does not contain satirical references to it."[79] The typical manifestation of this phenomenon, however, is a Russian Francophile, such as Fonvizin's Ivanushka in *The Brigadier*. By choosing instead to represent a foreign visitor, Catherine highlighted foreign influence rather than domestic insecurity.

The Turks, angered by Russian military actions in Poland, declared war on Russia on 25 September 1768. For Catherine, conflict with the Turks meant the opportunity to demonstrate Russia's martial might, and achieve important territorial goals in the south (the Crimea) and in Poland.[80] The war was domestically difficult, causing large taxation and budgetary problems that are alluded to in the play, as when the drunken Vypivaikova complains of being unable to find sugar or wine due to the ongoing war (164). But the conflict was also a turning point in Russia's military and national confidence. The brilliant naval victory at Chesmé in July 1770 by the Russian Baltic fleet gave Catherine a feeling of "bellicose superpatriotism."[81] By the time the war ended in 1774 with a peace treaty financially and territorially very favorable to Russia, Russia's status had changed: she was a military power to be reckoned with.

If the German visitor is essentially an aggressive military man, and the Frenchman a pedantic intellectual, the Turk Durfedzhibasov is much less clearly defined. In contrast to the other two foreigners, Durfedzhibasov is silent for much of the play. The majority of his dialog occurs in scene 2, when the Russian

---

[78] Another example would be Catherine's play *The Deceiver* [Obmanshchik], whose title character is clearly connected to the Italian alchemist Cagliostro.

[79] Welsh 49.

[80] Alexander, *Catherine the Great: Life and Legend* 129.

[81] Alexander, *Catherine the Great: Life and Legend* 133.

characters question him. His speech in this section is difficult to understand. He speaks with many grammatical errors and his own Turkish versions of Russian words; for instance, he uses the word "bach'ka" throughout as the word "bat'ka" (colloquial Russian for father).

> DURFEDZHIBASOV. I am a Turkish nobleman. My father is a great man. He here ... he himself ... *(gesticulates with his hand to the right and to the left)* this and that ... and he demands that everybody worship him ...
> PERILOV. What does that mean? He here ... and there ... and this way and that ... and commands: does he really command everywhere and everything there?
> DURFEDZHIBASOV. Yes, yes. The Sultan doesn't eat without my father. My father has many small ... like this ... *(shows the size of the biggest and smallest sheep, and how they walk)* big ... it walks on four legs—and small like this, small ... and big ...
> PERILOV. What is that?
> DURFEDZHIBASOV. White, like the earth in winter ... and they speak like this: eeh-eh! beh! ... beeh! ...
> MEREMIDA. Perhaps these are sheep?
> DURFEDZHIBASOV. Yes, yes, mother, sheep ... my father has many ... sheep ... the Sultan doesn't eat without my father ... my father is a great man ....
> MIKHAILO. So, does your father supply lamb for the Sultan?
> DURFEDZHIBASOV. My father is a famous nobleman and I'm his son.
> TEFKIN. Unimpassioned evidence of his Turkish prominence. (163–4)

Besides hearing the Turk's broken and simplistic speech, we learn that he (like the German) is asserting his connections to nobility in order to improve his chances of seeing the prominent nobleman of the play's title. A cultural clash is apparent—the Russians in the play are measuring wealth in terms of dowries or property, while Durfedzhibasov counts affluence and prestige by the quantity of sheep.

As many foreign visitors at a loss for words might do, Durfedzhibasov employs gestural language to compensate for his lack of speech. First, he emphasizes the power of his father by gesturing "*with his hand to the right and to the left*" in explaining how he commands everyone to bow to him. Then, the Turk "*shows the size of the biggest and smallest sheep, and how they walk*" (163). This image, of Durfedzhibasov demonstrating the gait of the many big and small sheep, is potentially quite comical. Note that he describes them as walking on four legs. If the actor playing Durfedzhibasov were to imitate the sheep to make his listeners understand his meaning, then Catherine would have had a literalization onstage of the image from La Rivière. Whereas the French economist saw the Russians as running about on all fours, Catherine herself depicts the Turks this way.

Durfedzhibasov never speaks again until scene 4, when he repeats phrases he has already said: "My father is a great man! I'm my father's son" (169); "I am a Turkish nobleman ... The Sultan doesn't eat without my father ... My father has a lot of beeh! beh!" (170). In the Turk's final line during a cacophony when all the characters speak at once, he again repeats "I am a Turkish nobleman. My father has many be-eh! be-eh! Give me lands ... give me some people, a rank, sheep, horses, cows, poultry ... and every kind of animal" (175). Catherine portrays each of the three foreigners in the play in his own uniquely negative light. The Turk's association with animals, combined with his sub-verbal bleating, creates a character who is inferior and conquerable.

Linguistic competence in the Russian language is an essential element of Catherine's characterization of the three foreigners. "Language, to Catherine, was a human artifact; its growth and development could not be left to take place naturally but had to be stimulated and guided by the conscious intervention of the ruler."[82] Catherine herself knew German and French from her childhood in Germany, and learned Russian as a young princess destined to wed the young Grand Duke Peter. Her reign was a crucial turning point in the elevation of the Russian language as a literary, diplomatic, and educational medium. Although she is not herself considered to be an accomplished speaker and writer of Russian (and never thought herself a poet), she was passionately interested in promoting Russian. She even went so far as to investigate a theory of the Slavic origins of world languages, compiling comparative word lists and dictionaries from around the globe.[83]

We have already seen that both Donnershlag and Oranbar fill their Russian speech with phrases and exclamations in German and French, respectively. Their Russian grammar and word choice is often incorrect. The Turk, however, is the most extreme case. The Turk's Russian language abilities are much more limited than the other two characters, so that he speaks haltingly, in a Russian even more broken and grammatically incorrect than the Frenchman's. His case endings are often faulty, and overall the speech is dominated by suffixes ending in an "em" sound: "Ia Turetsk dvorianin. Moi bach'kam velik chelovekam. On tam ... on sam ... i tak i siakom" (163).[84] That linguistic tentativeness and error is the primary identifying trait of the character, making him seem to be an ignorant simpleton. After the first line he speaks on stage, Mikhaila responds with "You, sir, are of course not Russian?" (163). In this play, being "not Russian" is worse than being foolish, greedy, or insidious. Again, rather than acknowledging the difficulties of speaking in a second language, the play treats the lack of Russian as a clear fault and as a comic effect. (This strategy reappears in 1786 in Catherine's adaptation of *Merry Wives of Windsor*.) The Russians in *Prominent Nobleman* do not let such errors go unnoticed. Even Vypivaikova, who spends the play searching for a drink of vodka or wine, is chauvinistic when it comes to her language. After a particularly mangled interchange between the German and the

---

[82] Rogger 113.

[83] Pallas published the *Sravitel'nye slovari vsekh iazykov i narechnii* in 1787.

[84] I am a Turkish nobleman. My father is a great man. He here ... he himself ... this and that ...

Frenchman, Vypivaikova exclaims, "How unintelligible this is! How they ruin our language!" (166).

The Frenchman's lack of vocabulary is also derided in the following exchange. Oranbar's Russian words are just barely understandable.

> ORANBAR. [...] it was necessary to begin *par raser la campagne.*[85]
> PERILOV. Tell us again in Russian. I truly don't understand French.
> ORANBAR. At once; it was necessary to begin to shave through the field ahead.
> PERILOV. To shave a field? Here they mow grass with a scythe: perhaps in France, there is such a shortage that they shave the grass with a razor ... but how can you shave it with a razor? (167–168)

Here, Perilov turns Oranbar's linguistic gaffe against him, insulting the French in the process, as he compares the strong Russian scythe to the ineffective French razor. Catherine herself commented, on the xenophobia of her age, that,

> Nowhere but in Russia are there such masters skilled in noticing the weaknesses, the laughable features, or the shortcomings of the foreigner; you can be assured that they will not allow him to get away with anything, because, naturally, every Russian, in his heart of hearts, does not like any foreigner.[86]

When Mr. Faktotov, Khrisanf's representative, appears in scene 4, the petitioners stop their in-fighting; each of the nine pleads directly to Faktotov, in turn. When he replies that he cannot understand them since they are all speaking almost at the same time, Catherine gives this very interesting stage direction: "*they all speak at once and each in his own language*" (170). Although she only writes out the Russian line that they all speak ("I want to see Mr. Khrisanf, I need to speak with him"), the onstage effect would have been striking: the same words simultaneously in French, German, Turkish and Russian! When this babel subsides, Faktotov asks them to speak successively, and they again talk one at a time—in Russian. In a short stage direction, Catherine has created a metaphorical demonstration of her ideal: out of the competing tongues, the Russian language is victorious. In fact, the plot goes on to justify this interpretation. In the remainder of the play, Faktotov only listens to the Russians one by one: Vypivaikova, then Pretantena, then Meremida, then Urtelov. The foreigners' needs are a lesser priority, and they do not speak again except in a final climactic scene of simultaneous babel on hearing that Khrisanf has left the premises. No one has been helped, but at least the Russians have been listened to, and their language has certainly won out.

In *Prominent Nobleman*, language is access to power, yet the most silent character is also the most powerful. We know little about Khrisanf, but he is endowed with wealth, wisdom, and prestige by the behaviors of the other

---

[85]   To raze the countryside.

[86]   Quoted in Kamenskii 58. Source is Catherine II, *Zapiski imperatritsy* 376–77.

characters toward him (or toward his absence). His servant Mikhaila even calls him a "saintly man" (162). According to Mikhaila, the "locusts" are only there to be able to gossip about their brush with greatness: "we, they say, were at Khrisanf's. He was in such a caftan ... he was happy or disturbed ... he whispered with so-and-so for a long time" (162).

Khrisanf is clearly a Catherine figure. His influence permeates every aspect of the play; he is the ultimate arbiter, symbolizing the equitable and just distribution of wealth and imperial favor. His onstage absence metatheatrically echoes Catherine's own authorial absence; because her plays were presented anonymously at the court theatre in 1772, she hovered over the action of the play without ever materializing—like the Prominent Nobleman.

Catherine saw language as a tool for her Empire's growth, prestige, and power. In her play, all of the petitioners are cranks and idlers, but those who are non-Russian get the brunt of the satire. Their mauling of the Russian language seals their fate, and underscores their powerlessness. If language, culture, and the nation form a three-legged stool that supports society, Catherine clearly perceived Russia not as the Turk's four-legged beast bleating "be-eh, be-eh," but as a fine and upstanding world power.

The genre of comedy itself, which dominates Catherine's dramatic output, reflects her own vision of her reign: by the end, her characters were justly rewarded or punished, and a happy closure echoed the sense of national well-being she deliberately projected. The resolutions of these five comedies of 1772 reflect Catherine's vision of the order and satisfaction under rule by an enlightened despot.

Chapter 3
Later Comedies

The gap in Catherine's dramatic writing between the years 1772 and 1785 is understandable, given the variety of concerns facing the busy Empress. Catherine's personal life remained turbulent throughout this period. After many years with lover Grigorii Orlov at her side (1759–72), she dismissed him and replaced him with the much younger Aleksandr Vasilchikov. Her love affair with Grigorii Potemkin began sometime in 1774, and they were probably secretly married that year. By 1776, the two moved into a more platonic arrangement, although Potemkin remained an extremely powerful and trusted adviser. Catherine began a string of younger "favorites," such as Petr Zavadovskii, Semen Zorich, Ivan Rimskii-Korsakov, and Aleksandr Lanskoi, her lover from 1780 to 1784. Lanskoi's sudden death in 1784 was a great blow to Catherine, and sent her into a deep depression. Catherine also had worries about succession. Hoping not to pass the throne to her own son Paul Petrovich, she pinned her hopes on an heir, and was disheartened by the April 1776 death of Paul's first wife, Grand Duchess Natalia, in childbirth. Paul married Maria Fedorovna later that year, and produced the first male heir, Aleksandr, in 1777.

The Pugachev Rebellion (1773–74) was a large-scale crisis that threatened to undermine the Empress's legitimacy as a ruler. With the resolution of that rebellion and the conclusion of the Russo-Turkish War in 1774, Russia entered a period of peace that lasted until 1787. The July 1783 annexation of the Crimea was a triumph, but the long-anticipated Tauride tour was postponed from 1785 to 1787, evidently giving her the desire to write comedies again.

Although she wrote no more comedies for many years after 1772, Catherine remained a prolific author in various genres.[1] Her writing for the rest of the 1770s was primarily legislative, including the massive *Provincial Reform* of 1775. In 1780, spurred by growing Freemasonry in Russia, she published a lengthy essay called *Secret of the Anti-Absurd Society, Discovered by an Outsider* [Taina protivo-nelepago obshchestva, otkrytaia ne prichastnym onomu]. In the early 1780s, she made two contributions to a journal called *Colloquium of Lovers of the Russian Word* [Sobesdenik liubitelei rossiiskago slova], edited by Princess Dashkova. Catherine's *Notes Concerning Russian History* [Zapiski kasatel'no rossiiskoi istorii], first published in serial form in 1783–84, was her expanded

---

[1] An unpublished fragment of a play in French called "Mr. Lustucru" probably dates from 1776. It seems to have been edited by Elagin. See Pypin 4: 115–117.

version of the ancient Russian historical chronicles; *Facts and Fictions* [Byli i nebylitsy] was a series of satirical feuilletons.

She intended another group of writings for her first two grandsons (born in 1777 and 1779): *Selected Russian Proverbs* [Vybornyia rossiiskiia poslovitsy, 1783], a collection of proverbs composed by Catherine herself; the primer *Russian Primer for the Instruction of Youth* [Rossiiskaia azbuka dlia obucheniia iunoshestva chteniiu, 1781] including a section on "Elementary Civic Education" [Grazhdanskoe nachal'noe uchenie]; and two tsarevich stories, one of which she later adapted as a comic opera.

In the period from 1785–90, Catherine the Great took up her pen again to write works for the stage. She wrote six operas, two historical dramas (one unfinished), ten full-length neoclassical comedies (five of which were published), at least five French proverb plays, two adaptations of Shakespeare plays (one unfinished) and several play fragments. Khrapovitskii's diary allows us to track the composition process during this period of extraordinary writing activity. Her first published plays since 1772 were the first two plays of her anti-Masonic trilogy: *The Deceiver* and *The Deceived One*.[2] She next changed genres, writing her first three comic operas (see Chapter 5), before completing the trilogy in June 1786 with *The Siberian Shaman*. She then entered into a period of Shakespearean experimentation for the duration of that year (see Chapter 4). The long-awaited Crimean tour occupied her from January through June of 1787, after which she wrote a French proverb play ("The Busy-Body," August 1787) followed by a closely-related full-length comedy: *A Family Broken Up by Intrigue and Suspicions* [Razstroennaia sem'ia ostorozhkami i podozreniiami, 1787]. Her final published comedy was *The Misunderstanding* [Nedorazumeniia], written between January and June of 1788; she also composed several more French proverb plays that year. She ended her two-year flurry of writing in late 1788 with *The Woeful Knight Kosometovich*, not writing again until two years later. Her final work was the comic opera *Fedul and his Children*. This chapter will focus on her published comedies—five full-length and five proverbs—from 1785–88. Two of her first dramatic endeavors after her thirteen-year hiatus were the first two plays of a trilogy with a markedly political purpose.

The Latin proverb "Ridendo castigat mores" (Improve morals through laughter) was the curtain motto at the Hermitage Theatre, Catherine's court theatre built in

---

2   At least three unpublished comedies may also date from this prolific period: *What Jokes are These?* [Chto za shutki?]; *Thinking One Way and Acting Another* [Dumaetsia tak, a delaetsia inako]; and *Dranov and his Neighbors* [Dranov s sosedi]. These were published for the first time in Pypin, volume 3, based on manuscripts now held in the Russian State Archive of Ancient Acts in Moscow (Ekaterina II Fond f. 10, opis 1). The title page of *Thinking One Way* indicates that it was written in March 1785, which predates the composition of *The Deceiver*. Pypin also publishes a few fragments of plays found in these archives, including one called "Brun" (referred to by Khrapovitskii in a diary entry of 31 July 1787).

the 1780s.[3] Catherine wrote her anti-Masonic trilogy as a comic means of reform, a warning against the growing influence of the Freemasonry in Russia.[4] The trilogy was one of her weapons against Masonic orders and mysticism; later in her life she used more direct preventive measures such as censorship and imprisonment. *The Deceiver* [Obmanshchik] and *The Deceived One* [Obol'shchennyi] were written in late 1785, although Khrapovitskii's diary does not mention their composition process. *The Deceiver* premiered at the Hermitage on 4 January 1786; *The Deceived One* followed closely after, on 2 February 1786. Catherine seems to have taken a break to write her first three comic operas that spring, not completing *The Siberian Shaman* [Shaman Sibirskoi] until summer. According to Khrapovitskii's diary, the Empress gave him the play for corrections and amendments on 16 June 1786.[5] The play was first performed on 24 September 1786, also at the Hermitage Theatre. All three plays played also in the public theatres in Moscow; *The Deceiver* played numerous successful public performances in both cities[6] and was also performed in German in St. Petersburg and Hamburg. Catherine's correspondent and friend Dr. Johann Zimmermann (court physician at Hanover) gave the German translation to the celebrated actor F. L. Schröder, who presented the play at his Hamburg Town Theatre in May 1786, casting himself in the leading role of Kalifalkzherston.

The trilogy complements the concerns and style of her earlier neoclassical comedies such as *Oh, These Times!* Catherine again set her sights on superstition, this time by portraying Masonry, alchemy, and shamanism as deceitful professions that prey on the gullible. *The Deceiver*, *The Deceived One*, and *The Siberian Shaman* all contain quite similar elements, most noticeably the intermingling of two plots: that of a young woman's marriage and of an outside deceiver or charlatan whose deceptions are uncovered. The engagement of the young woman and the revelation of the charlatan's chicanery combine to create the comic ending to each play. All three plays have some form of mysticism as their topic, although the specific satirical target varies from Masonry (or a version called Martinism), to Cagliostro's alchemy, to shamanism.

The trilogy also reached the reading public in many editions. *The Deceiver* and *The Deceived One* were first published in St. Petersburg in 1785;[7] *Shaman* followed in 1786. Zimmermann, who wrote to Catherine about the influence of

---

[3]   Pypin 1:x.

[4]   Catherine herself did not specifically call the trilogy "anti-Masonic," although the published German translation of 1788 was subtitled "Three Comedies against Enthusiasm and Superstition." The term has been commonly applied by critics.

[5]   Barsukov 11.

[6]   On Russian-language productions, see Annenkov entries and El'nitskaia 456. On the German-language production, see Bakmeister 10:251.

[7]   Pypin 1: 287 and 341 notes that there are no extant copies of these first editions in the Imperial Public Library. *The Deceiver* was published in a second edition in 1786 in St. Petersburg. All three plays also appeared in Dashkova's *Russian Theatre* in 1787.

Masonry in France and Germany, flatteringly urged her to make them available to the German reading public, stating how important it was

> to see the greatest Sovereign in the universe laugh publicly at all these follies and to preach an example to all the women in Paris, to the legions of men of letters, to the largest part of the German court, even to princes, and even perhaps to several kings present and future! The two Russian comedies entitled *Le Trompeur* and *Les Trompés* will be epoch-making in Europe. It's not the South that enlightens the north, but the north that enlightens the South; it's from the banks of the Neva that the light arrives to us. I beg and conjure Your Imperial Majesty to have these two Russian comedies translated into French and into German. [...] A German comedy-writer who puts [these follies] on the stage would be stoned. Nevertheless it's by comedies and not by edicts that sovereigns remedy these follies.[8]

German translations of each play were published separately in 1786 in St. Petersburg and Riga: *The Deceived One* as *Der Verblendete*,[9] *The Deceiver* as *Der Betrüger*, and *The Siberian Shaman* as *Der Sibirische Schaman*.[10] In 1788, C. F. Nicolai published the entire trilogy in German in Berlin and Stettin as *Three Comedies against Enthusiasm and Superstition* [Drei Lustspiele wider Schwärmerey und Aberglauben]. The anonymous author of a review of this edition, published in 1800 in a London periodical devoted to German literature, expressed gratitude to Catherine for her clear-sightedness:

> The great princess, who composed these plays, deserves therefore the thanks of all Europe for having so successfully attacked superstition and fanaticism, this pest of social happiness [...] all bespeak the august writer to have possessed a most intimate knowledge of the follies of the times, and reflect infinite honour on her zealous endeavors to promote morality, and the progress of mental illumination.[11]

Catherine addressed the "follies of the times" in all three plays.

Beyond their surface neoclassical plot concerns (such as the proper marriage of a young woman), the three plays that form the anti-Masonic trilogy are set against a very specific background of contemporary political pressures, trends, and intrigue. If Catherine's reign is usually considered to have moved from a period of relative openness and freedom to one of paranoia and severity, one can certainly chart a change in atmosphere by looking at the case of Novikov. In the 1760s, Novikov was a prolific writer and editor of several satirical journals; by 1792 he had been arrested and imprisoned by Catherine. Her changing attitude toward him

---

[8] Letter dated 15 February 1786. Pypin 1: 343.

[9] Pypin 2: 340 mentions another possible edition from Leipzig.

[10] C. G. Arndt, Catherine's cabinet translator, was awarded 300 rubles for his translation of *The Deceived One*, according to Khrapovitskii's diary entry on 23 February 1786. Barsukov 7.

[11] Anonymous. "Review of *Drey Lustspiele*."

and his literary endeavors was partly a result of his increasing involvement in Rosicrucian Freemasonry in both St. Petersburg and Moscow. Although Catherine eventually resorted to more direct measures, the trilogy was her means of publicly exposing—via comic/satiric strategies—the philosophical and social shortcomings of this secretive social structure.

Freemasonry was introduced to Russia sometime in the 1730s via Western European Masonic contacts in London. By the 1780s, however, the Rosicrucian Order, brought first to Moscow in 1782 by Moscow University professor I. G. Schwartz, was to dominate all other strains of Freemasonry in Russia. Catherine distrusted the myriad forms of Freemasonry; in her writing, she uses the terms Masonry, Martinism, and Rosicrucianism interchangeably, along with references to alchemy, Theosophy, and shamanism.[12] In principle, the Empress opposed the mystical belief system espoused by the Masons; the occult imagery and emphasis on primal instinct were anathema to her Enlightenment sensibilities.[13] But on a more pragmatic and political level, Catherine feared the Masons because their secret hierarchical structure undermined rigid national boundaries. Her biographer John Alexander cites also Freemasonry's "contacts with foreign courts (especially Prussia), [and] its apparent ability to mobilize substantial funds."[14] One potential Masonic convert was Catherine's own son, Grand Duke Paul, avidly interested in the secretive society; his contacts with Prussian king Frederick William II, also a Freemason, must have been severely troubling to Catherine. Too, Freemasonry in Russia was, with some exceptions, almost exclusively a male province, thus excluding Catherine.[15]

Catherine's relationship to Freemasonry cannot be understood without reference to Novikov. Novikov has been made out, both by nineteenth-century and Soviet-era Russian historians, as a heroic figure fighting against Catherine's tyrannical censorship. Kenneth Craven points out, however, that his relationship with the Empress began cordially, and, more significantly, that "[t]he introduction of enlightenment to Russia owes most to the collaborative publishing achievements of Catherine II and Nikolai Ivanovich Novikov."[16] From the mid-1760s, then, Novikov was a well-respected member of the Russian literary scene as he and the Empress freely traded satirical barbs in their respective journals. After joining the Freemasons in St. Petersburg in 1775, he moved to Moscow in 1779 when his connections helped him to obtain a post as director of the Moscow University

---

[12] Martinists were the followers of Louis-Claude, Marquis de Saint-Martin, author of the 1775 *Des Erreurs et de la Verité*, published in Russian in 1785. The term "Martinism" was often incorrectly associated with the Moscow Masons. On the distinctions between these groups, see Madariaga, *Catherine the Great: A Short History* 197–8 and Ryu 217.

[13] Baehr 124.

[14] Alexander, *Catherine the Great: Life and Legend* 299.

[15] See Smith 28–30.

[16] Craven 173.

Press. From this influential position, Novikov began to pursue Freemasonry with greater fervor; his press produced a substantial number of Masonic materials, and he was appointed a Chief Director of the Theoretical Degree of Rosicrucianism. Catherine, an ardent believer in the enlightening power of the written word, also began to fear that power, particularly in the years leading up to the French Revolution. She did not sit idly by to see Novikov's Masonic views promulgated in print; by 1786, she was impounding many of his publications, egged on by her informer, the archpriest Petr Alekseev.[17] She dismissed Novikov from his directorship in 1788, and ordered his arrest for insurrection in 1792.[18] This chapter will later suggest that Catherine's shaman character in her *The Siberian Shaman*, written in the midst of a controversy surrounding Novikov's publishing output, is in part a reference to him, thus linking shamanic "cults" to Masonic ones. The trilogy was not Catherine's first literary attack on Masonry. Her *Secret of the Anti-Absurd Society* is "a satire on Freemasonry and Masonic organizations and parodies Masonic rituals, emblems, and doctrine."[19] The work, probably written by Catherine in French in 1780 and translated into Russian by Khrapovitskii, was backdated with a 1759 publication date, possibly to avoid the appearance of being a direct commentary on contemporary issues.[20]

In 1779, the year of Italian alchemist Cagliostro's visit to St. Petersburg, Catherine wrote the following in a letter to Grimm:

> [Do you know that] Freemasonry is one of the greatest aberrations to which the human race has succumbed [?] I had the patience to plod through both published and manuscript sources of all the tedious nonsense with which they busy themselves [...] . And when they encounter one another, how can they keep from splitting their sides with laughter?[21]

Six years later, Catherine had decided to marshal that laughter in a different direction by writing a series of comedies.

The plots of all three plays are quite similar. In all cases, the male head of a family is under the influence of an outsider, an abnormal attachment that threatens to disrupt the daughter's wedding to the man of her choice. All three plays bear a strong resemblance to Molière's *Tartuffe*; in that play, Orgon's devotion to the falsely religious Tartuffe throws his entire family into disarray, and the daughter

---

[17] Dixon 105.

[18] When Paul acceded to the throne in 1796, Novikov was released from prison. For a fine exegesis of Novikov's position as an Enlightenment figure, see Jones.

[19] Catherine II, *Taina*. Gukovskii 67.

[20] For a discussion of the dating controversy, see Shchebal'skii, "Dramaticheskiia" 112–13.

[21] From a letter to Grimm of 7 December 1779 published in Russian in Catherine II, "Pis'ma Ekateriny Vtoroi k baronu Grimmu" 61–2. English translation from McArthur 531–2.

Marianne barely escapes being married off to the titular hypocrite, whose arrest leads to the restoration of order. In her unpublished preparatory notes for the composition of *Shaman*, Catherine wrote the following, which applies equally to all three plays:

> The first act provides knowledge of the frame of the mind of the characters.
> The second act—continues the knowledge of the characters, but also begins the action.
> The third act—the continuation of the action, the beginning of the obstacles or the imbroglio.
> The fourth act: Imbroglio.
> The fifth act: Catastrophe.[22]

Within this general pattern, Catherine focused each play of the trilogy on a different aspect of her overall theme: the dangers of mysticism, pseudo-science, and irrationalism for the gullible public.

The Deceiver

The Deceiver, the first play of the trilogy to be performed and therefore probably the first written, is an explicit indictment of Freemasonry. The antagonist is Kalifalkzherston, who has insinuated himself into the Samblin household. Kalifalkzherston offers to act on behalf of Dodin, the suitor to the Samblins' daughter Sofia. From the play's first scene, Kalifalkzherston is associated with the Martinists, although Catherine cleverly avoids stating the name exactly:

> MAR'IA. There is yet another way; my master knows ... only very secretly ... such people ... how do you say ... Mif ... mish ... mid ... myt ... miar ... mart ... marty ... I almost said with marmosets ... I cannot remember.
> DODIN. Ha, ha, ha, what are marmosets? Imitative apes, they are quite the poseurs ... what kind of people ... are they affected?
> MAR'IA. I myself don't know, only when they speak between themselves, we truly understand nothing. (250)

There is a pun here, between the Russian word for Martinists (*martinisty*) and the word for marmosets (*martyshki*). There is also wordplay in the name Kalifalkzherston, an allusion to the famed Italian alchemist Count Alessandro Cagliostro (1743–95), whose name in Russian was spelled "Kaliostro." Catherine wrote to Zimmermann that *The Deceiver* "represents Cagliostro," who, like the Freemasons, symbolized for Catherine the infiltration of the illogical and irrational into Russia.[23] Cagliostro, despite his reputation as an impostor and a swindler,

---

[22] Quoted in Pypin 1: 418.
[23] Pypin 1: 342. Letter's date is 10 January 1786.

was a very popular figure with connections in the highest circles of European nobility. When he visited St. Petersburg in 1779, Catherine saw him as a dangerous influence, saying "I have never seen him near or far, —nor have I had any temptation to do so, for I do not love charlatans."[24] But the theories and rites of Cagliostro and his wife Lorenza initially impressed many members of St. Petersburg's Masonic circle, including Catherine's literary advisor I. P. Elagin. There are conflicting stories about why Cagliostro left the capital in March 1780, but their common theme is an accusation of deception.[25] Five years later Catherine would write him into her play.

When the charlatan Kalifalkzherston enters, in *The Deceiver*'s second scene, he silently gestures and pantomimes different emotions and actions:

KALIFALKZHERSTON   *(enters lost in thought and arguing with his hands, as if declaiming).*

DODIN. It's dangerous to stand near him, I bruise.

KALIFALKZHERSTON *(continues to speak fervently with his hands).*

DODIN. Something lies heavily on his heart.

KALIFALKZHERSTON *(does a gay pantomime).*

DODIN. What is he so happy about?

KALIFALKZHERSTON *(does a sorrowful pantomime).*

DODIN. Grief appears out of the blue so quickly after joy.

KALIFALKZHERSTON *(bows on both sides, to no one).*

DODIN. Now's the time for civility.

KALIFALKZHERSTON *(in surprise).*

DODIN. Either he has gone out of his mind, or he is feigning. *(Dodin coughs).*

KALIFALKZHERSTON. A sound of a mortal voice startled my ear here. (250–51)

This sequence resembles the shaman's more ambiguous silent movements in II.2 of *The Siberian Shaman* (see below). In this case, making gestures without sound or words is suspicious behavior, connoting insanity or devious deceit. Catherine's stage directions in the third scene state that Kalifalkzherston is *"feigning that he is conversing with an invisible being,"* making it utterly clear to the reader that the character is deliberately performing a sham (253).

When Kalifalkzherston confides to Samblin that the invisible person he was speaking with was Alexander the Great, audiences may have been reminded of Cagliostro, of whom Zimmermann wrote: "All of Paris has believed, and Cagliostro has made the Cardinal de Rohan believe that he dines with Caesar and sleeps with Queen Cleopatra."[26] Another strong reference to Cagliostro in *The Deceiver* is the use of the diamond-studded icon. Kalifalkzherston cajoles Samblin into giving him the diamonds from Mrs. Samblina's icon for an alchemical

---

24   Quoted in Anthony, *Catherine the Great* 298.
25   See Smith 151.
26   Pypin 1: 343. Letter's date is 15 February 1786, addressed to Catherine.

experiment. Later in the play, the family learns that Kalifalkzherston has absconded with this valuable icon, which is finally returned by the faithful suitor Dodin who apprehended the shyster. The diamonds would have immediately recalled Cagliostro, who was notorious for his alleged involvement in the French "Diamond Necklace Affair." In this 1785 incident, Cagliostro was implicated, along with Cardinal Rohan, in an alleged plot to sell a false necklace to Marie Antoinette; Cagliostro was subsequently imprisoned in the Bastille. Douglas Smith argues that these events, more than the upsurge of Masonry in Moscow, were the impetus for Catherine's creation of the trilogy.[27]

Perhaps also alluding to Cagliostro's popularity in France, the play makes a simultaneous critique of Gallomania and foreign tutors, two favorite topics of Russian neoclassical comedy. Madame Gribuzh (whose name may derive from "gribouillage" or scribbling) is a Frenchwoman, hired as Sofia's companion, who speaks throughout the play in strongly accented Russian. According to the servant Mar'ia, Gribuzh is indulging Sofia with frivolities like makeup. At the end of the play, the family learns that Madame Gribuzh has fled with Kalifalkzherston, evidently another French convert into the cult of false mysticism and greed.

The tutor to Samblin's unseen son is also French. Roti, whose name indicates "roasted," speaks sometimes in French and sometimes in Russian with a strong French accent. Unlike Madame Gribuzh, Roti is mostly skeptical about Samblin's devotion to Kalifalkzherston. In one instance, however, when Kalifalkzherston revives Mrs. Samblina by having her friend Kvarkov play music and sing for her, "*Samblin, Madame Gribuzh, and Roti indicate in pantomime to Kalifalkzherston their surprise at his art*" (260). These three characters show their gullibility through pantomime, again associating silent motions with foolishness. Later, when Samblin reprimands Roti for not teaching his son some of Kalifalkzherston's ideas, the Frenchman is frank: "He's out of his mind" (269). Samblin later reminds the tutor of his origins as a gambler from the streets; in this way, Roti falls within the typical Russian comic role of the under-qualified tutor.

But in other ways, Roti acts like a comic version of a hero, a reflection of the equally skeptical Dodin. Roti's shining moment comes in IV.4, when, in an attempt to convince Samblin of Kalifalkzherston's insincerity, Roti imitates the deceiver's gesticulations and "pretending, as if in conversation with an invisible being, he gives Kalifalkzherston a slap in the face" (278).[28] Roti mocks Kalifalkzherston by making use of the villain's own pantomimic style.

By including these two French characters, one a gambler pretending to be a tutor, one a pettifogger pretending to be a friend, Catherine connected the play's dominant theme of deceit to the issue of foreign influence, here in a family setting. Catherine saw Masonry as a dangerous foreign import. In 1902, A. V. Semeka

---

[27] Smith 153.

[28] Chetteoui notes that this scene must be an allusion to an incident between Elagin and Cagliostro (89n).

thoroughly analyzed the trilogy in terms of its Masonic content, and argued that Catherine sought to promulgate the negative image of the Mason as a foreign influence harmful to the Russian spirit.

The Deceiver, like the later *Siberian Shaman*, focuses on the outrageous antics of the deceiver himself. As in *Siberian Shaman*, the fraudulent character proves his powers by feigning the cure of the female head of the family. In this case, Kalifalkzherston shrewdly ascertains the cause of the quarrel between Samblina and her friend (paramour?) Kvarkov, and proceeds to "cure" her by having him sing to her. Such cures are yet another nod to Cagliostro, who, besides conducting seances and demonstrating his knowledge of alchemy, also spent some of his time in the Russian capital treating illnesses. For instance, he cured the son of Prince Golytsin by keeping him for fifteen days.[29] Ruth P. Dawson examines the issues of marriage and family stability as they relate to occultism in this trilogy, observing that in both *The Deceiver* and *The Siberian Shaman*, it is the female characters who are ill and must be cured, although the male father characters are the true dupes.[30]

Besides his miracle cure, Kalifalkzherston talks of his life in ancient Persia, acts the expert on everything from marriage to Seneca, and has an offstage cauldron that explodes. The scene in which the butler informs Kalifalkzherston of a disaster in his experiments delighted Catherine's correspondent Zimmermann: "The cauldron that goes fchu, fchu, fchu and then bursts, almost, beg pardon of Your Majesty, burst my diaphragm."[31] Once Kalifalkzherston leaves in Act IV, it takes the earnest suitor Dodin to convince Samblin that his friend was a scoundrel, using a messenger-speech formula typical for Catherine's plays. Dodin's transformation from an unwitting member of Kalifalkzherston's circle to the savior of the family is the triumph of rationalism; Samblin's realization shows that the Masonic spell can be broken. In the February 1786 issue of the journal *The Growing Vine* [Rastushchii vinograd], two articles refer to the play. In one, a "Letter to the Creator of the Comedy *Deceiver*," the writer praises the playwright for revealing the foolishness of the times.[32] In the same issue, a poem praises the play's author for raising "[t]he curtain, concealing the deception of people's minds/Where fraud's temple is built with the shroud of loud words."[33] In *The Deceived One*, Catherine again focused on a foolish father who almost leads his family into ruin, and "fraud's temple."

---

[29] Chetteoui 37. See Chetteoui 35–38 for an overview of Cagliostro's curative adventures in St. Petersburg.

[30] Dawson, "Writing as a Woman."

[31] Quoted in Pypin 1: 410. Letter's date is 7 April 1786.

[32] Anonymous. "Pis'mo k sochiniteliu" 6.

[33] Anonymous, "K sochiniteliu komedii Obmanshchik" 43. Translated in Smith 150.

The Deceived One

This second play of the trilogy centers on "the deceived one" Radotov (whose name derives from the French *radoteur* or driveller). The complex plot features two young women, Radotov's daughter Taisa and his niece Sofia, each of whom has a suitor (Vokitov and Gribin, respectively). Each suitor in turn has a confidant, Tratov and Bragin. The servant girl Mar'ia also has a suitor in Tef. Even the antagonist is multiple: Protolk and Bebin are the ringleaders of a small group of swindlers that also includes Barmotin and Dadiakin. Protolk's name derives from both *protolkat'sia* meaning "to force through" and *tolkovat'* meaning "to interpret or explain," thus connoting a pushy know-it-all. Barmotin may derive from the verb "to mutter" (*bormotat'*).

At the play's outset, Radotov's wife complains to her brother-in-law Britiagin, the play's reasonable *raisonneur*, that since her husband brought some strangers into the household, he has been moody, insensitive, and incomprehensible. The chief conflict of the play is Radotov's intention to marry off his daughter and niece to two of the peculiar outsiders, Protolk and Bebin. The impending imperilment of a daughter, forced by her father to marry an inappropriate groom, is a classic plot of the *commedia dell'arte* and is another link to Molière's *Tartuffe*. The play's stakes are considerably heightened by the threat of the girls' marriage to these scoundrels.

In Act IV, the group of mystics brings a child to assist them in a magical experiment; the child symbolizes the Masonic propensity to take advantage of the naïve. This same frightened child later returns to the house to give the messenger speech that reveals the trickery of the thieves, who have fled the house with the valuable contents of Radotov's chest. Given such tangible proof, Radotov comes to his senses and admits that his curiosity and fascination got the better of him. The play ends with more than the usual number of betrothals (for Taisa, Sofia, and the servant Praskov'ia). The *raisonneur*, Britiagin, makes a final metatheatrical jest: "If it were really so, that a Comedy was ordered to be made from Protolk, from Barmotin, then I will purposefully come out of the country, please, write me beforehand." He goes on to conclude more seriously:

By the philosophizing of each century its descendants will judge it ... In general, they ascribe praise only to those centuries that distinguish themselves with common sense, not with ravings ... supervision is without doubt in the hands of the authorities ... we should thank Providence that we live in an age when gentle means of correction are chosen. (340)

Zimmermann wrote to Catherine that, "The speech by Britagin (sic) at the conclusion of the play deserves to be engraved in marble."[34]

---

[34] Quoted in Pypin 1: 344. Letter's date is 28 May 1786.

In contrast to *The Deceiver*'s Sofia (and *Shaman*'s Prelesta), the two young heroines in *The Deceived One* are much more directly influenced by the corrupting forces around them. A mother-in-law who perhaps reminded Catherine of her own relations with aunt-in-law Empress Elizabeth, Radotova Mat' (Radotov's Mother) blames Radotova Zhena (Radotov's Wife) for the fact that her granddaughter Taisa is under the spell of these "devils":

> my granddaughter Taisa came to my chamber, saw that on a table in front of me stands a glass with flowers, she began to kiss the leaves; I asked, what for? she said, that on each leaf a little soul resides! ... and that many thousands fit on the head of a pin! ... I fainted from fear! (294)

Others in the family also encounter Taisa's strangeness. When the serving girl Praskov'ia tends to a candle that a butterfly has almost extinguished with her wings, Taisa is horrified:

> TAISA. Akh, what have you done?
> PRASKOV'IA. Nothing ... I saved the butterfly so that it wouldn't burn its wings.
> TAISA. You don't understand at all what kind of trouble you could have created! and that the butterfly has a little soul, which it was necessary to purify ... with flame. (312)

From Catherine's perspective, Praskov'ia reacts to the physical world around her in a sensible manner, preserving the practical function of the candle while keeping the butterfly alive. For Taisa, nature is fraught with symbolic meaning. The deluded Taisa would sacrifice, for the sake of her mystical beliefs, this poor butterfly—a symbolic representation of herself.

Taisa's cousin Sofia is equally bewitched, although by her devotion to fashion:

> To tell the truth (*curtseys*) my desire is to have a new dress with a trim so wide (*shows to all sides*), and so thick (*indicates fourteen inches*), and that all around me would dangle the largest possible flowers, beads, fringe, tassels, ribbons, feathers, and other such agreeable things. (301)

By giving the two cousins similar symptoms, Catherine connects the cult of mysticism to the cult of fashion, asserting that each is an empty and temporary form of escapism.[35]

Just as the two girls are more vulnerable than Catherine's typical heroines, so too are the play's male confidants more directly embroiled in the play's action. Both confidants disguise themselves, becoming deceivers as they endeavor to assist their friends' causes. Tratov has decided to pose as a mystical advisor in

---

[35]   See Schmid's thesis connecting the girls' initiation into social speech in the trilogy with the initiation into the secret societies.

order to become Taisa's tutor and therefore plead the cause of his friend Vokitov. Tratov instructs her in nonsensical numerical and natural concepts, and manages to make her believe that she has been drawn to Vokitov by an unknown force; Praskov'ia's aside speaks the plain truth: "for me, this force is called, I think, L-o-v-e" (316). Tratov, although part of the lovers' subplot, is another version of the false teacher, a reflection of the insidious influence that Protolk has over Taisa's father.

Gribin's friend Bragin also feigns an interest in the newcomers' teachings, and seeks Barmotin's tutelage. Bragin goes so far as to infiltrate their private rites, and takes part in an offstage initiation ceremony that the spying Praskov'ia says looks like a game of blind man's bluff. Bragin returns from this event completely drunk (his name is perhaps related to the noun "*braga*" meaning homebrewed beer), but still manages to give Gribin important information about Sofia's impending marriage. Tratov's and Bragin's motivations are benign and altruistic, and the results of their impersonations are positive. Yet their actions are nonetheless deceitful, and they must dabble in mysticism to accomplish their goals. Catherine here is allowing for a contextual use of deceit: as long as the two men keep their wits about them (which the drunken Bragin only barely succeeds in doing), they can use these scoundrels, the true deceivers, for good ends.

The play's father figure is not so clever. Radotov, in the play's first scene, is portrayed by his wife as a formerly sensible husband and father who has completely succumbed to the bizarre teachings of the men he has taken into the house. Praskov'ia also notes that his formerly outgoing and gregarious manner has changed to one of solitude and seriousness. But a male character, Radotov's brother-in-law Britiagin, is the first one to make a thorough diagnosis. Explaining that Radotov is "deceived," Britiagin reveals that under the influence of these men, Radotov is dabbling in alchemy, and that his head has been filled with "Cabalistic fantasies," to the point that he even sought out a Jewish teacher-cum-ragman (307). We neither hear the name of or meet any of these strangers until the third act, when Barmotin enters to show Radotov the rings he has traded for, and ends up (in a very amusing scene that concludes the third act) instructing Bragin about how "never [to] look anywhere with your eyes" (318). The ringleaders Protolk and Bebin do not appear until IV.6, when they arrive to perform a magical experiment for Radotov. Their entrance is preceded by another very funny scene featuring the drunken Barmotin and Bragin, who are the first to return from some kind of ritual, which seems to have featured much drinking, eating, and carousing. They discuss the group's alchemical preparations, before being joined by Radotov, Protolk, Bebin and a small child of seven or eight years old. Protolk then clearly assumes the role of leader, and directs the child to stamp his feet and then tell what he sees. This ritual eventually forces Dadiakin to confess his guilt in coveting a roast pig at dinner, a revelation that suitably impresses the gullible Radotov. In the fifth act, Bragin soberly reports to Britiagin that, "They intend to secretly set up different charitable institutions, such as schools, hospitals, and similar things, and that's why they try to attract rich people" (328).

In 1786, having just written *The Deceiver* and *The Deceived One*, Catherine ordered an investigation into Novikov's activities in Moscow, to determine whether he and his Mason friends had established any schools or hospitals; as Isabel de Madariaga points out, the report concluded that he had not.[36] Nonetheless, Catherine's concern was genuine. The aspirations of Protolk and his group to create charitable institutions as a front for their activities will have more disastrous societal consequences than their dabblings in alchemy; not only the family will be affected.

Douglas Smith points out Catherine's perspective as seen in *The Deceived One*:

> The Masons are not united by any shared love of morality, by a desire to strengthen the frayed bonds of humanity, or by a joint commitment to further the common good. Rather, what unites them are the vices of vanity, gluttony, folly, and greed. [...] Unlike earlier images of Freemasonry as the devil's attack on society's religious foundations, Freemasonry here appears as a purely secular phenomenon—an elaborate ruse used by clever rogues to rob the gullible rich.[37]

Just as Kalifalkzherston reveals himself to be a mere thief, Protolk and his band are nothing more than con artists who prey on Radotov's curiosity and naïveté in order to trick him. These charlatans and petty criminals seem far removed from the real freemasons in Russia, many of whom were some of the nation's leading statesmen, writers, and artists. But for Catherine there was no difference. Her concerns had in fact changed little from 1772, when she wrote *Oh, These Times!*, featuring the gullible Mrs. Marvel. In *The Deceived One*, Britiagin connects Radotov to his credulous cousin in the other play:

> Remember, not too many years ago, how much you laughed at our first cousin, Mrs. Marvel, and now in your prejudices you resemble her exactly ... She had her unique ways of thinking, and her own choice expressions .... Like you, people hardly understood her! (296)

In the 1770s, Mrs. Marvel was a representative of backward and old-fashioned superstition. Now, in the 1780s, Catherine saw such behaviors among the highest classes of Russian and Western European society. Her trilogy sought to expose the deceivers and the deceived.

---

[36] Madariaga, *Catherine the Great* 116. Novikov's close friend, the Moscow freemason S. I. Gamaleia, is also implicated in the play. Chetteoui notes some of Gamaleia's specific ideas in the reports of Radotov's behavior in the play's first scene (98n). Welsh finds in Barmotin a clear reference to Gamaleia, but does not explain why he singles out this character (23).

[37] Smith 148.

Audience Enlightenment in *The Siberian Shaman*

How was Catherine inspired to write a satirical treatment of shamanism to conclude her trilogy? *The Deceiver* and *The Deceived One* are much more explicitly critical of Masonry itself, associating it with alchemy and foolhardy mysticism. In representing the native practices of Siberian peoples, linked since the 1552 conquest of Kazan to Russia's identity as a colonizing force, Catherine expands her focus eastward. For Catherine, mysticism was not only found in the elite temple-parlors of Europe, through Masonry, but also in the temple-huts of Siberia, through shamanism.

From early in her reign, Catherine had struggled to defend her empire from charges of backwardness and barbarity. After reading Chappe d'Auteroche's *Voyage to Siberia*, Catherine wrote her 1770 *Antidote* in response and defense.[38] In it, she stressed Russia's civility, both in social customs and economic and political structures. At the same time, however, Catherine was aware of the significance of shamanism to Siberian culture. The historians and cartographers of her own Free Economic Society were exploring distant points in Siberia in the 1760s and 1770s, bringing back information about shamanistic rituals and practices (see Fig. 3.1).[39]

One other source of information was Diderot's *Encyclopedia*. In the letter Catherine wrote in French to Zimmermann, dated 7 April 1786, after remarking on her plays *The Deceiver* and *The Deceived One*, she writes of *The Siberian Shaman*: "[...] the article on Theosophy in the *Encyclopedia* furnished the framework for it."[40] That article, ostensibly a definition of Theosophy, is a lengthy diatribe against barbarity.

> Here is perhaps the most remarkable kind of philosophy. Those who professed it regarded human reason with pity; they had no confidence at all in its obscure and deceptive glimmer; they claimed to be enlightened by an interior principle, supernatural and divine, which was burning in them, and which would fade in and out [...] which violently seized their imagination, which agitated them, which they did not control, but by which they were controlled, and which conducted them to the most important and hidden discoveries about God and nature; that is what they called theosophy [...]. It follows from the preceding that the Theosophes were men of an ardent imagination; that they corrupted Theology, obscured Philosophy, and took advantage of their chemical knowledge, and it is difficult to say whether they have more harmed than served the

---

[38] The full French title is *Antidote, ou examen du mauvais livre intitulé Voyage en Sibérie fait en 1761;* see volume 7 of Pypin for the complete text.

[39] Flaherty 118. One particularly noteworthy published account is Pallas, *Reise durch verschiedene Provinzen des Russischen Reichs*. Because Catherine and the Imperial Academy of Sciences directly supported his work, she is certain to have been familiar with Pallas's accounts of specific shamanistic customs.

[40] Quoted in Pypin 1:409. Note that this letter to Zimmermann predates her giving the copy to Khrapovitskii for amendment, and also predates the premiere.

Fig. 3.1 Tungusic Shaman. Illustration from: *The Costume of the Russian Empire*. London: W. Miller, 1803. Plate XLVII. The engraving was reprinted from Johann Gottlieb Georgi's *Beschreibung aller Nationen des Russischen Reichs*. St. Petersburg: C. W. Müller, 1776–80

progress of human knowledge. There are still some theosophes among us [...] who have taken a violent dislike to Philosophy and to Philosophers, and who would succeed in extinguishing among us the spirit of discovery and of research, and in plunging us again into barbarism [...].[41]

The entry makes clear the dangerous nature of such practices, the threat to the reason and the progress of the age—the opposition of Theosophe to Philosophe is clear. Certainly Catherine's own sentiments were similar.

Although the "Theosophy" entry does not mention shamanism, the *Encyclopedia*'s entry on "Schamans" (sic) briefly but succinctly delineates the Enlightenment perspective:

It's the name that the inhabitants of Siberia give to impostors, who there serve the functions of priests, jugglers, sorcerers, and physicians. These shamans claim to have credence over the devil, whom they consult to know the future, to cure illnesses, and to play tricks which appear to be supernatural to an ignorant and superstitious people; for this they use tambourines which they hit with force, while dancing and turning with a surprising rapidity; when they have made themselves insane from the strength of the contortions and from fatigue, they claim that the devil manifests himself to them when he is in the mood. Sometimes they finish the ceremony by feigning to pierce themselves with a knife, which intensifies the astonishment and the respect of the foolish spectators. These contortions are ordinarily preceded by the sacrifice of a dog or of a horse, which they eat while drinking a good many brandies, and the comedy finishes by giving money to the shaman, who prides himself on his disinterestedness no more than other impostors of the same sort.[42]

The Encyclopedists' need to establish the shaman as compelling dissembler reveals their fascination with the Asiatic Other as well as their desire to create a European identity through difference.[43] Perhaps it was the very presence of these two essays, published in volumes 14 and 16 of the *Encyclopedia*, that linked shamanism to theosophy and thus to Masonry in Catherine's mind.[44] Perhaps those final lines—"the comedy finishes"—provided the associative spark that brought together shamans and comedy.

Despite Catherine's evident distrust of shamanism as charlatanism, *The Siberian Shaman* employs a slightly different strategy in the characterization of its "deceiver." The play presents a contradictory portrayal of its title character, for although Catherine most often indicates his fraudulence, he sometimes appears genuine. While at times the spectator witnesses events that clearly indict the

---

[41] Diderot 16: 253–61.

[42] Diderot 14: 759.

[43] See Flaherty Chapter 5, on Diderot's interest in shamanism.

[44] Catherine had drawn heavily on the *Encyclopedia* twenty years earlier as she formulated her *Great Instruction* [Nakaz] (Alexander, *Catherine the Great: Life and Legend* 101).

shaman as an impostor, at other times the audience is cast in the same role as many of the onstage characters: that of impressionable onlooker. By providing a contradictory and ambiguous portrait of the play's representative of mysticism, she asks each audience member to assume actively the responsibility for discerning that character's trustworthiness; these same spectators could then apply those skills of judgment in their own lives as subjects of Catherine's Empire.

The plot of *Siberian Shaman* revolves around the Bobin family (Bobin, Bobina, their daughter Prelesta, and Kromov, Bobina's brother), who move from Irkutsk to St. Petersburg, bringing with them a Siberian shaman named Amban-Lai. Visitors arrive: they are the Drobin family (Sidor, Flena, and their nephew Karp—whom they are anxious to wed to Prelesta). Although Bobin is proud of Lai's powers, claiming that the shaman cured Bobina, the servant girl Mavra reveals to another visitor, Bragin, that the cure was a hoax.

The tale of the shaman and his deceptions is paralleled by the story of Ivan Pernatov and Prelesta.[45] The romantic intrigue of the play is a familiar neoclassic construction: back in Siberia, Prelesta had loved Ivan, a man whom the Bobins did not consider wealthy or prestigious enough for their daughter. Prelesta, lonely and homesick for Irkutsk, grows ill, and the Bobins enlist Lai to cure her. Ustinia Mashkina, an affected old woman who is traveling with the Pernatovs, arrives on the scene. Ustinia pretends that she and Ivan will soon marry, thus increasing Prelesta's illness. Although Lai tries to cure Prelesta, his healing is revealed to be a sham, and in the end he is arrested for his trickery. In the closing scene, Bobin gives permission for Prelesta to marry the man she truly loves: Ivan (who, it turns out, has acquired a substantial inheritance).

A twenty-first century reader may be tempted to reject *Siberian Shaman*'s anti-mystical stance, and might instead be impressed by the shaman's rituals and by his apparent wisdom. While it is true that a large chasm separates eighteenth-century spectatorial conceptions of the Other from those of the present, the play does present certain paradoxes in the portrayal of its title character. On one hand, Catherine's intentions for the play and for the character of the shaman should be obvious. Clearly, Catherine saw her shaman character as a fraud. In her own words, the play is

> a huge blow against the enthusiasts. Imagine a man who has passed through 140 different degrees; why, if you please? to achieve such a degree of intellectual beatitude that instead of answering the people who speak to him, he behaves in all sorts of eccentric ways, cries like a cat, sings like a rooster, barks like a dog, etc. etc. etc. Yet for all this, he is no less a pimp and a rogue.[46]

---

[45] The surname Pernatov may derive from the adjective *pernatyi* (feathery). Prelesta is a speaking name with several possible connotations. Although in general usage, the word *prelest'* means loveliness, or charm, in the eighteenth century, other synonyms included *obman* (deception) or *soblazn* (seduction) (Gribble).

[46] Pypin 1:411. From a 30 September 1787 letter in French to Grimm.

On the other hand, within the play itself Catherine often paradoxically depicts the shaman as intriguing, perhaps wise, and possibly even genuine. Given Catherine's goals of exposing and rooting out superstition, how are these moments of seeming magic reconciled with the image of the shaman as a fraudulent interloper? I will analyze the play's strategies act by act, with particular attention to Act II, in which the shaman creates a trance performance that metatheatrically implicates the spectator.

In Act I of *Siberian Shaman*, Catherine employs the same strategy that Molière used to introduce his famous faker Tartuffe—she postpones bringing her title character onstage until Act II (in Molière's play, Tartuffe does not appear until the second scene of the third act). The audience must therefore form initial impressions based upon the reported observations of other characters. The Bobins, who have brought the shaman with them from Siberia to St. Petersburg, explain the exotic details of his origins to Kromov and to Sanov, a visiting friend. Born in China, the shaman was orphaned, reared by a Tungusic *dvoedanets*[47] and then sent to study with Mongolian shamans. When Bobins explain that Lai miraculously cured Bobina of her illness, the characters report their varied perspectives:

SANOV. Supposedly he can tell a person's character just by looking at his face ....
KROMOV. Some describe him as a wise man.
BOBIN. He is shrewd, perceptive, and virtuous ....
KROMOV. Others ... call him a sorcerer ....
SANOV. The stupid and ignorant, when they lack common sense, see sorcery everywhere. (353)

Just as in *Tartuffe*, the audience is exposed both to the devout believers (in this case, the Bobins), as well as to skeptics like Sanov. Before we have even met the shaman ourselves, however, Catherine adds a final blow to his credibility. In the act's final scene, Bragin (who we later learn is a friend of the young man Ivan Pernatov) questions the two servants about the shaman. Mavra and Prokofii reveal that they substituted water for the shaman's miracle cure—Lai's reputed healing of Bobina is a hoax. Mavra comments that the shaman is either intentionally blinding the Bobins, or "they wanted to deceive themselves" (358). The play will return to this theme repeatedly—that the shaman himself is only fulfilling the desires of those around him to believe in him. The deceived are as culpable as the deceiver.

The second act of *Siberian Shaman* is in many ways startling and unexpected; its first scene is atypical of eighteenth-century comedy. In it, stage action— without dialog—comprises the entirety of the scene:

Act II. Scene 1. The stage presents the Shaman's chambers in the Bobin house. Lai, dressed in a short caftan or in a dressing gown, is sewing boots; having sewed several,

---

[47] Literally, one who pays two tributes; in this context, most likely referring to one who paid *iasak* (tribute) to both Russia and China (Dal').

he puts on Shamanic clothes and sits motionless on a chair with a rapt visage; before him or near him stands a table with an open book; several minutes later [Act II, scene 2] *begins.* (360)

Russian neoclassical comedy, like its French counterpart, is primarily a dialog form. Characters enter and exit a central site of action; that action consists of conversations (declarations of love, revelations of intrigue, displays of foolish thinking). Rarely do playwrights display non-conversational activities, such as duels. The genre itself is dependent on the intellectual clash of personalities—of wits rather than swords. Catherine's comedies are no exception, and indeed much of her writing suffers from the awkward insistence that major events must take place offstage.[48] The stage space is a site for reportage and reaction, rather than for events and action.

Too, neoclassical Russian writers rarely show a solo character in a scene. When a character does appear alone, it is almost exclusively to deliver a revelatory soliloquy, as when a lover, left alone, presents true inner feelings, or a wily servant discloses recent plans. Conventionally, the soliloquy is the doorway into the truth of a character, and the mode of the typical solo scene is almost exclusively verbal. Thus from the first moment of II.1, the scene is unusual. We see several successive actions of the shaman, none of which is accompanied by dialog. If we compare the scene to a typical soliloquy, we would assume, despite Amban-Lai's silence, that he communicates through his actions, and that what he communicates is genuine. First shown in a dressing gown, he sews several boots—he thus confirms an earlier description by Bobin: "Well, sometimes he reads a Chinese book ... or mends his clothes ... or sews boots" (353). After sewing several boots, he dons his shaman's clothes and sits motionless.

What is the duration of these actions? The implication is that they are slow and sequential, appropriate for the behavior of someone alone and unwatched. Yet of course, Lai is watched; we the spectators find ourselves not in the position of quietly listening confidants (as with a soliloquy) but of silent voyeurs, seeing into the private chambers of someone we have not yet met. If Lai's silent sewing is genuine, then perhaps so too are his subsequent actions: putting on shamanic clothing, sitting motionless "with a rapt visage" (*s voskhishchennym vidom*). At this moment in the play, Catherine does not indicate that the shaman is feigning or crafty; he does not open his eyes to see if his foolish dupes are coming. Instead, Catherine gives a very specific durational note: that II.2 begins "several minutes later." Thus the shaman sits, unmoving, rapt, alone for several minutes—the same shaman whom, at the close of the previous scene, the seemingly trustworthy maid Mavra revealed to be a faker and a charlatan. Catherine thus offers two contradictory sets of information, from two very different sources. Both the initial

---

[48] Cf. scene III.3 of *The Deceiver*: when the alchemist Kalifalkzherston's cauldron bursts offstage.

praises and criticism of Amban-Lai are relayed to us by other characters; it is on the basis of Mavra's verbal recollection of past events that the audience is led, at the end of Act I, to mistrust him. But rather than giving us hearsay, in II.1 Catherine gives us visual evidence. We must judge the shaman by what our own eyes see: a demonstration of a shaman assuming his ritual attire and entering a trance state—a series of actions that, in the scene itself, has no connotation of disingenuousness.

One possible explanation is that Catherine relies too heavily on Mavra's narrative account of the shaman's deception, misjudging the voyeuristic power of this solo scene. In this view, to show a scene in which the shaman appears to be genuine is a dramaturgical error, a misjudgment. But scene II.1 may be a deliberate strategy whereby Catherine casts her audience in the role of observer. We, like the Bobins, rely on what we see of Lai's behavior. Using a scientific model of observation, Catherine allows us to judge Lai as one of her court explorer-historians might have—through a viewing of external behavior. And from that viewpoint, the trance itself does appear to be authentic. If we think so, we have been allied with the Bobins, and must await the unfolding of events, to see how we too have been duped.

In the solo scene of the shaman alone in his room, the spectator is in a state of doubt and suspense. But in the following scene, watching Lai interact with the Bobins and their guests, that same spectator forms predictable alliances with the normative family members, with whom she or he can identify. Catherine directly contrasts the shaman's behavior with that of the other characters. To achieve this juxtaposition, Catherine employs the metatheatrical tactic of the play-within-the-play, or rather in this case, the shamanic ritual-within-the-play.

This ritual can be seen through the lens of metatheatricality. The court ethnographer Peter Pallas compared the shamans' rituals to such dramatic forms as farces or pantomimes.[49] Reading Amban-Lai's shamanic ritual with twenty-first century eyes, we are also inclined to view his actions as the elements of a performance. The metatheatrical element becomes apparent when we contrast the ritual performance's style with the highly formalized, rigid conventions of the neoclassical comedy *Siberian Shaman* in which the ritual is contained. That contrast is yet another source of humor, and of commentary.

Amban-Lai's shamanic ritual takes place in two scenes in Act II: scenes 2 and 4, separated by a brief scene when he is offstage. In the former scene, Lai is in a trance state but is not yet verbally communicative. The comic premise of the scene is simple—to get him to talk. Bobin explains that they must find something that will seize hold of his imagination. Lai responds to their attempts non-verbally, with gestural statements. When Sanov asks to listen to his wisdom, Lai "*does a pantomime as if someone is tickling him*" (362). They show him a crutch; he shakes his head to the right and to the left as if saying "no." They show him the

---

49 Flaherty 73.

clock, and he *"nods his head forward and to the side, in the manner of Chinese dolls"* (362). Lai's silence contrasts with their banter as he moves, gestures, runs, pantomimes, nods. The comic suspense builds. Finally, when Bragin shows him a purse full of money, Lai stretches out his hands and begins to speak. At this moment, the ritual-within-the-play commences, and Catherine has succeeded in comically revealing the hidden charlatanism of her shaman, who even in trance is drawn to money.

The performance begins, and is presented in three distinct sections: Amban-Lai's initial verbalization (after he is shown the money), his return into the room with a drum, and the "ballet" performed by his followers at the end of the scene. These events are clearly distinguished from his behavior in the remainder of the play; in later scenes, he converses in (somewhat) comprehensible Russian, and in general, assumes a more "civilized" demeanor.

In the first part of the ritual/performance, when Amban-Lai finally breaks the silence, he approaches four of the men present (note that only men are brought into the shaman's chambers), and for each has a different animalistic verbalization: to Sidor Drobin, he barks like a dog;[50] to Karp Drobin, he meows like a cat (which Sanov mistakes as Chinese); to Kromov, he sings like a rooster; and to Bragin he clucks like a hen. By vocally imitating various animals, the shaman is both physically expressive and irrational; he is everything that the other characters are not, with their rigid and predictable bodily movements, their prescribed diction, their stiff formality. He then pushes the others apart, and leaves the room. Throughout this initial sequence, the visitors each attempt to force Lai to communicate on their terms, refusing to accept his utterances as serious or communicative. Kromov asks Lai if he is pretending, and Bragin states that Amban-Lai must be joking.

After a brief scene with the dumbstruck men, Lai returns in scene four of Act II, entering with the same rapt visage indicative of the trance state, this time holding a shamanic drum. Catherine's theatrical strategy shifts once again; no longer do we see Lai interact with the family members. In this second segment of the ritual, Lai strikes his drum, runs around the room, sings, howls, and screams various vowel sounds before collapsing—many of these elements are accurate to actual shamanic practice. The stage directions specify that the men are frightened by his actions. Would a spectator, perhaps a member of the nobility, safely ensconced in a seat in the Hermitage Theatre in 1786, have been frightened as well? A. F. Anisimov, a present-day Russian ethnographer of Evenk culture, found that one actual shaman's performance to be "so deftly accompanied by motions, imitations of spirit-voices, comic and dramatic dialogs, wild screams, snorts, noises, and the like, that it startled and amazed even this far from

---

[50] The word for barking used here is the Russian word *lai* meaning barking; thus it is a pun on Lai's name.

superstitious onlooker."[51] To what extent could such a display onstage have produced a comic effect; to what extent did it provoke wonder and fear in its audience, thus further underscoring its credulity?

The third segment of the ritual is described in a single sentence. *"His followers leave him after a short ballet"* (364). The presence of shamanic followers (referred to later by Sidor Drobin as *"pliasuny"* or dancers) comes as a surprise to the reader of this play. How and when do they enter the scene?[52] Paradoxically, while the stage directions seem to imply a shamanic, ritualistic dance, the Russian word *"balet"* connotes European high art. Whatever dance Lai's followers performed must have been read against the background of its setting: a "civilized" Russian domestic interior rather than a shamanic tent. As in her description of Lai alone, here Catherine does not specify that this dance is comic in nature, although humor might result from the perception of incongruity.

In scene 5, when Lai awakens from his trance, he speaks intelligible Russian to those around him; for the first time in the play, the audience can judge the shaman's own statements. He explains that he cannot remember what transpired during the trance, and that his goal is to use silence as a means toward the attainment of non-existence. The shaman brags about his marvelous book, in which he claims everything is written, including information about the frame of mind (*umonachertanie*) of each person in the room. The shaman's book may be in a larger sense a commentary on Catherine's age, the age of Encyclopedists in which all knowledge was being cataloged, printed and disseminated. The very idea of a "shamanic book" must have seemed an oxymoron to Catherine—a book having connotations of the rational and quantifiable, shamanism having very much the opposite. But Novikov was making just such mystical books available to Catherine's subjects; thus Lai's book can also be seen as a reference to Novikov's Masonic publishing efforts.[53]

After Lai impresses the gathering with his observations, they leave and Catherine shows us yet another view of Lai: with his guard down, in conversation with the butler. In marked contrast to the philosophical discussions of the previous scene, the two men discuss boots:

BUTLER. Amban, don't you want a glass of vodka?
LAI. Give it to me, brother ... I'm tired.
BUTLER. Will the master's boots be done soon?
LAI. They would have been done a while ago ... but you can see how busy I am.

---

[51] Anisimov 101.

[52] Their possible presence in II.1 complicates the reading of this scene as a gestural soliloquy. Were these followers present when Lai was alone in his chamber?

[53] One possible visual clue that the Amban is being satirized as a Freemason is the presence of the open book. A Bible, opened to a particular passage as a source of wisdom, is a traditional part of the setting in a Masonic lodge. Mackey 113.

BUTLER. Yes, brother ... you undertook too much.... You should sew boots a little
more diligently .... (367–68)

This exchange again puts wisdom in the mouth of a servant character; the butler
sees through the shaman, as does Mavra. Just as the shaman can reveal someone's
true nature by consulting his book, the butler "reads" Lai by calling him brother
and treating him as a boot maker rather than as an esteemed sorcerer, even scolding
him. The solidarity between the two men—both working men—is evident, and the
scene subtly serves to demystify Lai.

Thus, within the first two acts of her play, Catherine has created contradictions
in the representation of her title character: between the reported and witnessed
perceptions, between his trance persona, his public demeanor, and his
(presumably) more genuine behavior alone in his room and in interaction with the
butler. Rather than behaving as a type, Lai is an unstable presence in the play; it is
up to the spectator to resolve this instability into the single moral perspective
required by the play's genre.

In Act III, Catherine introduces yet another unseen but crucial character: the
Bobins' daughter Prelesta. Her story is thus intertwined with the shaman's.
Because she is suffering from an undetermined illness, the Bobins ask Lai to heal
her. The shaman is reluctant, explaining his theory that, "In all flesh there are two
forces of attraction, one for the elements, and the other for the bodies. Healing an
illness depends on the expulsion or increase of one or the other" (374). However,
he soon goes off, first to the Pernatovs to heal the ill woman traveling with them,
then on to Prelesta.[54] Before his return in Act IV, then, the shaman has met with
Ivan Pernatov (Prelesta's true love) in an offstage scene—and *Siberian Shaman*'s
two plots intersect.

In the third scene of Act IV, when Lai returns, Sanov praises him for having
cured the Pernatov woman by attributing the cause to jealousy between the
husband and wife. Again, Catherine points out Lai's natural shrewdness; if his
cures lack magic and mystery, he is an excellent judge of character. As he himself
explains:

Passion's paintbrush sketches on the face of every person: happiness, joy, anger, grief,
jealousy, envy, falsehood, vengeance, indecision, stubbornness, steadfastness—all affect
the exterior [...] when one knows what motivates people, is it hard to perceive this or
that detail in external appearances? (385–6)

If understood from a spiritual perspective, these words attest to the power of Lai's
abilities; a rationalist, like the playwright herself, interprets these words rather as a

---

[54] Dawson examines the issues of marriage and family stability as they relate to
occultism in this trilogy, observing that in both *The Deceiver* and *The Siberian Shaman*, it is
the female characters who are ill and must be cured. ("Catherine the Great: Playwright of
the Anti-Occult.")

con man's credo, a shyster's scheme for exploiting naïveté by way of a few careful observations. The play constantly oscillates between these two perspectives, but in the end comes down on the side of rationalism and a view of Lai as a con artist who easily persuaded others to accept his pronouncements as supernatural if "they wanted to deceive themselves."

Such strategies fall through for the shaman in IV.4, when Lai and Prelesta meet face to face and alone. The scene is unusual in that few young heroines in neoclassical comedies are left alone with men; most women of marriageable age appear together in scenes with their maids and their mothers, and only rarely meet alone with their fiancés—except in happy denouement scenes. But no character raises an objection to leaving Prelesta alone with the shaman; his status as a healer seems to override his ethnic and class differences. Perhaps also because of those differences, he is clearly not a suitor and therefore not a threat to chastity. Lai's plan is simple: his cure for Prelesta's illness is a letter in which Ivan Pernatov professes his love for her. Prelesta is scornful and stubborn, however, refusing to read his "prescription," and speaking disparagingly of his handwriting: "Well, but if you scribbled it in Mongolian, I won't understand it!" (387). When she does realize that the prescription is a letter from Ivan, she refuses to read it, convinced that he is engaged to Ustinia. Ultimately her father enters and reads the letter to himself. When Bobin realizes Lai's duplicity in proffering a cure by means of a love letter, he angrily orders the shaman to leave.

The shaman does not appear in the remainder of the play; through an escalating series of reported stories, the audience learns of several offstage events: that a group of followers has assembled in Lai's chambers, forming a shaman school of sorts; that many curious people have gathered in the courtyard of the house, all eager to learn more about the famed shaman; later, that Lai has been arrested for swindling a widow out of her fortune. The audience sees none of these events firsthand; nor does Lai return to defend his behavior. At the play's conclusion, then, the shaman is revealed as a sham. In a parallel plotline, Ustinia Mashkina is also shown to be a fake; her feigned engagement to Ivan is unmasked as a fraud. Catherine ties together her two plotlines by explicitly acknowledging the parallels between Ustinia's deception and Lai's lies. In the play's all-important moralistic closing pronouncement, Kromov compares Ustinia to the shaman Lai:

> You resemble these Shamans; both you and they, following rules you've invented, at first deceive only yourselves, but then deceive everyone else who puts their faith in you. (406)

In these final moments, Catherine contrasts both Lai and Ustinia with Prelesta, the play's heroine. In the last scene, Bobin carefully coaxes Prelesta into revealing her love for Ivan. By speaking a third-person tale, she is able to give voice to her wish to marry Ivan over Karp Drobin. Although through much of the play Prelesta has appeared shallow and foolish, the scene emphasizes her sweetness and modesty.

Where she is naïve, Lai is shrewd. Where she is modest, Lai is the opposite; where she underestimates her own rights and powers, he overestimates his; where she gains her happiness, he, like Ustinia, loses all.

What, finally, is Catherine's case against Amban-Lai, her Siberian shaman? As a monarch, she regarded shamanism (along with Masonry and alchemy and other practices she saw as anti-rationalist) not only as the highest form of folly but as a dangerously infectious form of insubordination to the goals of her reign. Yet as playwright, she employed a subtle strategy of characterization; rather than rigidly determining the audience's perceptions of the shaman from start to finish, she allows his role to remain ambiguous, shifting constantly until the denouement, and the final revelation of his duplicity. The fixity of that conclusion (the shaman's arrest) provides a needed moral and interpretive anchor to the play.

In employing this unique strategy, Catherine was able to cast her spectators, who were also her political subjects, in the role of active truth-seekers. In essence, the play became a kind of rehearsal for "real life." Her ideal spectator-subjects would learn the tools by which to recognize deception, possibly having themselves been deceived by aspects of the shaman's performance. Catherine thus implicates the audience in the narrative and metatheatrical structure of her play.

If read against a background of Catherine's battle against Freemasonry—its organizational structure, its political power, its impact on the world of publishing in Russia—the comedy *Siberian Shaman* can be seen as the last installment in the trilogy's critique of Novikov and his Masonic circle. The shaman himself is another parody of Novikov, who through his high status in the Rosicrucian Order and his publishing efforts, sponsored a range of inquiry outside the bounds of Catherine the Great's version of the Enlightenment. From Catherine's perspective, his Masonic ideas were just as nonsensical as a dog barking; like a shaman, Novikov was capable of entrancing the people—her people—through his strange ideas. In Catherine's view, the shaman Novikov deceived those who wanted to deceive themselves; part of the enlightening strategy of her trilogy was to awaken her audience from the trance of his mysticism.

Five Proverb Plays

A Potemkin Village. The phrase conjures up visions of false façades and thriving towns with happy peasants, conjured for the benefit of a touring monarch. The term was born during Catherine's extensive and elaborate 1787 tour of the Crimea, which she embarked upon in January 1787, a few months after the premiere of *Siberian Shaman* (see Fig. 3.2). Some of Catherine's critics alleged that her former lover Grigorii Potemkin, now Governor-General of the Crimea, had enhanced her visit by arranging advance construction of elaborate facades, to hide any unpleasant evidence of poverty or discontent. Potemkin's critic Georg Von Helbig, who had coined the term "Potemkinsche Dörfer" (Potemkin Village), even claimed that towns seen along the Dnieper river cruise were "composed of façades—painted screens on pasteboard—that were moved along the river and seen by the Empress five or six times."[55] Although Sebag Montefiore and other historians have demonstrated that Potemkin did not engage in such large-scale deception, certainly Catherine engaged in this six-month tour partly to witness in person Potemkin's publicly doubted Crimean achievements. And, as Montefiore points out, every state visit today sees "houses repainted, streets cleaned, tramps and whores arrested, banners festooned across streets."[56]

Thus, although Potemkin Villages never existed per se, the Empress and her coterie were treated to a carefully orchestrated display, with mock sea battles, flourishing shops, new fortresses and churches, and demonstrations of Kalmyk cavalry. Even if it wasn't a pasteboard façade, Potemkin created a massive show with the intention "to portray the Crimea as an earthly paradise"[57]—an accepted artifice, a reminder to suspend disbelief. And to promote a particular rendering of reality. In this way all theatrical plays are Potemkin Villages. Plays are deceptions, and while not all playwrights aim to defraud, on some level all authors intend that their visions take precedence over reality, if only temporarily.

This same Crimean tour, in addition to serving as a high-profile demonstration of Catherine's dominion over this new region, also yielded a flurry of new theatrical activity. By 1787, Catherine had been writing plays for fifteen years. All but one were in Russian.[58] But after returning from her long journey, Catherine and a select group of highly placed friends wrote a group of one-act comedies in French between 1787 and 1788. Catherine herself composed five one-acts (and may have co-written at least one other).[59] The genre of these short plays was that of "dramatic proverb," in which a lightly comic story is resolved with a final moral punchline. These proverb plays differ from the rest of Catherine's dramatic writings in their use of French, and also in their lack of availability to the public. If staged in a theatre at all, most were presented only in the Hermitage Court Theatre for a select group of invitees. But their original context was a more intimate space: various private rooms and chambers, where their enactment was less a formal performance and more a playful game, by and for a private inner circle.

That "proverb circle," born of the lengthy tour of the Crimea, consisted of several friends and advisors who had accompanied her on the trip. Among the

---

55 Montefiore 380.

56 Montefiore 381.

57 Dixon 43.

58 The French fragment "M. Lustucru."

59 "L'Amant Ridicule" by the Prince de Ligne was probably co-written with Catherine sometime between the end of the Crimean tour and November 1787. See Pypin 4: ii; Hyart 92. Further in chapter, I will discuss the additional possibility raised by Hyart that Catherine penned most of "L'Insouciant," attributed to Dmitriev-Mamonov. Pypin seems to agree, as he included the play in his edition of Catherine's works.

Fig. 3.2 **Catherine in recognizably Russian traveling costume, after Mikhail Shibanov. Original portrait was done during Catherine's visit to Kiev in 1787, as part of her Crimean tour**

traveling group were three ambassadors: Count Louis-Philippe de Ségur (France); Alleyne Fitz-Herbert (England); and Count Louis Cobenzl (Austria). Charles-Joseph de Ligne, the Austrian general and trusted advisor to Joseph II, represented the Holy Roman Emperor before he joined the tour himself. And Aleksandr Dmitriev-Mamonov, Catherine's favorite from 1786–89, was at her side throughout the journey.

Upon her return to St. Petersburg, Catherine invited members of this group to write their own proverbs, to be staged in her private Hermitage Court Theatre. The plays were then published in a very limited edition, *Recueil des Pièces de l'Hermitage*, in St. Petersburg in 1788–89, with no attributions. A later edition, *Le Théâtre de l'Hermitage de Catherine II*, published in Paris in 1799, attributes plays to Catherine, Ségur, Cobenzl, de Ligne, and Dmitriev-Mamonov.[60] Other included authors are Count Stroganov (a Senator), Ivan Shuvalov, Baron d'Estat (a French attaché), and Mlle. Aufrène (Aufresne).[61]

As always with Catherine's comedies, serious concerns underlie their frivolous surfaces. While the proverbs share many similarities with Catherine's full-length comedies, their brevity allows them to be both more didactic and more humorous. Catherine titled one of her short plays "The Rage for Proverbs." In it, a Madame Tantine, overcome with a mania for these short little entertainments, forces everyone around her to write and perform them. For a while, Catherine and her inner circle experienced this rage for proverbs. If her other dramatic writings were meant to be entertaining lessons for the general public, Catherine and her cohorts wrote these short dramatic confections to examine, teach, and amuse themselves.

"A dramatic proverb is a short play, usually in one act, in which the title is illustrated or proven by the plot."[62] Clarence Brenner traces the history of the development of the dramatic proverb back to mid-seventeenth-century French salons, where an interest in proverbs led to the "*jeu de proverbes*," a parlor game that required the players to speak entirely in proverbial sayings. This game transformed into the dramatic proverb, which initially consisted only of a scenario with improvised dialog. The salon audience's goal was to guess which proverb, implied by the play's action, would be cited in its closing lines.[63] Once elite social life transferred to the court under Louis XIV, a similar guessing game, charades, became a more widespread entertainment. In the late seventeenth century, however, a few dramatic proverbs were written by women authors with

---

[60] This edition consists of nineteen plays. The earlier 1788 edition published in Russia contained all the same pieces, except that Catherine's historical play *From the Life of Riurik* did not appear, and the fourth volume contained five additional plays not published in the French edition. The Russian edition did not list authors for any of the works.

[61] The most pages in either edition are occupied by Ségur, whose tragedy *Coriolan*, three-act comedy *Crispin duègne*, and three proverbs occupy more pages than Catherine's plays, or the plays of all the others combined (Hyart 94).

[62] Levy 8.

[63] Levy 8.

connections to education: Mme Durand, who published ten proverbs in 1699, and Mme de Maintenon (second wife of Louis XIV), who wrote forty proverbs for the girls at Saint-Cyr (not published until 1829).

With the eighteenth century came a new age of "Theatre of Society," with private stages in aristocratic homes. By 1765 there was a renewed interest in dramatic proverbs, which lasted until the Revolution. In 1768, a collection called *Théâtre de la Societé* published one of Collé's dramatic proverbs. That same year appeared the first collection of proverbs (thirty-three) written by the real genius of the form, Carmontelle. In his preface to his 1773 edition, he gives the following explanation of the form's necessities:

> The dramatic proverb is thus a type of comedy that one makes by inventing a subject, or by using some features, some little story, etc. The words of the proverb must be enveloped in such a manner so that the spectators don't guess it, it's necessary, when they [the players] say it, that they [the spectators] cry *ah! that's right*: as when someone tells the solution to a riddle that one hasn't understood.[64]

Numerous collections appeared, and a journal called *Mercure de France* published dramatic proverbs almost monthly from 1768 to 1778.[65] Despite this public exposure, proverbs written for the society milieu were done almost exclusively on private stages. Comic actor Abraham-Joseph Fleury complained that their popularity competed directly with productions at the Comédie Française.[66]

Proponents of a new educational literature for children also favored dramatic proverbs. A trend toward the "Théâtre de l'Éducation" dominated the last three decades of the eighteenth century. Among its authors were Moissy, Garnier and also Mme de Genlis. The latter's collections such as the four-volume *Theatre for the Use of Young Persons* [Théâtre à l'usage des Jeunes Personnes, 1779–80] included proverbs meant to be acted by children as a means of instilling morality and virtue.

The genre overall did not have great impact on Russian theatre, but did, for a short time, occupy the interests of the Empress and her innermost circle, just as its popularity was waning in France. The rage for proverbs in Russia began with Catherine's close circle of friends and favorites, on the long journey from St. Petersburg to the Crimea and back again.

Catherine's tour of the Crimea was the result of her acquisition of territory there in 1783; Potemkin had been a major force in that achievement, and now, as governor-general of the "New Russia," was in charge of demonstrating Russia's new strengths (new towns, new fleets) in that region. Initially planned for 1785, the tour was postponed twice. Lasting from January to July of 1787, the tour

---

[64] Quoted in Brenner 16.

[65] Brenner 25.

[66] Hawkins 2: 260.

included three months in Kiev, followed by a river journey on the Dnieper beginning in April. On 12 May, Catherine and the Emperor Joseph arrived together in Kherson, where they were treated to a fireworks spectacle. By 17 May, they departed for the Crimea. The return was via Poltava, and then Moscow, returning to Petersburg by 11 July. By August, she was at war with Turkey, a conflict that would last until 1791.

Although she worked at her usual pace throughout the travels (rising at 6 a.m., working until 11 p.m.), there was time, following the conclusion of afternoon travel at 7 p.m., when Catherine would receive her foreign envoys for some conversation until about 9 p.m.[67] Count de Ségur noted in his memoirs that,

> A thousand different amusements, the curious and striking narrations of Catherine, the intellectual, although rather melancholy reflections of Mr. Fitz-Herbert, the whimsicalities of Cobentzel, who made us play with him at proverbs, in which he excelled, in the bed-chamber of the Empress, gave an agreeable variety to the passing hours.[68]

Elsewhere Ségur remembers, "we amused ourselves sometimes, in the evening, by playing *au secrétaire*, by making enigmas, charades, and bouts-rimés."[69] After their return to St. Petersburg in July 1787, Catherine seems to have maintained and expanded her proverb circle. She herself composed five new proverbs between August 1787 and October 1788, resulting in several court theatre productions and the publication of fourteen proverbs by Catherine, Ségur, and others in 1788.

The presence on the Crimean tour of Catherine's latest "favorite," Alexander Dmitriev-Mamonov (1758–1803), shows an interplay of literature and love. Her lover since 1786, the twenty-nine year old Mamonov rode daily at Catherine's side in the six-seat carriage that also accommodated her maid of honor Anna Protasova. She wrote often to her correspondent Friedrich Melchior Grimm of her "Red Coat" ("M. l'habit Rouge").[70]

Mamonov, then, was certainly a part of the amusing evenings that led to the traveling group's "rage for proverbs." His play *L'Insouciant* was included in the published collection of proverbs (both editions). Hyart points out that only three members of the published group were native French speakers: Ségur, M. d'Estat, French attaché to the imperial cabinet, and Mlle Aufrène, daughter of actor Jean Aufrène, a performer with the French Theatre in St. Petersburg.[71] For others, such as Cobenzl, Shuvalov, Stroganov, Mamonov, and Catherine herself, French was not the native tongue. Among Mamonov's attractive qualities, however, were his

---

[67] Madariaga, *Russia in the Age* 370.

[68] Ségur, *Memoirs* 3: 111–12.

[69] Ségur, *Memoirs* 3: 17.

[70] Madariaga, *Russia in the Age* 356. For example, see a letter dated 3 October 1788 in Grot, "Pis'ma imperatritsy" 465.

[71] Hyart 97.

education, wit, and fluency in French.[72]   Catherine may have invited him to participate in the collection to show off these traits.

Mamonov's *L'Insouciant* is a three-act comedy about Lev Naryshkin, Catherine's mischievous friend from her days as a Grand Duchess, and another traveler on the southern tour. Within Catherine's inner circle, Naryshkin was the court jester, about whose presence on the journey Ségur wrote: "and if, by chance, the conversation became rather languid, Narischkin, the Master of the Horse, soon excited laughter and repartee, by his tricks and buffoonery."[73] Khrapovitskii, a friend of Mamonov's, hints in his diary that *L'Insouciant* may have been finished by Catherine in September. Hyart makes this case by noting that Khrapovitskii recopied the play, a practice reserved only for the Empress's work.[74] Later, in November, Khrapovitskii writes of another proverb, finished by Catherine because Mamonov "grew lazy."[75]

Mamonov was also one of the Empress's favorite audience members. Khrapovitskii's diary notes that on 23 April 1788, "The evening was passed at A.M.D.M.'s [Aleksandr Matveevich Dmitriev-Mamonov]; there they played 'The Flatterer and the Flattered'."[76] We also know that Catherine planned two of her comedies ("Voyages of M. Bontems" and "There's No Evil without Good") for presentation in Mamonov's chambers on 30 August (his nameday for St. Alexander). Khrapovitskii's diary tell us that Mamonov was ill that evening, but that the plays were later done in his chambers for Mamonov's birthday celebration on 19 September 1788. Whether she composed them specifically for this occasion or not, it is significant that Catherine perceived her own dramatic proverbs as worthy presents for her lover.

"The Busy-Body"

Catherine's five dramatic proverbs share certain traits: they are all short, in French, take place within an upper-class French milieu, and each ends with the pronouncement of a French proverb. Catherine composed the first one ("The Busy-Body" [Le Tracassier]) sometime in August 1787, just after her return to St. Petersburg. Another play ("The Flatterer and the Flattered") followed in April 1788, and the final three were written between August and October 1788. As "The Busy-Body" opens, Rodencour sees Moncalme, his nephew, in innocent dialog with the chambermaid, and begins to tease Moncalme about this encounter. Rodencour endeavors first to plant suspicions in Moncalme, that his beloved

---

[72]   Madariaga, *Russia in the Age of Catherine the Great* 355.
[73]   Ségur, *Memoirs* 2: 258.
[74]   Hyart 92.
[75]   17 November 1788; Barsukov 197. The proverb was called "Don't Pay Taxes for Nonsense" [Za vzdor poshliny ne platiat]. See also Pypin 3:iii.
[76]   Barsukov 77.

Marquise is in love with the marquis of Souche. Then, alone with the Marquise, Rodencour tells her that Moncalme and the maid Marton were having a "tête-à-tête." For her part, the Marquise is taken in enough to be quite upset with her chambermaid Marton, creating a scene with some spark. Although the Marquise's father arrives with another suitor (the silent count A) and Rodencour makes several other suggestions of possible matches, in the end the Marquise chooses Moncalme. Marton gives the closing proverb: "Un tiens vaut mieux que deux tu l'auras," the French equivalent of "A bird in the hand is worth two in the bush."

Rodencour, the titular Busy-Body, is certainly the play's most interesting character. We do not learn anything of his motivations, all we see is his meddlesome insinuations of lustful impropriety. Rodencour makes observations of physical behavior:

> See how she [Marton] plays with her apron ... with her ribbons. ... She doesn't know what to do with her hands ... where to look ... she arranges her glances ... her face ... Bravo, bravo, Marton. ... Here's how one fools the world ... (6)

He then interprets these gestures to mean something suspicious. To Rodencour, the body seems uncontrollable and betraying:

> the marquis has eyes, ears, a mouth.... The Marquise has them too.... From eyes depart winks; from the mouth, remarks; sentiments that enter into the ears and from there go right into the heart (7)

One disappointing aspect of the playwriting is that Moncalme never seems to believe for a moment in the falseness of his beloved Marquise. Rodencour's attempts to rattle him seem to fall on deaf ears, and Moncalme remains as steady as his telling name.

Many of Catherine's other villain characters in her longer comedies are blinded by ignorance or superstition. Compared to the rational Moncalme, Rodencour is almost demonic in his persistently skewed interpretations of observable fact. He is a precursor to the dissension-stirring Dvorabrod from the full-length play *A Family Broken Up by Intrigue and Suspicions*, which Catherine began writing just a month later; indeed, Rodencour is the French telling name for roaming the court (equivalent to Dvorabrod in Russian). On 31 May 1788, Catherine had written to Grimm with this comparison: "there is no one who hasn't encountered such men, and above all in the court; this play was written to unmask them; he's Rodencour, he's Hauslöffer, he's Dvorabrod in Russian."[77]

The meddlesome Rodencour is not ignorant, but his interpretation of reality is warped by a misguided belief that everyone around him is faithless and flirtatious. In Moncalme's words, "But, my dear uncle, you have a way of envisioning things

---

[77] Grot, "Pis'ma imperatritsy" 450.

that continually fill your mind with visions, suspicions, and chimeras" (7). In this way, Rodencour can be compared not only to the villains of other Catherine comedies, but to the naïve patriarchs and matriarchs who are led astray by the irrational.

The proverb itself is only tangentially related to the main plot, which predominantly emphasized the theme of a meddling busy-body. In the original French, the proverb implies something held right now is better than something imagined for the future. Rodencour's imagination often runs wild based on observations of behavior; the proverb advises us to eschew those flights of fancy in favor of the concretely held.

"The Flatterer and the Flattered"

Catherine's second proverb, "The Flatterer and the Flattered" [Le Flatteur et les flattés], makes clear reference from the first to the Aesopian tale of the Fox and the Crow. In that tale, the Fox flatters the Crow by praising his beauty. In Jean de La Fontaine's French version of the tale, Renard (the fox) convinces Corbeau (the crow) to sing, which causes him to drop the cheese he had held in his mouth. Catherine's character Corbec appears in black, and the flatterer Renard in "well-worn yellowish outfit." Corbec does not hold cheese, but he is the recent heir to his uncle's fortune, and Renard admires the air of freedom about him, while warning that it could attract compliments from adulators. Renard then proceeds to enumerate Corbec's "beautiful and good qualities," including his health, his appetite, and his good sleeping habits. Corbec criticizes his wife's reliance on "remedies" of various sorts, and when she appears on the scene, she is portrayed as a cranky spouse who complains about her husband's control of the servants. They quarrel, and when the husband leaves, Renard sympathizes with Madame de Corbec by flattering her with comments about her beauty and education. The Corbecs, both enchanted with Renard, plan to give him lodging, clothing, and money, which he takes before leaving. In a metatheatrical touch, he says that he must leave because he is "engaged to represent the fable of the Corbeau and the Renard."

> M. RENARD. Assuredly it's a small thing; but the ending is moral.
> M. de CORBEC. Moral! Moral! There's nothing more boring than these eternal moralizations, in my view.
> Mme. de CORBEC. Oh my dear, I ask you for the favor of knowing the moral; I don't know how to do without it. I'm crazy about it. I read and re-read moral tales, all because of their titles. (32)

Renard then leaves the couple, who entertain the idea that he might have been mocking them.

The theme of flattery seems a natural one for an Empress writing to entertain her courtly circle. As the anonymous *Monthly Review* critic, writing of the Paris edition, commented, "Her Imperial Majesty has manifested great experience in courtly adulation, and a thorough knowledge of the disinterested motives with which it is offered at the shrines of wealth and power."[78] As with *The Busy-Body*, the contrast is between normative yet gullible victims and a schemer who overdoes, whether by skepticism or flattery.

Renard speaks the proverb, which comes near the end of the play, as a bit of advice to the Corbecs: "every flatterer lives at the expense of whomever listens to him; this lesson is well worth a cheese" (11). This phrase, along with several others from the play, is an exact rendering of several lines from La Fontaine's French verse version of the tale:

> *Le renard s'en saisit, et dit: "Mon bon monsieur,*
> *Apprenez que tout flatteur*
> *Vit aux dépens de celui qui l'écoute:*
> *Cette leçon vaut bien un fromage, sans doute."*
> *Le corbeau, honteux et confus,*
> *Jura, mais un peu tard, qu'on ne l'y prendrait plus.*

> The Fox was on it in a trice.
> "Learn, sir," said he, "that flatterers live
> On those who swallow what they say.
> A cheese is not too much to give
> For such a piece of sound advice."
> The Crow, ashamed to have been such easy prey,
> Swore, though too late, he shouldn't catch him twice.[79]

In the play, we see Catherine's use of these familiar French lines:

M. RENARD. *Le tout dépend de la façon dont elle est dite. Par exemple, si je vous disois:* (à M. de Corbec). *Mon bon monsieur, apprenez que tout flatteur vit aux dépens de celui qui l'écoute; cette leçon vaut bien un fromage, sans doute.*

M. de CORBEC. *Oui, oui, je me souviens du reste. ... N'est-ce pas: le Corbeau, honteux et confus, jura, mais un peu tard, qu'on ne l'y prendrait plus?*

M. RENARD. *Vous y êtes. C'est un badinage de société ... Il vous plaira de m'excuser.*

M. RENARD. All depends on the way it's told. For example, if I said to you: *(to M. de Corbec)* My dear monsieur, learn that every flatterer lives at the expense of whomever listens to him; this lesson without doubt is well worth a cheese.

---

78 Anonymous, "Review of *Théâtre*" 506.

79 La Fontaine 69.

M. de CORBEC. Yes, yes, I remember the rest. ... Isn't it: the Crow, ashamed and confused, swore, but a little late, that he wouldn't get caught again?

M. RENARD. That's it exactly. It's a little society banter ... it will please you to excuse me. (32)

Another striking phrase from La Fontaine appears earlier in the script, when M. Renard calls M. Corbec "*le phénix des hôtes de ce bois*" (the phoenix of the denizens of this forest). In the French verse,

[...] *si votre ramage*
Se rapporte à votre plumage,
Vous êtes le phénix des hôtes de ces bois.

If but your voice be half as good,
You are the Phoenix of the wood! [80]

The *Monthly Review* claimed that Catherine wrote the play to win a wager, asserting that it was easy to write proverbs and "that La Fontaine's fable of the Crow and the Fox would answer the purpose as well as anything else."[81] Of course, given the theme of the play, how might she expect her audience of friends and courtiers to deliver a verdict, except to admit she had won?

"The Voyages of M. Bontems"

Much of the dialog in the third play, "The Voyages of M. Bontems" [Les Voyages de M. Bontems], belongs to Crispin, the valet of Bontems (a dandyish young man with the telling name "Good Times"). Crispin relates their various fantastical adventures to Mme. du Poid (the aunt of Bontems) and her servant Marton, while Bontems silently listens. At the end of the play, Bontems's father appears, upset at his son's gambling debts. His military conquests revealed to be fiction, Bontems runs away, leaving Crispin to be beaten by the father. The maid Marton gives the final proverb: "*A beau mentir qui vient de loin*" (He who comes from afar lies well).

Crispin's tall tales provide the play's interest. Some of them are the stuff of Wonderland: "Well, for example, we were, my master and myself, in a country where it was day during the night, and night during the day, warm in winter, and cold in the summer" (37). He later claims that he and his master survived by eating pebbles, which are sown with rye and wheat. He attempts to legitimize his own stories by calling them history. When indignantly protesting his mistreatment

---

[80] La Fontaine 69.

[81] Anonymous, "Review of *Théâtre*" 506. The author does not explain a source for this anecdote.

by Bontems *père*, he says "To treat a historian this way! Without respect for history!" (44).

As she gives the final proverb, Marton claims that she had not been taken in by Crispin's tall tales. Referring to his beating by Bontems *père*, she teases:

MARTON. Monsieur Crispin, I give you compliments on the well-merited recompense that you have just received.
CRISPIN. I think you are mocking us.
MARTON. Me, to tell the truth, I am not your dupe at all, my friend; I've long known the proverb that says: He who comes from afar lies well. (44)

While the military braggadocio of Gustav and his brother Charles may have been on Catherine's mind, the theme of lies and travel connects also to the Crimean tour. Even before the trip, both Catherine and Potemkin were facing accusations of exaggeration and hyperbole in the publicly available information about the Tauride region. Part of the likely strategy of Potemkin's fantastical presentations along the tour route (fireworks, mock military battles, regiments of "Amazons") was to refute charges of mendacity with fantasy, with events and sights extraordinary yet true. The Empress and the Governor-General must have known this proverb, and the necessity, when coming from afar, to invert it by telling the truth well.

Toward the end of the play, as Bontems *père* arrives, Crispin tells of their sea adventures on a ship with "two masts and one oar. [...] No, no, it was two oars and one mast" (41). Crispin's hyperbolic boasting, particularly of naval successes, can be seen as a satire on Gustav III and his brother the naval commander Charles, Duke of Södermanland (later Charles XIII). The Russo-Swedish War had begun in June 1788, and Catherine had already written her comic opera *Woeful Knight Kosometovich* about "brother Gu" in July (see Chapter 5). Catherine wrote "The Voyages" in August of that same year. Khrapovitskii makes an uncharacteristically interpretive comment about the latter play when he writes "here is much salt related to the Swedish war."[82] A few days later, Khrapovitskii made the Empress smile by noting that "Crispin in the recitation of naval combat lies more agreeably than Prince Charles does."[83]

Despite such private interchanges, Khrapovitskii was disturbed at the Hermitage Theatre premiere of *Woeful Knight* in January 1789, worried that its critique of Gustav would be found offensive by Cobenzl and Ségur.[84] Apparently a fully mounted operatic production was more diplomatically worrisome than a proverb to be seen by just a few within an inner circle. And indeed, Ségur writes

---

[82] Barsukov 134; Entry's date is 21 August 1788.
[83] Barsukov 140; Entry's date is 28 August 1788.
[84] Barsukov 247; Entry's date is 30 January 1789.

disparagingly of *Woeful Knight* in his memoirs, but was content to have his own plays and proverbs appear alongside "The Voyages" in print.[85]

Another satirical target of "The Voyages" was Mercier de La Rivière. Although it had been over twenty years since the legal theorist had come to St. Petersburg, full of pretensions to reforming Russia, Catherine was not content with her earlier spoof of him in *A Prominent Nobleman's Entrance Hall* (1772). He makes a small appearance in "The Voyages" in Crispin's tale:

> My adventures! Listen to me then: One fine day I found myself between the sky and the earth, you see well that we were three: the sky high above my head, the earth underneath my feet, and myself all alone between them both; luckily, they weren't quarreling at this moment; around me reigned a deep silence, there weren't any people or animals or trees or houses or rivers. (37–8)

In the original French, that final line reads "à l'entour de moi régnoit un profond silence, il n'y avoit ni hommes, ni animaux, ni arbres, ni maisons, ni rivières." Since La Rivière wore out his welcome in Petersburg with his arrogant pontificating (Catherine called him "a chatterer"), this little allusion to a deep silence with no "rivières" calls him to mind. Many in Catherine's inner "proverb circle" knew very well her disgust at La Rivière's pretensions. Count de Ségur's memoirs reveal that she had told him in detail the story of the much-earlier visit of La Rivière, when he had arranged his rooms into the department of finance, the department of commence, etc. (See Chapter 2 for more detail on his visit.) What's more, Count Cobenzl's own dramatic proverb *Gros-Jean*, included in the same published collection, is clearly also about La Rivière.[86] So probably many in the circle would have caught this little joke about silence and rivers.

Such satirical references in the proverbs again raise the issue of *na litso* satire. In her comedic work destined for public stages, Catherine for the most part remained faithful to her early ideal of *satira na porok* (satire of general vices). As she herself wrote, "Comedy must be amusing, but not injurious, have mockeries but not insults; it allows salt, but not gall and vinegar."[87] Why then did Catherine write these proverbs with satire directed at individuals? As I argued in Chapter 2, Catherine's exceptions to her own rule in her comedies and operas were all allusions to foreigners: Cagliostro, Mercier de La Rivière, and Gustav III. The same holds true in her proverbs, which feature the latter two figures.[88] As well,

---

[85] Although the editorship of the Paris volumes is usually attributed to Jean-Henry Castéra, Hyart makes an argument that Ségur himself was behind its creation (102).

[86] Pypin 4: iii–iv.

[87] Quoted in Drizen, "Imperatritsa Ekaterina II" 154.

[88] The extant exception would be the comic portrayal of the Russian Naryshkin, in "L'Insouciant," a play that is attributed to Mamonov but may have been partly written by Catherine. Two non-extant proverb plays by Catherine seem to have made reference to Princess Dashkova. Khrapovitskii's diary from 23 October 1788 notes, "received, for

the limited public exposure to the proverbs—seen only in small showings in select persons' chambers or for small groups in the Hermitage and in a limited edition publication—meant that they could not be construed as harmful to the larger public. Given Khrapovitskii's trepidation about the Hermitage production of the comic opera *Woeful Knight*, it's clear that once the audience size grew and the event was more public, the stakes were higher. On this occasion, Ségur, her fellow author of proverbs, complained to see the Empress "demeaning herself in this manner, and lessening her character, by giving too much way to a childish resentment."[89] The world of the proverb was more private and more safe.

"There's No Evil Without Good"

"There's No Evil without Good" [Il n'y a pas de mal sans bien] was paired with "The Voyages of M. Bontems" as a performance for Mamonov. Catherine also sent the plays as a pair to Grimm, telling him that he should write some proverbs himself and that she already had enough material for at least two volumes.[90] In the first scene, we learn that Maigret has recently married and become thin (his name derives from *maigrir*, to grow thin). He has come on behalf of his nephew to ask Grosdos ("fat back") to present the nephew as suitor to Madame Richard's daughter Rosalie. Grosdos, after finally convincing the mother, tries to present Maigret's nephew's case to Rosalie, who rejects him. In the end, we discover that Maigret has other girls in mind, and had only started with the closest neighbor.

The highlight of the play is its first scene: Maigret explaining to Grosdos how he gets along with his wife. The humor does not derive from plot, but purely from the verbal play of reversals as Maigret reveals the downside to each compliment Grosdos pays about the former's wife. It is the single best-written comic scene in Catherine's dramatic work.

GROSDOS. I'm truly impatient to see Madame Maigret.
MAIGRET. She hardly goes out and doesn't receive anyone at her place.
GROSDOS. And why's that?
MAIGRET. She attends constantly to the affairs of her house.
GROSDOS. Sounds like she has a good mind.
MAIGRET. Oh! No, she has no mind at all; but on the other hand she doesn't lack good sense.

---

copying, in Russian, a proverb 'After a fly with an axe' [Za mukhoi s obukhom]. Very clear that the rivalry between Postrelova and Duryndin is about princess Dash[ko]va with Nar[yshkin]" (Barsukov 178). The next day he writes that Catherine had recognized the necessity to "soften the severity" of the names, and delete Postrelova's bragging about her travels. A note on 22 August 1789 refers to a different "unplayed comedy in which Dashkova is clearly presented" (Barsukov 304).

[89] Ségur, *Memoirs* 3: 313.
[90] Grot, "Pis'ma imperatritsy" 465. Letter is from 3 October 1788.

GROSDOS. So you can pride yourself, I think, on having peace in your house.
MAIGRET. Not exactly.
GROSDOS. How's that?
MAIGRET. My wife, to tell the truth, is sometimes a little jealous.
GROSDOS. Apparently she loves you passionately.
MAIGRET. She would like very much for me to believe her.
GROSDOS. Do you have reason to doubt her?
MAIGRET. Her passion, yes, but not her friendship.
GROSDOS. Between a man and a wife, that's always something.
MAIGRET. Moreover, we hardly speak.
GROSDOS. Why?
MAIGRET. Because my wife is a stutterer.
GROSDOS. Even better, then you will hardly quarrel.
MAIGRET. On the contrary, it's precisely when she's angry that her tongue loosens
    itself.
GROSDOS. Here's what's very sad for you.
MAIGRET. Not at all; it's then that I'm free like a bird. As soon as my wife begins to
    scold me, I leave the house to have elbow room.
GROSDOS. But there comes a time when you must return home?
MAIGRET. By that time my wife has forgotten, because she has no memory at all.
    (50–51)

The verbal play is classic, reminiscent of Aristophanes, or Molière; the tradition
would continue into vaudeville. The dialog inverts the play's closing proverb, a
demonstration that there is no good without evil. The same inversion appears in a
one-liner of Grosdos, who symphathizes with the nephew's need to find a wife to
take care of his house and children: "When one is rich, one doesn't lack obstacles"
(51), a complaint that seems particularly Russian in its melancholic interpretation
of good fortune.

Hyart refers to the play's main theme as "the refusal expressed by a girl to
marry a husband imposed by her mother, a theme that reflects the preoccupations
of Catherine."[91] Since the heroine Rosalie, however, is portrayed as a capricious
and affected young miss, the play does not wholeheartedly argue for a young girl's
right to choose. On her entrance, she "curtseys in an extremely gauche manner"
(55). Girls refusing arranged marriages had been a staple of western drama since
the renaissance, so this plot is not an innovation on Catherine's part. The short
comedy is distinguished, rather, by some very humorous exchanges, particularly
satirizing marriage and women's changeability.

While she might not be the model of an independent young woman, Rosalie
does show some spirit. When her mother scolds her for her spontaneous
exclamation of surprise and joy at the news of her suitor, Rosalie protests:

ROSALIE. But, mama, you'd always like me to be still as a log.

---

[91] Hyart 90.

Mme. RICHARD. How would you rather be?
ROSALIE. I would like to be natural, astonished when there's something astonishing, gay or sad according to the occasion. (56)

She later asserts herself by forcefully refusing to consider the nephew's proposal. She at first rejects him, mistakenly thinking he is still married. When she finds out he is a widower, she is shocked that he wants to remarry so quickly: "he wouldn't love me more than he loved the first one. It's a villainous man who won't mourn his wife" (57).

Finally, Grosdos, upon hearing that the nephew will not be upset at the negative outcome of his suit, gives the proverb: "There is no evil without good" (*Il n'y a point de mal sans bien*) (62). Grosdos refers to the benefits of Maigret's nephew not marrying Rosalie. The theme is also introduced early as we learn that Maigret has become thin from illness: "I'm only more sprightly [...] . They won't mock my red and puffy cheeks anymore" (49). We also hear of the nephew's wife's death.

MAIGRET. He has become a widower.
GROSDOS. I'm so sorry to hear it, I imagine he must be very distressed by this loss.
MAIGRET. Oh, yes; but he consoles himself, because his wife was very nasty. (51)

The proverb is not a moral pronouncement, but a comment on perspective. In this short play, marriage is not about love, but about convenience and mutual benefit. The play's lack of sentimentality only adds to its humor.

"The Rage for Proverbs"

"The Rage for Proverbs" [La Rage aux Proverbes] treats societal modes and manners, and scarcely attempts a plot. Dantée, despite his lack of wealth, seeks Rosalie's hand from her aunt Tantine. Tantine's servant girl Marton explains that her mistress is obsessed with proverbs: making them, playing them, and demanding that others make them. Marton counsels Dantée that to win Rosalie, he should make a half-dozen; she implies that Tantine will value the proverbs over the suitor's wealth.

The comic centerpiece of the play is Tantine's instruction to Rosalie. In her lesson on how to be a proper young lady, Tantine advises Rosalie to appear languid and exhausted rather than vivacious, to say "ze" rather than "je" as a first person pronoun, to employ superlative adjectives ("appalling, terrible, horrible, dreadful" (74)), and to faint in front of as many people as possible. In action, these affectations frighten off Dantée, as well as the other gentlemen visitors Vieuteau and Jeunet.

Tantine's lesson is Catherine's most scathing portrayal of mannered affectation. Rosalie herself is a model of adolescent immaturity, as when she claims that she is never happy: "I would always like to have what I don't have, and as soon as I have it I don't think of it anymore" (76). Her attitude, however, also reflects such changeability within courtly society. Jeunet (presumably younger ("jeune") than Vieuteau, whose name hints at age) then represents a more reasonable attitude, shunning affectation and urging Rosalie against the pretensions of society, as when he reacts to her accent by asking if she burnt her mouth on her porridge.

The closing proverb, again spoken by Marton as in two others of Catherine's five proverbs, is that "to promise and to keep a promise are two things" (*promettre et tenir c'est deux*). Marton calls it a "confounded proverb" (84), and aims her own anger at Jasmin, Dantée's valet. In the play's first scene, Jasmin had promised Marton "herds, jewels, furniture, silver, a coach, etc." (67) in exchange for helping to bring Dantée to see Madame Tantine. Not only does Marton not see any riches, but Tantine receives no proverbs, the other significant unfulfilled promise in the play.

The words "promettre" and "promis" appear throughout the short play with noticeable frequency (about two dozen times) in many contexts. For instance, Jeunet promises Rosalie she will be perfect if she follows his advice, and then criticizes Tantine for not keeping promises (74–5). Tantine promises she won't sulk, Vieuteau can't keep his promise of talking to Tantine (82), and even Dantée's aunt has promised to leave him her wealth. The play is full of what Marton calls "pretty promises" (84), certainly a fitting image for Rosalie, who herself is pretty but empty.

One of the most explicitly metatheatrical of Catherine's plays, "The Rage for Proverbs" jests at Catherine's "proverb circle" by poking fun at proverbs and their devotees. Madame Tantine is similar to many of Catherine's stage aunts and grandmothers; in her advice to Rosalie about the importance of superficiality and empty manners, she could not be more different from the author. Yet Tantine shares her creator's passionate desire for proverbs, and in her remarks we seem to hear the Empress herself onstage: "It appears to me that there is nothing so jolly as proverbs, which are easy to make and to play" (79).

The genre itself is also ridiculed, however, with Tantine admitting how little effort is needed for the creation of proverbs:

MARTON. Madame claims that there's less science to it than to cooking a pastry.
JASMIN. Still they need to be good.
MARTON. We don't look at them that closely, no we don't; our own are sometimes detestable, witness the one they will play today. (70)

The play does not contain any fully developed proverbs-within-the-play, although Jasmin does explain two scenarios for Dantée to enact for Tantine. These little guessing games are more like parlor games than scripts.[92] At one moment it seems a real proverb will be created onstage, at Jeunet's line "Yes, madame, you're right; viva proverbs! Nothing is so good as they." Taking Rosalie's hand, he says, "Let's make a proverb, mademoiselle." But instead of acquiescing, Rosalie fashions her own dramatic moment by fainting.

Besides Tantine's quest for proverbs, the script's metatheatricality emerges in two other ways. The first is in the first scene, as Jasmin does an elaborate demonstration of the physical abnormalities of his master's Aunt Cantin. Through pantomime, he shows her crooked nose, her crooked mouth, and other deformities of her eye, arm, foot, and back. For each of her behavioral traits he makes a little show:

JASMIN. She holds herself like this. *He bends his back and juts his head forward.*
MARTON. I think you're joking.
JASMIN. She walks like this. *He walks amusingly.*
MARTON. I've never seen the like.
JASMIN. She speaks like this. *He imitates.*
MARTON. Her conversation must be very amusing.
JASMIN. For each speech that she says, she coughs like this. *He coughs.*
MARTON. But will you finish?
JASMIN. She laughs like this. *He laughs.* You are laughing, I think?
MARTON. It's hard to resist the urge to laugh, in seeing what you say of this Madame Cantin. (68–9)

Here Catherine is able to achieve contradictory goals: making her audience laugh, and also making them question their laughter. Jasmin's tasteless pantomime is reminiscent of the *na litso* debate; to what degree should we resist the urge to laugh at satire aimed at a specific individual?

The second metatheatrical moment comes as Jeunet starts to apply rules of playwriting to the scene in which he himself is a character. When Dantée agrees to follow Madame Tantine's orders, Jeunet objects on the grounds that "when all the world is in agreement, there's no conflict in the scene" (78).

JEUNET. If Monsieur Dantée had said that he wouldn't play, or make proverbs, this would have been in perfect conflict with the opinion of madame, but now that he promises to follow her orders, there's no more conflict; I bet that madame, who is an author herself and who knows the importance of conflict in the circumstances and speeches in scenes and who knows the rules of art, must find it bad that he would be of the same opinion as her, and I bet that the monsieur is harming madame's amusement.
VIEUTEAU. You're joking, Monsieur Jeunet, I think.

---

[92] Never in the play does Catherine use the word "write" in reference to the proverbs; she uses "make." So perhaps the proverbs desired by Tantine are this type of short charade, rather than literary creations.

JEUNET. Not at all, Monsieur Vieuteau. All scenes with no conflict become insipid, boring; ask madame.

VIEUTEAU. But we're not playing a comedy here, Monsieur Jeunet.

JEUNET. Oh yes, Monsieur Vieuteau: it's from society that all good comedy takes its models, isn't that right madame? (78)

Jeunet continues to speak about well-made plays even as he departs the house by making an excuse about going to see a fire: "I like to see the beginning, the progress, and the end" (83). Marton borrows from Jeunet's conceit, when, puzzled by Dantée's sudden exit, she says, "this ending doesn't conform to the beginning" (84).

The significance of these metatheatrical references to writing and playing plays and proverbs lies in the context. The primary audience for "The Rage for Proverbs" was the "proverb circle" itself—her lover Mamonov, her friend Ségur, those in the know about the rage for proverbs and the literary issues revolving around it. Another author in the collection was Mlle. Aufrène, daughter of the celebrated French actor Jean Aufrène. Khrapovitskii suggested to Catherine "that the young Aufrène would play well the role of Rosalie."[93] In that case, even the actress onstage would have been a part of the "proverb circle." With her final proverb, Catherine managed to poke fun at mannered society, at her own select group, and even at herself.

While the five (or more) proverb plays written by Catherine in 1787–88 share some of the traits of Catherine's other dramatic writings (smart maids, foolish girls, gullible victims), their limited audience gave them a freedom not seen in her longer comedies. At times Catherine is able to spoof particular real-life persons; at other times she is free from unwieldy plot constraints, and can focus on humorous dialog. Yet if the plays were meant to be seen by only a select audience, why did Catherine allow them to be published in Russia in 1788–89? The answer lies in the numbers: apparently, only thirty copies were printed, probably as gifts for a select coterie.[94]

Although the proverb plays' clearest context is that of the "theatre of society," Catherine also clearly saw their educational potential; in this way, the proverbs can be compared to the comic operas. Her first three comic operas were written before the proverbs, in 1786, as fantasy tales for the entertainment and education of her grandsons. She wrote *Woeful Knight Kosometovich* in July 1788, just before writing the final three proverbs. On 14 December 1789, Khrapovitskii's diary reports that two proverb plays ("Voyages of M. Bontems" and "The Rage for Proverbs") were performed in the Hermitage Theatre "for Their Imperial Highnesses." Catherine may have enjoyed watching her grandsons see a send-up of their grandmother's literary obsessions.

---

93 Barsukov 173; entry from 14 October 1788.
94 Filov 2: 326.

Catherine wrote to Grimm about her newfound love of dramatic proverbs: "it rains them here and we have decided that it's the unique means to restore good comedy to the theatre."[95] Ironically, by 1787, the popularity of dramatic proverbs had waned considerably in its birthplace of Paris, vanishing completely with the revolution against the aristocracy. Nor did the form take root in Russia in any significant way. Yet these vignettes offer a window into the world of court society, teaching us what made them laugh from the banks of the Dnieper to the Crimea to St. Petersburg and the Hermitage.

A Family Broken Up by Intrigue and Suspicions

Catherine's career as a writer of neoclassical comedy concluded with two final works in Russian. After returning from the Crimea in mid-1787, Catherine wrote another full-length comedy from September to December, *A Family Broken Up by Intrigue and Suspicions*. It shares themes with the French proverb "The Busy-Body" written the month before. *Family* was first performed at the court theatre on 29 December 1787, and had at least one performance at the public theatre. It was published twice in Russian in 1788, first as a separate edition, and then in Dashkova's *Russian Theatre*. Like the anti-Masonic trilogy, it was also translated into German and published in 1788, as *Der Familen-Zwist durch falsche Warnung und Argwohn*.

Written after the productions and publication of the three anti-Masonic plays, it bears a strong resemblance to them in plot and theme, but lacks their pointed critique of mystical charlatanism. Rather, *Family* features a quite ordinary antagonist, the meddlesome Dvorabrod, who sows the seed of discontent among a happy family. The plot features Dobrin's impending proposal to Prelesta, daughter of the Sobrins and sister to Ivan Sobrin. Act I scene 5 concludes with the four family members in a tearful embrace, joyfully looking forward to the future marriage and the purchase of a new house for Prelesta. The first hint of problems to come is Dobrin's uncle Takkov's appearance at the house with amnesia from a blow to the head, and no apparent recollection of Dobrin's marriage plans. Next, a family friend Predyn arrives with Dvorabrod, who immediately begins to breed an atmosphere of dissension in the house. Dvorabrod comments on his house, which Sobrin seeks to purchase: "First: in it there are many entrance-halls and not a small number of exits ... secondly, it is arranged for an agreeable family ... *(looks back at Sobrin and his wife)*. And so for a disagreeable family, it is equally comfortable" (73).

From that point on, Dvorabrod starts on his campaign to poison the relationships in the house. He accomplishes much of his plan in Act II, and then, in Act III, adds more complications that escalate the distrust and anger between the

---

[95] Letter is from 4 October, 1787. Grot, "Pis'ma imperatritsy" 418.

characters. The turning point does not come until Act IV, when, after a bitter fight, Sobrin and Sobrina begin to figure out the cause of their discord. Unlike the trilogy, in which the villains are apprehended by offstage police, Sobrin confronts the deceiver directly. He unravels the web of deceit, expels Dvorabrod from the house, and reinstates the marriage. As in *The Questioner*, the servants also decide to marry at play's end. Thus the play's title turns out not to be true: the family is not "broken up" by Dvorabrod, but in fact its stability is further assured by marriage.

The telling name Dvorabrod can indicate either someone who wanders from house to house, or someone who roams the court (*dvor* can mean either an ordinary homestead or the court itself). In the German translation he is Hauslöffer, "a name indicating a person who goes from house to house carrying news and gossip."[96] After sending Grimm a letter on 3 March 1788 in which she claimed her comedy *Family* was "good and very good," Catherine wrote the following to him on 31 May:

> Ah! finally the Hauslöffer has had your approbation. Hauslöffer is a parasite who runs from house to house, who haunts antechambers, who catches news and meals, who tries to make himself necessary and chooses the means as he finds them; he's a rogue who, in stuffing heads with suspicions, believes he has reached his goal, which is to give himself the respect and attract the attention of those he draws near to.[97]

While Dvorabrod himself embodies the vice of meddling and rumor-mongering, the play also critiques the multiple vices of which the Sobrin family is falsely accused: for example, gambling (Ivan Sobrin); adultery (Mrs. Sobrina and Predyn); debt (Dobrin); and lack of parental trust (Sobrin). Although the audience knows throughout the piece that the characters in fact do not possess these traits, the vices themselves are cast in a negative light, thus giving the play a highly moralistic tone. Gullibility is the single vice, central to Catherine's early comedies and to her anti-Masonic trilogy, possessed almost without exception by the characters in *Family*. The play could have been easily called *The Deceiver*, since Dvorabrod manages to fool everyone. The forgetful uncle Takkov is not taken in by Dvorabrod, but his own amnesia-induced bumbling is a reflection of the others' vulnerablity. The theme of deceit runs throughout the play; Dvorabrod's chief accusation is that the family members are deliberately misleading each other. For example, Dvorabrod convinces Sobrin that Dobrin is deeply in debt, and therefore taking advantage of the family. Sobrin also believes the lie that his wife and Predyn are cheating on him. Trofim is deluded into thinking that Mavra is playing him false with Dobrin, and even calls her "Deceiver!" (90). Dvorabrod, the Deceiver, has many to deceive.

---

96   Dawson, "Writing as a Woman" 31.
97   Grot, "Pis'ma imperatritsy" 450.

Two characters are less entangled in Dvorabrod's web: Mavra and Mrs. Sobrina. Although Mavra never believes one of his lies, even the usually clever servant girl is vulnerable: Mavra quarrels heatedly with Trofim without realizing that Dvorabrod is to blame. Mrs. Sobrina, however, seems more aware of the stranger's influence from her first encounter with him, when she counters his insinuations with: "You have told me so much that if I were suspicious, these things would occupy my thoughts for several days" (96). In Act V, she is the first to suggest that the family's problems are Dvorabrod's doing, and expresses her distrust of him: "only I don't like Dvorabrod ... he has told me a lot of nonsense: some I didn't understand, the others I laughed at, and the third I let pass past my ears" (107). In *Family*, it is the men who are the deceived ones.[98]

The play's structure reflects its focus on intrigue. Since Dvorabrod must be left alone with each family member to plant thoughts of doubt or suspicion, *Family* has an unusual number of two-person scenes. As in *Siberian Shaman*, there is a scene in which the deceiver is left alone with the play's young heroine. Here, in II.4, Dvorabrod slowly draws Prelesta in, telling her that there are rumors about her in the city. His scorn for her is apparent in an aside, a rare revelation of Dvorabrod's thoughts: "O! how the female gender is born sly!" (79). As he lets out the idea that Dobrin is unfaithful, his words become halting, with numerous ellipses to indicate slow and deliberate speech: "He ... he is a fair young man ... if a bit frivolous ... foolhardy ... uncontrolled ... " (80). Later in III.7, Dvorabrod is left alone onstage for a brief soliloquy. Again, his speech is halting and his thoughts are almost incoherent; rather than revealing the reasons for his devious actions, his rambling words show the workings of his mind.

In the final act, when Dvorabrod is being upbraided and revealed as a charlatan, his speech is again choppy, and he alternates between whispering to individuals and laughing out loud:

SOBRIN. What do you think? Who proposed the beginning of Prelesta's lack of
    fondness? ... Who led her into doubt?
DOBRIN. I don't know ... and am afraid to ask.
SOBRIN. Mr. Dvorabrod of course.
DVORABROD *(Takes Sobrin by the caftan)*. I don't know ... don't know ... ha, ha,
    ha!
DOBRIN *(to himself)* Could it be that Dvorabrod is my rival!
SOBRIN. He told Prelesta God knows what ....
DVORABROD. I! ... I was only joking ... ha, ha, ha!
DOBRIN. What did he say then?
SOBRIN. *(to Dobrin)* That you love another ... that he is a obviously a witness to this
    ...
DOBRIN. But, Mr. Dvorabrod, if the matter is so, and you evilly slandered me, then the
    time has come to say here loudly what I heard from you.

---

[98] Dawson, "Writing as a Woman" 29–51.

> DVORABROD. From me ... ha, ha, ha! Utter attacks. *(to Dobrin in a whisper).* For
> pity's sake, why say in front of people what was said alone? (118)

Dvorabrod's inner motivations are never clearly shown to the audience; he has no confidant and in his single soliloquy he gives no reasons for his actions. He is merely a villain for the sake of villainy, who does not share even the greed of the trilogy's deceivers. Nor does he meet any particular justice; unlike the trilogy's charlatans who are apprehended by police, Dvorabrod is simply asked to leave the house. Catherine indicated to Grimm that the Dvorabrod type was very prevalent at court; one "lesson" of the play may be that such types must be found out and eliminated for the good of the whole. Catherine wrote of the Dvorabrod character in a letter to Zimmermann on 6 May 1788: "they say of him that he is newer in the theatre than in the universe."[99]

Dvorabrod's importance as a character is reflected by the fact that he was played by the most famous Russian actor of the century, Ivan Afanasevich Dmitrevskii (1734–1821). Dmitrevskii was the most prominent Russian actor of this period, whose many foreign influences included Lekain, Talma, and Garrick. He also played other roles in Catherine's plays.[100] Noted for his declamatory style and "intelligent but unemotional approach to acting,"[101] Dmitrevskii was famous as the wise Starodum in Fonvizin's *The Minor*. A versatile actor in both comedy and tragedy, Dmitrevskii also played the title roles in Molière's *Misanthrope*, and in Sumarokov's *Dmitrii the Impostor*. Like Dvorabrod, such characters are on the fringes of society; the misanthrope Alceste denounces the deceit around him, while Sumarokov's villainous Dmitrii seeks vengeance on those who seek to usurp him.

The archive containing the manuscript of *Family* also contains a list of the roles in the play with the names of the actors who presumably played them.[102] The role of Sobrin was portrayed by the comic talent Anton Krutitskii. The son Ivan Dobrin was played by "him who played Mitrofanushka," a notation which may point to Vasilii Chernikov, who premiered the role of Mitrofan in Fonvizin's *The Minor* in 1782. Predyn was played by Piotr Alekseevich Plavil'shchikov (1760–1812), a playwright and actor with "athletic good looks and a noble countenance which made him ideally suited for the impersonation of positive heroes, kings, and moralizers in tragedy."[103] Several years earlier, Plavil'shchikov had played a role

---

[99] Quoted in Pypin 2: 128.

[100] Dmitrevskii acted the title role in Catherine's *The Beginning of Oleg's Reign*. He also played in comedies by Catherine from 1785–86, such as *The Misunderstanding*. Vsevolodskii-Gerngross, *I. A. Dmitrevskii* 56.

[101] Golub, "Dmitrevsky." Past acting styles are difficult to determine. Victor Borovsky disagrees with Golub, referring to Dmitrevskii's "natural and simple delivery." Borovsky 77.

[102] Pypin 2: 129.

[103] Golub, "Plavilshchikov."

similar to Catherine's Predyn: the *raisonneur* Pravdin in *The Minor*.[104] The similar matchups between actors and roles reveal how closely Catherine's plays followed the conventions and styles of her period.

Family extends the logic of the anti-Masonic trilogy to criticize a more prevalent kind of deceiver. Catherine used the public performance space to attack forces that might de-stabilize the court. Catherine wrote to Grimm that her goal in writing the play was to "unmask" such parasites, whether in the court or in the family.

The Misunderstanding

Catherine probably wrote her final published comedy, *The Misunderstanding*, in early 1788. Its only publication was in 1789 in volume XXI of Dashkova's *Russian Theatre,* and its first performance was 9 September 1789. A note to Khrapovitskii, on 5 September 1789, reveals Catherine's involvement in the play's staging: "Tell Dmitrevskii and Krutitskii in the second act not to notice the words of Potachkin, but to speak between themselves, as if they weren't there."[105]

In contrast with the full-length comedies that precede it, *The Misunderstanding* lacks a deliberately deceitful charlatan; the marriage of the young woman (Sbyslava) is here imperiled by mistakes and misinterpretations rather than by cunning. Sbyslava's aunt Gostiakova is reminiscent of the foolish ladies of Catherine's early comedies. Her problems with her mills and factories and her mistreatment of her laborers are linked to her faults in raising Sbyslava. Gostiakova's confused conversation with the girl's beloved Druzhkov brings on the central misunderstanding of the play. As in many of the early comedies, there is no mother. Sbyslava's father Razsudin, however, is a model of reason and integrity, and while he is temporarily deluded by his sister's conviction that Druzhkov has another lover, he sensibly ends the play by pledging his daughter to Druzhkov. Herta Schmid, as part of her overall thesis that Catherine's later comedies imply an audience that is metaphorically "not of age," argues that *The Misunderstanding* praises fatherly authority. For Schmid, the play is less a laughing comedy than a sentimental and conservative warning about the dangers of a loss of authority.[106]

The ridiculous aphorism-spouting tutor figure, Potachkin, provides the play's comic moments. Described as a "pedant, flatterer, and hypocrite," Potachkin is also a would-be playwright, who is readying plans for a performance in honor of the marriage festivities. In comic scenes with the servants, he assigns the Butler to

---

[104] Later, in 1790, he would also play the rival prince Vadim in Kniazhnin's historical play *Vadim of Novgorod* (see Chapter 4).

[105] Catherine II, "Sobstvennoruchnyi pis'ma" entry 117, col. 2089.

[106] Schmid 122–3.

"play the ass" by portraying Silenus, uncle to Bacchus; the servant Prokofii will be assigned the role of Mercury, with wings on his costume, and accompanied by a rooster. Potachkin even recites numerous stilted and nonsensical verses from the play, but is abandoned by his listeners. At the close of Act III, he is left alone onstage, complaining balefully: "Bah! All have gone ... such is the fate of our brother poet: you sweat while creating, but they don't want to listen to you" (178). While Catherine is certainly winking at her own labors as an artist, Schmid believes that Catherine is also satirizing the penchant for fantastical-mythological productions then prevalent in school drama.[107] In contrast to Potachkin's dreamed-of production, Catherine's own comedy seems more rooted in reality, more sensible and useful for its Russian audience. Even though Catherine had begun writing her own comic operas two years before creating *The Misunderstanding*, those operas are not based in classical mythology as are Potachkin's. They instead draw on Russian folk imagery. Even in operatic fantasy, Catherine wished to keep her viewers closer to home.

With *The Misunderstanding*, Catherine returned to the less overtly political style of most of her 1770s comedies. Gostiakova[108] is reminiscent of Sanctimonious, Grumbler, and Tattler in their bumbling interference; they are fools but not charlatans. But Gostiakova's mismanagement of her factories and ill-treatment of her laborers make her a more barbarous figure. Her potentially destructive nature is revealed in her plan to destroy the ancient palaces in her forest to sell off their bricks for a profit. Her Butler argues that "it is a shame to smash the palaces, they are ancestral and very sturdy" (147). Gostiakova's damaging spirit links us to the three deceivers of her trilogy and to Dvorabrod. In what was probably her last completed comedy, Catherine had no tolerance for those who would smash palaces.

The flurry of Catherine's dramatic writing from 1786–88 encompasses a wide variety of genres, themes, and styles. The next two chapters will consider her experiments in Shakespearean style and in the genre of comic opera. The later comedies considered in this chapter, long and short, almost all come back to a central theme of charlatans preying on the gullible through trickery, flattery, and misinformation.[109] As the French Revolution loomed, Catherine grew more wary of dissent. The dangers of dissension in the family reflect Catherine's campaign against chaos in the nation.

---

[107] Schmid 122–23.

[108] Her name derives from the word "guest," which in one connotation can also mean "thief" (the uninvited guest). Dal' 1: 386.

[109] The only exceptions are her last two proverbs, *No Evil Without Good* and *The Rage for Proverbs*. *The Misunderstanding* also lacks a real villain.

Chapter 4
The Shakespearean Influence

In his anonymously published *General Observations Regarding the Present State of the Russian Empire* (1787), Sir John Sinclair, English visitor to St. Petersburg, calls Catherine the Great "a hero in petticoats," who "knows the French Belles Lettres perfectly, and, anno 1786, was reading Shakespeare in the German translation. She also writes comedies herself; and in any part of the world would be accounted, in private life, a most accomplished woman."[1]

Although the majority of Catherine's dramatic writing, like most Russian drama of the period, was modeled on French neoclassicism, French dramaturgy was not the sole influence on Catherine's writing style. Not only was she reading Shakespeare in 1786 as Sinclair notes, she also completed three plays inspired by a Shakespearean esthetic that same year. Catherine humbly subtitled her version of *The Merry Wives of Windsor*, called *This 'tis to Have Linen and Buck-Baskets* [Vot kakovo imet' korzinu i bel'e], as "a free but feeble adaptation."

With *This 'tis*, the first Russian play to credit Shakespeare's influence on its title page, Catherine followed (and influenced) a growing Russian trend of the 1780s: a lively interest in English fashion, language, and literature was replacing the former domination of French culture.[2] As literary historian Marcus Levitt has noted, "The question to consider is not how eighteenth-century writers misunderstood or corrupted Shakespeare but how they adapted him to meet specific needs of their own."[3] Catherine's rejection of the French model, by imitating Shakespeare rather than Molière or Racine, was an act with both cultural and political connotations. The approbation of Shakespeare had the potential to simultaneously express pro-English and anti-French sentiments, all in the name of Russian cultural pride.

Later in 1786, after completing *This 'tis*, Catherine finished two more scripts inspired by Shakespearean style. Although Catherine primarily wrote comedies or light operas, these Shakespearean experiments had a more serious tone. *The Beginning of Oleg's Reign* [Nachal'noe upravlenie Olega] and *From the Life of Riurik* [Iz zhizni Riurika] were modeled on English chronicle plays; their setting, however, was ninth-century pre-Christian Russian history. *Riurik* was written as a drama, but *Oleg* is most often classified as an opera due to its many songs and choruses. Both scripts bear the same self-conscious inscription: "an imitation of

---

[1]   Quoted in A. G. Cross, "A Royal Blue-Stocking" 94.
[2]   See Simmons 792.
[3]   Levitt, "Sumarokov's Russianized 'Hamlet'" 319.

Shakespeare" (219). A third history play, *Igor*, was never finished. Later in 1786, Catherine began one final Shakespearean exercise, an incomplete adaptation of *Timon of Athens* called *The Spendthrift* [Rastochitel'], bringing the total number of her Shakespearean experiments to five.

Shakespeare was a source of curiosity to Russian *literati* of the late eighteenth century, but the stylistic features of his plays were by no means an accepted means of dramatic expression. Catherine took the lead in self-consciously asserting the value of a Shakespearean model. Although Russian secular drama's origins were in imitation of Racine, not Shakespeare, Russian playwrights paid close attention to the French and German theoretical debate (led by Western European theorists such as Voltaire and Lessing) about Shakespeare's artistic merits. As early as 1748, Aleksandr Sumarokov, the first professional Russian playwright, had written an adaptation of *Hamlet*. He preserved the play's basic plot, but transformed the play into a neoclassical tragedy, complete with confidants, and did not credit Shakespeare's influence. Although English was not a well-known language among Russian courtiers and writers, readers of French could read summaries of Shakespeare plays in La Place's editions (1746–49). A German speaker living in Russia could read Shakespeare in translation from sources such as Wieland's 1762–66 edition of twenty-two plays, or later in Eschenburg's twelve volumes of the complete Shakespeare plays (1775–82).

In 1772, the first Russian translation of part of Shakespeare's work appeared: a single speech from *Romeo and Juliet*. It was not until 1783 that a full play, *Richard III*, was translated, and in 1786, Karamzin published a Russian translation of *Julius Caesar*, including a preface.[4] In September of that year, Catherine wrote to her correspondent Friedrich Melchior Grimm that she had "gobbled up" the German translations by Eschenburg.[5] This rapid consumption seems to have inspired her Shakespearean phase.

Catherine experimented at a time when the influences of growing Romanticism in Western Europe had scarcely been felt. It would not be until decades later that Aleksandr Pushkin would write his sprawling historical epic *Boris Gudunov* (1825), using Shakespearean temporal and spatial structures, and a wide array of characters from peasants to Tsars. Catherine was ahead of her time in her admiration of Shakespeare and her disregard for the "usual theatrical rules." While these scripts are not typical of Catherine's work, and do not in fact signal a new trend in Russian theatre of their era, *Riurik* and *Oleg* in many ways anticipate the European Romantic project in drama: in the rejection of the genre rigidity of neoclassical tragedy, in the glorification of a medieval historical setting, and in the deliberate championing of Shakespeare as a dramaturgical paradigm.

---

4   For information on these early translations, see Lirondelle, *Shakespeare en Russie* 29; Veselovskii 95.

5   Letter's date is 24 September 1786. Grot, "Pis'ma imperatritsy" 383. Eschenburg's translation of *Merry Wives* seems to have been Catherine's primary source for her version.

From Fat Falstaff to Francophile Fop: *This 'tis to have Linen and Buck-Baskets*

Before writing her historical plays, Catherine began with a genre closer to her previous writing experience: comedy. The diary of her literary secretary Aleksandr Khrapovitskii indicates that a play called *The Basket* was complete by 15 June 1786: "I compared the comedy *The Basket* with the original of Shakespeare."[6] The play was Catherine's Russian version of *Merry Wives*. Its later title, *This 'tis to Have Linen and Buck-Baskets*, comes from one of Ford's lines in *Merry Wives*: "This 'tis to be married! This 'tis to have linen and buck-baskets!" (III.v.130–131). Catherine's *This 'tis* was first published by the Academy of Sciences in St. Petersburg in 1786 in a single edition, and again in 1787 in Dashkova's *Russian Theatre*. The play premiered in St. Petersburg, either in the last half of 1786, or the beginning of 1787.[7]

The Merry Wives of Windsor resembles a typical eighteenth-century Russian comedy in many ways, and was therefore a logical choice for adaptation by Catherine. Shakespeare's play features a combination of exaggerated fools and normative lovers. Its central story is also typical of Catherine's own comedies: the undoing of a rogue paralleled by a marriage plot in which a young girl avoids several inappropriate suitors and marries the man of her dreams in a happy denouement.

But Catherine also made many alterations to help the comedy conform more precisely to a neoclassical esthetic. She emphasizes the instructive point of the plot, that her Falstaff-substitute Polkadov is being punished for his excessive Gallomania and his lustfulness. She also eliminates subplots, cultural and geographical specificity, and most soliloquies. Such changes led Soviet critic Grigorii Gukovskii to write, "Catherine's play was more like a comedy by Sumarokov rather than anything by Shakespeare."[8] Despite her conscious attempt to follow a Shakespearean model while satirizing Francophilia, Catherine instead ultimately crafted a typical neoclassical comedy, still strongly influenced by the French mode. While seemingly rejecting the French neoclassical model, she remained safely within its boundaries.

French customs, manners, and culture were widespread in Catherine's court. She followed the lead of Peter the Great in championing European (particularly French) cultural and social values; she herself was a devoted enthusiast of pre-revolutionary French Enlightenment philosophy. Yet from the 1763 conclusion of the Seven Years' War near the beginning of her reign, Russia's relations with France were strained. Catherine had also been outraged by Chappe d'Auteroche's

---

[6] Barsukov 11.

[7] It also played in Moscow on 7 and 8 April in 1787, and again on 8 November 1788 in St. Petersburg. Vsevolodskii-Gerngross, *Ot istokov* 442.

[8] Gukovskii 86.

Voyage en Sibérie, published in Paris in 1768. She zealously defended Russia by writing her *Antidote* as a reply to Chappe d'Auteroche in 1770. Thus, despite mutual alliances and treaties in the 1770s and 1780s, relations with France were uneasy and competitive. One of Catherine's goals was to further Westernization while at the same time preserving and nourishing Russian culture, language, and traditions. The prevalent Gallomania, particularly among the nobility, was thus troubling to her. As she encouraged a Russian cultural pride, she had little use for disdainful Francophiles who compared the two countries unfavorably.

Imitating Shakespeare may have enabled Catherine to battle France on two levels, while still remaining "at peace": by poking fun at Gallomania within the action of the play itself, and, more significantly, by seeming to reject the French model of dramaturgy in favor of Shakespeare. Although she accomplished her first goal, her comedy scarcely rejected neoclassicism. Catherine may have spoofed the French in the subject matter of her comedy, but she still bowed to the French style.

Although character names are Russianized, the plot of Catherine's play closely follows Shakespeare's main story. Iakov Vlas'evich' Polkadov (Falstaff) attempts to woo the wives of both Egor Avdeich' Papin (Page) and Fordov (Ford). The wives, Akulina Terent'evna Papina and Fordova (Mistress Page and Mistress Ford), thwart him three times, by hiding him in a linen basket, dressing him as a witch, and masquerading as goblins in the forest. K'ela (Mistress Quickly) aided the wives in their scheme. In the meantime, Anna Papina (Anne Page) is being courted by three suitors: Kazhu (Doctor Caius), Lialiukin (Slender), and Fintov (Fenton). Other characters include Polkadov's rascally friends Bardolin, Numov, and Pikov (Bardolph, Nym, and Pistol); the inn's Host; the judge Mitrofan Avakumovich' Shalov (Shallow); the matchmaker Vanov (Sir Hugh Evans); and a servant Zin'ka (Peter Simple). Catherine deletes three minor characters altogether: the Pages' son William, the servant John Rugby, and Robin, Falstaff's page.

Most of these Russian characters are quite similar to their originals: Fenton/Fintov is the devoted lover, Ford/Fordov is the comic cuckold, and so on. Yet Catherine made deliberate changes to several of Shakespeare's characters to reflect the Russian milieu and to promote her anti-French theme. Falstaff's transformation from Shakespeare's "greasy knight" into Polkadov, a Russian Francophile, is one of the most prominent changes in the adaptation. Catherine was not alone in satirizing Gallomania: the Francophile was a stock character in Russian comedy of the eighteenth century. Ivanushka in Denis Fonvizin's *The Brigadier* [Brigadir, 1769] epitomizes this type; he speaks in a Franco-Russian jargon, and boasts of his familiarity with the customs and manners in Paris. Catherine herself also included a Russian *petit-maître*, Firliufiushkov, in the cast of her early comedy *Mrs. Grumbler*.

In the very first line of Catherine's *This 'tis*, Shalov sets the stage for the worldly Polkadov: "Just because Polkadov may have been to Paris twenty times doesn't mean he has the right to make a fool of Mitrofan Shalov" (5). From his first entrance in I.3, Polkadov ostentatiously mixes French phrases into his speech, comparing St. Petersburg to Paris:

> Here are still such idlers [...] every trifle, *des simples tours de jeunesse*, they make into a calamity ... ask the female sex ... how courteous I was with them. ... *Chez nous à Paris* that is the custom ... (7)

Polkadov also brags about his affection for fine French products such as powder, tobacco, and wine (25) and later complains about the linguistic abilities of his companions Bardolin, Pikov, and Numov: "they speak ... neither French nor German" (13). He vainly assesses the Russians' lack of sophistication throughout the play, only increasing the humor when the other characters later dupe him.

Polkadov combines his affection for anything French with a self-perceived worldliness. In II.11, Fordov, disguised as Bruk, flatters Polkadov by alluding to his reputation:

> I heard that you, sir, have traveled all around and have become famous for your travels ... I have wished to meet you for a long time.... They say ... that all the women are crazy for you ... head over heels. (26)

Shakespeare's version of the same speech has quite a different beginning: "Sir, I hear you are a scholar" (II.ii.170). Catherine's change gives an additional implication: that Polkadov is a well-known ladies' man. Polkadov's characterization is complete as a Francophile, world traveler, and Don Juan.

Catherine also significantly alters the character of Falstaff by trimming his enormous size. In Shakespeare's II.1, Mistress Ford has a long speech, wholly absent from Catherine's scene, that makes several allusions to Falstaff's "greatness":

> I shall think the worse of fat men, as long as I have an eye to make difference of men's liking.... What tempest, I trow, threw this whale, with so many tuns of oil in his belly, ashore at Windsor? How shall I be revenged on him? I think the best way were to entertain him with hope, till the wicked fire of lust have melted him in his own grease. (51–62)

Whereas Mistress Page later replies, "Let's consult together against this greasy knight" (II.i.99–100), Anna Papina's closing line in II.3 omits the "greasy knight", saying merely "Let's go consult about what to do" (21). Mistress Page's line "I am glad the fat knight is not here" (IV.ii.31) becomes Akulina Papina's "It's very good that Polkadov isn't here" (41). In one of Falstaff's most picturesque speeches, his description of being dumped into the Thames, he himself refers to his own weight in several ways:

[...] and you may know by my size that I have a kind of alacrity in sinking; if the bottom were as deep as hell, I should down. I had been drowned, but that the shore was shelvy and shallow,—a death that I abhor; for the water swells a man; and what a thing should I have been when I had been swelled! I should have been a mountain of mummy. (III.v.10–17)

Catherine's Polkadov instead gives an unembellished account of the action: "they carried me out in a basket and threw me in the pond" (38).[9]

Falstaff's enormity is not his only missing physical attribute. Sir Hugh Evans, the Welsh parson, refers to the "peard" of the witch of Brentford (not knowing he is talking about Falstaff):

By the yea and no, I think the 'oman is a witch
indeed: I like not when a 'oman has a great peard;
I spy a great peard under his muffler. (IV.ii.178–180)

Catherine retains the incongruity of the image, while omitting the beard: "Only she truly looks like a witch; like a man in a woman's dress ... a very scarecrow!" (44).

Why did Catherine deliberately eliminate these attributes? In contrast to Shakespearean comedy, continental neoclassicism emphasized character action over character appearance, and eschewed specifics to focus on universality. Neoclassical comedies in Russia, although strongly dependent on exaggerated characters and stereotypes, therefore did not usually satirize characters' physical traits. In Catherine's own comedies, we learn much about the characters' foibles, obsessions, and values, but little about their appearances. Even when Catherine describes the title character of her shaman character in *Siberian Shaman* (also 1786), she mentions details about his clothing and actions, but nothing about his body or features. The characterization of Catherine's Polkadov is created by his behavior and dialog.

Catherine also omits a perhaps more important Falstaff characteristic: his blustering, bragging verbosity. Again, the effect is to draw attention to character behavior rather than innate personality. In Shakespeare's characterization, Falstaff is not only a "greasy knight," a drinker, and a chaser of women, he is also a broadly comic abuser of the English language, with a flair for bawdy metaphor and vivid imagery. In Shakespeare's V.v, the first time Falstaff appears in his disguise as Herne, his lengthy speech inflates his own egoism. The numerous mythological references heighten the humor, as Falstaff places himself in league with the gods, moments before his undoing at the hands of the false fairies and hobgoblins.

---

[9]   Catherine adds one reference to Polkadov's size, by indicating he will not be able to fit into the chimney (41). Simmons notes that this mention "has more point in reference to Falstaff than to Polkadov" (Simmons 797).

Now, the hot-blooded gods assist me! Remember, Jove, thou wast a bull for thy Europa; love set on thy horns. O powerful love! that, in some respects, makes a beast a man, in some other, a man a beast. You were also, Jupiter, a swan for the love of Leda. O omnipotent Love! how near the god drew to the complexion of a goose! A fault done first in the form of a beast. O Jove, a beastly fault! And then another fault in the semblance of a fowl; think on 't, Jove; a foul fault! When gods have hot backs, what shall poor men do? (V.v.2–12)

Catherine was much less interested in linguistic distinctions between her characters. Polkadov does begin the play by weaving French phrases into his speech, but after the second act he loses this habit, and speaks a very simplified, non-distinctive speech. In Catherine's final act, Polkadov, disguised and waiting in the park, speaks simply and concisely: "here alone ... in the forest ... every tree seems to be a wood-goblin to me" (49).

The merry wives trick Falstaff not only because of his actions but because of his irrepressibly lusty personality, as revealed through his hyperbolic dialog. In contrast, because Polkadov's language is simple and direct, his punishment is less a judgment on his inherent character traits than on his actions (the attempted seduction of the women). This shift emphasizes the didactic function of Catherine's version, helping her to achieve one of the principal goals of neoclassical comedy: to teach a moral lesson.

The changes to Mistress Quickly also highlight the anti-French sentiment of Catherine's play. Quickly, housekeeper of Doctor Caius, is transformed into the French merchant woman Madame K'ela. French critic André Lirondelle criticized Catherine's play for losing Mistress Quickly's picturesque nature and "her verbosity of a woman of the people."[10] Whereas Mistress Quickly's lively ramblings are humorous, Madame K'ela is amusing in a quite different way: her speech is broken and ungrammatical, and her Russian words are spoken with a strong French accent. When the audience first encounters her in I.14 she is immediately comical as she substitutes "kospodin" for "gospodin" and "shelovek" for "chelovek."

K'ELA. And your master has what name? [*Kospodin kak imia?*]
ZIN'KA. Ivan Avraamovich' Lialiukin.
K'ELA. Is he a good man? [*Dobr shelovek on?*] (17)

K'ela's nationality links her to the Francophile Polkadov and to the French doctor Kazhu. Kazhu's dialog has an equally comical French accent (his "ia snai, shto ia snai" should be "ia znaiu, chto ia znaiu" (17)); he is quite similar to Shakespeare's Doctor Caius who also has a strong accent ("By gar, it is a shallenge" (I.iv.102)). As the audience laughs at K'ela's and Kazhu's lack of Russian language, Catherine thus not only makes fun of the Francophile character Polkadov, but also shows

---

10   Lirondelle, "Catherine II, élève de Shakespeare" 181.

French nationals as foolish. In a transparent show of cultural pride, Catherine implies that ignorance of the Russian language is a shortcoming.

K'ela's dialog is not wholly comical, however. Late in the play, in V.6, Madame K'ela's invocation to the witches is in a sophisticated Russian verse, inconsistent with K'ela's earlier dialog. Several critics consider this disparity a careless error on Catherine's part.[11] But since the verse lines spoken in V.v by Mistress Quickly as Queen of the Fairies are also inconsistent with her linguistic character in the rest of the play,[12] Catherine's seeming inconsistency actually replicates an incongruity from Shakespeare's text.

Catherine changes Sir Hugh Evans from a parson to Vanov, the matchmaker (*svat*). Although he speaks most of the same lines as Evans, Vanov is Russian and hardly a comic character. The strong Welsh dialect of Shakespeare's Evans is consistently a form of humor: "be pold, I pray you; follow me into the pit; and when I give the watch-'ords, do as I pid you" (V.iv.2–3). Lirondelle notes that Catherine transfers this ridicule from Evans to K'ela, preserving the humor of errors in language.[13] Catherine may have felt that isolating three characters as French or Francophile (K'ela, Kazhu, and Polkadov) was sufficient for her purposes, and that satirizing an additional nationality would cloud the issue.[14]

Catherine adds her own touch to make her version of Slender a more familiar Russian comic type. Lialiukin punctuates most of his dialog with repetitive laughter:

> Hee! hee! hee! I had a father, Anna Egor'evna … hee! hee! hee! … Uncle will tell you many jokes about him … hee! hee! hee! … Uncle, tell Anna Egor'evna a joke about papa, such as when he grabbed the goose from a neighbor in the courtyard … hee! hee! hee! (35)

The frequent repetition of the same phrase— "hee! hee! hee!"—effectively shows his immaturity. Lialiukin characterizes himself as a juvenile: "hee! hee! hee! … only I am a minor and have not yet been in service … hee! hee! hee!" (35). Fonvizin's *The Minor* [Nedorosl', 1781], usually considered to be the "best Russian play of the eighteenth century,"[15] has a title character who is also a *nedorosl'* or minor. Fonvizin's minor Mitrofan, who has also not yet entered government service, is comical because of his ignorance. Although Lialiukin possesses none of Mitrofan's arrogance, in each play the minor is ridiculously considered to be marriage material for the heroine. In changing these four

---

[11]   Lirondelle, "Catherine II, élève" 181; V. Lebedev 19.

[12]   Craik 38–39.

[13]   Lirondelle, "Catherine II, élève" 180.

[14]   Of course *Prominent Nobleman* (1772) satirizes a Frenchman, a German, and a Turk.

[15]   Karlinsky 159.

characters, Catherine transformed Shakespeare's cast into the familiar types of Russian comedy: the Francophile, the foreigner, and the minor.

In addition to changing character traits, Catherine made *This 'tis* into a very compact version of *Merry Wives*. When Lirondelle compared the two scripts in 1908, he harshly criticized Catherine's alterations to and abbreviations of Shakespeare's original: "It seems that the empress wanted to lead a dramatic action like a war campaign."[16] As a published text, *This 'tis* is much shorter than *Merry Wives*, but is quite similar in length to Catherine's other comedies of the 1770s and 1780s. Her abridgement may therefore have been for the sake of the comfort of her Russian audience. Catherine focuses her plot on the central storyline of Falstaff's threefold mortification, while also retaining the story of Anne Page's betrothal. Such a dual plot, typical of neoclassical comedy, is frequently found in Catherine's comedies. The fate of a young girl's love is usually tied in some way into the main action of the play, and the resolution concludes that action while also allowing the girl to marry her true love. Each play in Catherine's anti-Masonic trilogy combines a satire on mysticism with just such a marriage plot.

In changing the play to fit a more neoclassical esthetic, Catherine eliminates an entire subplot: that of the thwarted duel between Caius and Evans, and their revenge on the Host of the Garter Inn (stealing his horses). Entire scenes are cut (II.iii, III.i, IV.iii). These *Merry Wives* subplot scenes are deeply Shakespearean in placement and tone; they parallel the main action, and provide an echo of the play's theme of revenge and reconciliation. Their loss does not affect the main thrust of the play, but it does sacrifice one layer of complexity.

Catherine also deletes some onstage comedy by not putting her Simple into a closet to hide. In Shakespeare's I.iv, Simple (Slender's servant) arrives at Doctor Caius's house to discuss Slender's suit for Anne Page. When Caius returns, Quickly shuts Simple in the closet. Caius then finds him, saying "dere is some simples in my closet, dat I vill not for the varld I shall leave behind" (I.iv.58–59). This small bit of farcical business is humorous because of comic irony: the audience knows more than the doctor. In Catherine's abbreviated version, Kazhu merely finds K'ela and Zin'ka (Simple) talking together. Catherine's Russian comedies typically avoid onstage physical business, preferring instead to discuss offstage events; in *This 'tis*, however, later scenes contain such actions as Polkadov being beaten in the linen basket, and a dance of fairies and goblins. Why, then, did Catherine choose to eliminate Simple's closet? Perhaps the wing-and-drop scenery of the Russian public playhouses simply did not allow for a working closet, whereas the Elizabethans could have used an onstage arras. In any case, because Shakespeare's version foreshadows the later scene with Falstaff hiding in the basket, Catherine's omission loses the parallel.

Another lengthy omission is the complete deletion of Shakespeare's IV.i, in which Evans questions his young pupil William Page. For Shakespeare's

---

[16] Lirondelle, "Catherine II, élève" 183.

audience, the pleasure of the scene must have been the witty wordplay, and perhaps also the sight of the young boy-actor speaking off-color humor:

> SIR HUGH EVANS. What is your genitive case plural, William?
> WILLIAM PAGE. Genitive case!
> SIR HUGH EVANS. Ay.
> WILLIAM PAGE. Genitive,—horum, harum, horum.
> MISTRESS QUICKLY. Vengeance of Jenny's case! fie on her! never name her, child,
>   if she be a whore. (IV.i.52–7)

The scene is reminiscent of a quizzing scene in *The Minor*, in which the young Mitrofan is questioned about grammar, history, and geography. Satirizing foreign tutors was an established comic strategy in Russian comedy by Catherine's era,[17] so it is surprising that Catherine eliminated the scene and character of William Page altogether. For Catherine's purposes, however, the scene is dispensable on several levels. Coming at the beginning of Act IV, as the tension builds toward Falstaff's second humiliation, the scene slows the action. Witty puns are a hallmark of Shakespearean comedy, but too much would have been lost in the transition from English to German to Russian. Catherine in general also eschews sexual humor. By cutting the scene, Catherine excised yet another small subplot, therefore creating a more streamlined neoclassical story.

Catherine also cuts the first scene of Shakespeare's Act V. In the original, Falstaff has learned of his third opportunity from Mistress Quickly. After she exits, Ford appears once more in the disguise of Master Brook. The audience is treated to the pleasure of hearing Falstaff again insult Ford to his face, without knowing it: "That same knave Ford, her husband, hath the finest mad devil of jealousy in him, Master Brook, that ever governed frenzy" (V.i.15–17). Catherine instead chooses to begin her fifth act with Shakespeare's V.ii: with Papin, Shalov, and Slender in the park hiding from Falstaff. This change lessens Brook's comic potential. Catherine also alters Shakespeare's final line:

> MISTRESS PAGE. Well, I will muse no further. Master Fenton,
>   Heaven give you many, many merry days!
>   Good husband, let us every one go home,
>   And laugh this sport o'er by a country fire;
>   Sir John and all.
> FORD. Let it be so. Sir John,
>   To Master Brook you yet shall hold your word
>   For he tonight shall lie with Mistress Ford. (V.v.232–239)

In *This 'tis*, this closing exchange is very simplified:

---

[17] Welsh 88.

AKULINA PAPINA. What is there to do? ... we thought we were making a joke, but meanwhile came an unexpected ending.

FORDOV. Let's go, let's go have supper. (54)

Catherine ignores the inclusiveness of Shakespeare's conclusion, in which the roguish Falstaff is invited to participate in the laughter and merriment that were so recently at his expense. She also once again eliminates the humorous potential of the Ford/Brook double identity. Without the rhyming couplet to punctuate the play's ending, Fordov's invitation to supper is a pale substitution for Shakespeare's original.

Both plays are almost completely in prose. On occasion *Merry Wives* contains passages in iambic pentameter (for instance, Fenton's speech in V.v.212–222) or speeches in rhymed couplets (Mistress Page's closing lines in Shakespeare's V.iii.21–22 or the V.v invocations to the fairies). Catherine's play, in contrast, contains only two sections in verse: Falstaff's letter to Anne Page and K'ela's song to the witches (20). Given Catherine's practice of leaving matters of poetic finesse to her assistants, these sections, particularly the song, were probably composed by Khrapovitskii.[18]

Besides avoiding verse, Catherine eliminates most language that is fanciful or poetic.[19] While Akulina Papina says only that Polkadov "*boitsia leshikh*" (is scared of wood-goblins) (47), Mistress Page develops a vivid and frightening tale of Herne the hunter, who

Doth all the winter-time, at still midnight,
Walk round about an oak, with great ragg'd horns;
And there he blasts the tree and takes the cattle
And makes milch-kine yield blood and shakes a chain
In a most hideous and dreadful manner. (IV.iv.27–30)

Her words paint a picture—the "spoken decor" of the Elizabethan stage made language central to the audience's experience.

Catherine also generally omits the sensual details that make Shakespeare's descriptions so vivid. In a climactic passage of the play, Falstaff gives a narrative of his journey in the buck-basket:

Being thus crammed in the basket, a couple of Ford's knaves, his hinds, were called forth by their mistress to carry me in the name of foul clothes to Datchet-lane: they took me on their shoulders; met the jealous knave their master in the door, who asked them once or twice what they had in their basket: I quaked for fear, lest the lunatic knave

---

[18] Lirondelle, "Catherine II, élève" 181.

[19] As Simmons points out, some of Catherine's omissions are due to her source: Eschenburg's German translation, which neither retained the blank verse passages nor fully rendered all of Shakespeare's allusions (797n).

would have searched it; but fate, ordaining he should be a cuckold, held his hand. Well: on went he for a search, and away went I for foul clothes. (III.v.89–98)

Catherine's version in her III.15 scene is quite similar to this point:

POLKADOV. They called the servants and ordered them to carry me out ... in the doorways we almost met with the jealous demon ... He asked, what's that basket? ... I trembled like an aspen leaf.... The servants said they were carrying dirty linen to the washhouse ... and they carried me out ... (39)

Note the addition of the aspen leaf, a rare evocative metaphor added by Catherine.[20] As Polkadov continues, however, he tells of being dumped into the water in a quite abbreviated way: "They carried me into the garden ... and there overturned the basket into the pond ... and on me not a thread remained dry ..." (39). In contrast, as Falstaff focuses on the details of that journey, Shakespeare draws his audience into the story, into the very basket itself:

But mark the sequel, Master Brook: I suffered the pangs of three several deaths; first, an intolerable fright, to be detected with a jealous rotten bell-wether; next, to be compassed, like a good bilbo, in the circumference of a peck, hilt to point, heel to head; and then, to be stopped in, like a strong distillation, with stinking clothes that fretted in their own grease: think of that,—a man of my kidney,—think of that,—that am as subject to heat as butter; a man of continual dissolution and thaw: it was a miracle to scape suffocation. And in the height of this bath, when I was more than half stewed in grease, like a Dutch dish, to be thrown into the Thames, and cooled, glowing hot, in that surge, like a horse-shoe; think of that,—hissing hot,—think of that, Master Brook. (III.v.99–112)

Shakespeare animates the scene through images of the "hissing hot" Falstaff "half stewed in grease." The two writers' versions are distinct in taste and characterization. Catherine's speech lacks the frank vulgarity and liveliness of Shakespeare's. Polkadov, who simply mentions that his clothes were wet, is no longer the fat knight Falstaff; he is merely a Francophile fop who has been inconvenienced.

Catherine's text, stripped of the visual and sensual imagery of Shakespeare's, is less expressive and less picturesque. She gives her audience the bare bones of plot and character; perhaps little else seemed necessary for the comedy's didactic purpose, a vestige of the French neoclassical style that still pervades the play.

All of Shakespeare's *Merry Wives* takes place in the general environs of Windsor, with each of its five acts divided into several different locations. A change of scene indicates a change of place, from Page's house, to the Garter Inn,

---

[20] In *2 Henry IV*, however, Mistress Quickly claims to be shaking like an aspen leaf (II.iv.109–110).

to a field, to Windsor Park, etc. Catherine instead uses French scene divisions, so that the entrance or exit of a character generally produces a new scene. An act ends when all characters leave the stage, and location is either not specified or remains the same for an entire act. For instance, all sixteen scenes of Catherine's Act I take place at the coaching inn (as compared to Shakespeare's four scenes in three locations), and all ten scenes of her Act V take place in the garden.

In Catherine's other neoclassical comedies, it is very unusual for a shift in place to occur mid-act; Catherine, however, was unable to fit the lengthy action of Shakespeare's third act into a single location. Her first and second scenes seem to take place on the street, her third scene moves to Fordova's chamber, and scene nine moves the action back to the coaching inn. Despite such variety, Catherine indicates in a note that the action of her entire play takes place in the "county of St. Peter at a coaching inn" (4).

By setting the play in St. Petersburg, Catherine could more easily achieve her instructive purpose. A comedy set in Russia and showing recognizably Russian characters would have more of a didactic impact than a play about the foibles of foreigners. For the transfer to Russia, Catherine cuts mention of places or practices specific to England. In many cases, however, she does not replace them with something Russian. The resulting effect is a vague universality typical of neoclassicism. In Shakespeare's play, six of the scenes take place in rooms at the Garter Inn. That designation was probably a punning reference to the occasion of the play's first performance, thought to have been the Garter Feast of 23 April 1597. At these festivities, the Knights of the Order of the Garter were elected, and most scholars agree that the play may have been commissioned specifically for an after-dinner entertainment.[21] Not only does Catherine not retain the name of the Garter Inn, she does not replace it with a Russian name. The play simply takes place "at a coaching inn" in St. Petersburg.

Catherine follows this pattern throughout the play. Rather than substituting a Russian place-name for a more localized flavor, Catherine replaces the English name with a non-specific noun. In Shakespeare's III.iii, Mistress Ford instructs her servants to carry the basket "among the whitsters in Datchet-mead, and there empty it in the muddy ditch close by the Thames side" (III.iii.12–13). Many audience members in the public playhouse or at the Garter Feast (which in 1597 took place in Whitehall Palace) would have been familiar with the environs of Windsor Park, and could visualize the servants' path through the meadow to the river. Fordova instead instructs Iona and Roman to "take the basket on your shoulders, and carry it away into the garden ... and turn it over at one go into the pond, in the middle of the meadow ..." (29). Catherine declines to mention the Neva river or any particular St. Petersburg park or meadow. Thus, her version of the play loses the enjoyable sense of familiarity, but gains a more neoclassical sense of universality.

---

[21] See chapters One and Two in Green.

Characters in *Merry Wives* mention Windsor nineteen times, often using the word in adjectival relationship to a noun: "Windsor stag;" "Windsor bell;" "Windsor chimney;" "Windsor wives." This repetition of Windsor as a modifier further creates a sense of a particular place, a distinct world. In contrast, Catherine does not ever mention St. Petersburg itself in the dialog of her play. Mistress Quickly's directive "Search Windsor Castle, elves, within and out" (V.v.55) is a metatheatrical allusion to the courtly occasion of the play's commission and first performance. In the case of *This 'tis*, the author was the monarch, and no further allusions to the crown were necessary.

Besides mentions of English places, Shakespeare's text is full of references and allusions to English cultural practices. Because the play is his only comedy set in England, written on the occasion of a traditional English feast, Shakespeare may have wished to emphasize the English-ness of the setting and major characters. In most cases, Catherine eliminates terms or concepts specific to England. For example, Falstaff says, "Let the sky rain potatoes; let it thunder to the tune of Green Sleeves, hail kissing-comfits and snow eringoes; let there come a tempest of provocation, I will shelter me here" (V.v.18–21). There is no Russian equivalent to the song "Greensleeves," a popular English love song of the late sixteenth century, so Catherine merely cuts it (as well as the rain of potatoes). Polkadov says much more simply: "but now although the thunder crashes ... although the hail flattens ... although the storm places everything upside down, I'm not afraid of anything" (49).

In one instance, Catherine turns an alteration to her advantage. In the original, Falstaff's letter to Mistress Page says "you love sack and so do I" (II.i.8). Catherine changes Polkadov's line to Akulina Papina into a contrast between the two characters, with a hidden nod to the original English setting of the play: "You feast on English beer, I on champagne" (20).

In some instances, however, Catherine chose to Russianize the dialog by including cultural indicators, making it clear that the play has been removed from its original English setting to somewhere in St. Petersburg. The character names are one obvious example of Russianization; Ford becomes Fordov, Anne Page is Anna Papina, etc. In accordance with Russian practice, characters use Polkadov's name and patronymic, Iakov Vlas'evich', when they address him directly. In a few cases Catherine creates new lines with Russian-related material. Catherine adds a new metaphor, comparing Polkadov to an aristocratic Russian wolfhound,[22] with Pikov's line: "A borzoi dog, sir, galloping after a hare, doesn't ask whether the grey hare is a yearling ... her business to fetch a catch" (22). The line has no equivalent in Shakespeare's text.

In Catherine's III.10, Lialiukin comments: "from here I will go play at *babki*" (36). *Babki* is the Russian children's game of knuckle-bones. This addition, which

---

[22] A few lines before in Shakespeare's text, Pistol had called hope a "curtal dog" (II.i.102), which may have inspired the dog reference.

has no equivalent in Shakespeare's text, accomplishes two things: it adds a Russian flavor and also further characterizes Lialiukin as juvenile. Since Gallomania is a key issue of the play, this overall sense of Russianness is necessary, although not emphasized. Catherine balances such Russianness with neoclassicism, just prior to a turning point in the history of Russian drama.

In another strategic move toward universality, Catherine also carefully excises any references to Christianity or its cosmology. She herself had an ambiguous relationship to the Orthodox Church, of which she was the official head. Her conversion to Orthodoxy from Lutheranism took place in 1744, as a condition for her marriage. Her coup against her husband was in part successful because he had alienated the Church, and was perceived as a "danger to the Orthodox faith."[23] Upon acceding to the throne, however, Catherine pursued a policy of secularization, gaining state control of church lands and in many ways reducing the autonomy of the Church. Catherine's own philosophy was based on the Enlightenment principle of wisdom gained through education and the pursuit of reason. Spirituality seems to have played little part in Catherine's life, although of course everyday court activities and ceremonies were intimately tied to church ritual.

Religious belief and imagery do not play large roles in Catherine's other comedies, although *Oh, These Times!* is a significant exception. Because Sanctimonious is a Tartuffe-like religious hypocrite, her monologues are filled with references to God, the devil, prayers, and icons. In *This 'tis*, Catherine omits virtually every reference to Christianity. In some cases, Catherine cuts entire lines, such as in her scene I.2, where she eliminates Evans's line "It is spoke as Christians ought to speak" (I.i.92), or in her V.5, where Mistress Ford's line "Heaven forgive our sins" (V.v.30) is completely gone. Other dialog is retained, but shortened to eliminate the Christian concepts. Mistress Page's line, "Heaven guide him to thy husband's cudgel, and the devil guide his cudgel afterwards!" (IV.ii.79–80), becomes Akulina Papina's "Let him scold him, this will be funny ... " (42). Page's speech

> The night is dark; light and spirits will become it well. Heaven prosper our sport! No man means evil but the devil, and we shall know him by his horns. Let's away; follow me. (V.ii.11–13)

becomes simply Papin's "It's very dark, let's go hide" (48).

Other longer speeches are altered so that the basic sense and flow of the line is preserved despite the removal of the slight religious reference:

---

[23] Madariaga, *Russia in the Age of Catherine the Great* 30.

SLENDER. I'll ne'er be drunk whilst I live again, but in honest, civil, godly company, for this trick: if I be drunk, I'll be drunk with those that have the fear of God, and not with drunken knaves. (I.i.164–67)

LIALIUKIN. I will never drink anymore ... with idlers ... with drunks ... with gamblers.... I will only drink with good men ... with polite men ... with courteous men ... with honest men ... not at all with others ... (9)

Fenton's speech at the end of Shakespeare's play reveals the inherent Christian ethos of the entire script:

The offence is holy that she hath committed;
And this deceit loses the name of craft,
Of disobedience, or unduteous title,
Since therein she doth evitate and shun
A thousand irreligious cursed hours,
Which forced marriage would have brought upon her. (V.v.217–220)

Fenton casts Anne Page's marriage to him as a holy act, arguing that forced marriage results in "irreligious cursed hours." Thus, true love is tied to morality—a sharp contrast to the adulterous shenanigans of Falstaff in the rest of the comedy. But Catherine's Fintov avoids any mention of religion, by focusing instead on Anne's wishes and their mutual love:

She is so timid that she cannot speak.... Please hear me out.... You both wanted her to marry against her wishes ... I have loved her for a long time, so, as she loves me ... now we are united forever. You, Egor Avdeich', were giving away Anna Egor'evna to Lialiukin; Akulina Teren'tevna was giving her away to Doctor Kazhu.... We made use of your preparations, and then came from the wedding to ask for your pardon and your blessing. (53)

Catherine's fight against mysticism may explain her scrupulous avoidance of religious concepts in the play. Whereas *Oh, These Times!* was composed in 1772, *This 'tis* was written the same year Catherine completed her anti-Masonic trilogy, her triple attack on con men who draw unsuspecting people into their schemes.[24] Because the deceivers of those plays are alchemists, freemasons, and shamans, the plays promote the secular virtues of reason and logic. Just as her early comedies castigate the superstitious, the anti-Masonic trilogy criticizes the gullible. Writing *This 'tis* during the same year, Catherine may not have wanted to address religious belief at all, safely preferring to censure accepted social ills such as Gallomania and adultery.

---

24 *Shaman* seems to have been completed in June 1786. See Barsukov 11 for the diary entry on 16 June 1786—one day after the entry on *The Basket*.

Shakespeare's and Catherine's scripts, written in very different eras, also differ in performance context and conventions. One key distinction was the presence of boy-actors in English professional troupes, in the roles of most female characters. Since actresses were featured on Russian Imperial and estate stages from the 1750s,[25] Russian audiences were accustomed to the correspondence of the actor's gender with the role. In performance, therefore, Catherine's version of *Merry Wives* was missing a layer of humor from its original production context. The climactic scenes in Shakespeare's comedy make use of the fact that Anne Page herself would have been played by a boy. Amidst the confusion of the fairy songs and the pinching of Falstaff, "enter Caius at one door and exit stealing away a Fairy in green; enter Slender at another door and exit stealing away a Fairy in white; enter Fenton and exit stealing away Anne Page."[26] Later, Slender complains about the mistaken identity:

> SLENDER. I came yonder at Eton to marry Mistress Anne Page,
> and she's a great lubberly boy. If it had not been
> i' the church, I would have swinged him, or he
> should have swinged me. If I did not think it had
> been Anne Page, would I might never stir!—and 'tis
> a postmaster's boy. (V.v.181–6)

Doctor Caius has a similar reaction to the jest: "Vere is Mistress Page? By gar, I am cozened: I ha' married un garcon, a boy; un paysan, by gar, a boy; it is not Anne Page: by gar, I am cozened" (V.v.200–202). The joke in both cases is that of course Anne Page herself is also a boy (actor).

Catherine retains the disguised boys in her version, although the laughing Lialiukin seems tickled by his discovery:

> Hee! hee! hee! ... I thought that I took the hand of Anna Egor'evna ... hee! hee! hee! ... and led her, hee! hee! hee! ... but instead of her ... hee! hee! hee! I grasped by the hand ... guess who ... hee! hee! hee! ... . I truly thought that it was Anna Egor'evna ... hee! hee! hee! ... but then I found out that it was a kitchen-boy ... hee! hee! hee! (52)

The humor of the mistaken identity and gender confusion remains, but the metatheatrical layer—the boy-actor as Anne Page—is lost in this context.

Another common performance practice on the Elizabethan stage was the soliloquy; in *Merry Wives*, Ford speaks four of them. Neoclassical plays in general avoided the soliloquy as a device, since a character speaking while alone onstage violates the principle of verisimilitude. Shakespeare was of course not bound by concerns about believability, and so used soliloquies often, usually to reveal a character's inner plans, motivations, or emotions. In Ford's case, each soliloquy

---

25 Schuler 3.
26 See Craik edition, Act V.v, p. 215.

gives further evidence of the growing tortures of his jealousy and plans for revenge. Catherine, however, omits most of these instances of self-reflection. At the end of Shakespeare's II.i, Ford reveals his doubts about his wife, and his plans to disguise himself as Brook. Catherine's scene II.8 is a simple exchange between Fordov and the Host, planning out the masquerade as Brook. Shakespeare's II.ii features, like Catherine's scene II.11, the irony of a Falstaff unwittingly talking to a disguised Ford. At the end of II.ii, Ford is much more incensed, so his second soliloquy is a jealous rampage about "the hell of having a false woman!" (II.ii.275). His line "I will rather trust [...] a thief to walk my ambling gelding, than my wife with herself" makes reference to the play's subplot, that of the false stealing of the Host's horses (II.ii.281–8). In cutting that plotline as well as the soliloquy, Catherine removes the imagery of the wife as a horse, but also loses the fierceness of Ford's rage at Falstaff.

Ford's next soliloquy in the middle of III.ii implicates Mistress Page and plans to reveal Page's cause for jealousy. His self-assurance will soon be seen to be ironically humorous, for in the next scene he will be duped by linen and buck-baskets. Catherine retains the exchange between Papina and Fordov, but chooses not to show the workings of Fordov's mind nor his prideful belief in the success of his search. By trimming off each of these speeches, Catherine preserves the basic plot yet leaves Ford's emotional reactions and mental processes to the audience's imagination. Whereas in Shakespeare's comedy, Ford's soliloquies make him a more sympathetic fool, Catherine's excision de-emphasizes Ford's character.

Catherine does retain part of Ford's final soliloquy, at the end of III.5. The speech shows Ford determined to avenge the wrongs Falstaff has done him. The speech, which is fourteen lines long, begins:

> Hum! ha! is this a vision? is this a dream? do I sleep? Master Ford awake! awake, Master Ford! there's a hole made in your best coat, Master Ford. This 'tis to be married! this 'tis to have linen and buck-baskets! (127–131)

In Catherine's III.15, she reduces Fordov's speech to the very brief statement: "I don't know whether I'm dreaming or in reality.... This 'tis to have linen and buck-baskets ... but now he won't be going to my house" (39). Perhaps Catherine broke the rules of neoclassicism and retained this quite small soliloquy because it contains the title image of her comedy.

One question remains about Catherine's alterations to Shakespeare's original. Why did she change the title from *The Merry Wives of Windsor* to *This 'tis to Have Linen and Buck-Baskets*? Catherine's version is consistently a lean and plot-oriented version of the script, with little emphasis on language or subtlety of character. Rather than focusing her play on the Merry Wives, she instead concentrates on the play's plot of deception, and therefore on the linen and buck-baskets.

This 'tis reflects a complex historical moment: the intersection of Enlightenment secularization, a new Russian cultural identity, and the older French playwriting style. Whereas Catherine can in one sense be seen as a pioneer in her choice of a Shakespearean model, the alterations examined here show a conservative approach: the transformation of the play into a neoclassical comedy. Catherine's goal throughout her reign at this crystallizing period in Russian history was to forge a Russian national identity, through language, culture, and literature as well as through military action. The irony was that this creation of Russia would be in part accomplished by a German-born princess, standing on the shoulders of an English writer, and making fools of the French.

Staged Histories

Having tried her hand at imitating Shakespearean-style comedy, Catherine turned next to his chronicle plays, perhaps feeling that a more serious work might offer her more literary freedoms. Shakespeare's history plays would have had a natural appeal to a monarch-playwright with a keen interest in political history. Catherine would have seen right away, with the insight of an outsider to English culture, that Shakespeare was offering a deliberately created version of the tales of English kings, told through the persuasive rhetoric of the stage. If she had been thinking only as a playwright, Catherine might have done well to dramatize the scandal of her own ascension to the throne, the intrigue surrounding her husband's death, the in-prison murder of claimant Ivan Antonovich (Ivan VI), and the endless parade of her own favorites—events certainly rivaling the Wars of the Roses. But thinking rather as a monarch, Catherine prudently turned her attention back many centuries, to the distant origins of the modern Russian state. She first took up the story of Riurik, the Norse conqueror who founded Novgorod and consolidated power in northern Russia. Catherine boasted to Grimm about the "historical exactitude" of both *From the Life of Riurik* (composed in August of 1786) and *The Beginning of Oleg's Reign* (written one month later).[27] Both plays bore the same bold inscription: "an imitation of Shakespeare, without preservation of the usual theatrical rules." The former was never staged; the latter was presented as an elaborate opera. Perhaps the operatic form made a production more viable, allowing Catherine to stray from the neoclassical precepts associated with non-musical tragedies.

Some critics have asserted that *Riurik* and *Oleg* bear little relation to Shakespeare: "in them there are no hints of the drama and historical chronicles of Shakespeare, except for the mentioned indication in the title."[28] But others, like myself, give Catherine more credit for innovations, noting the structural

---

[27] Letter's date is 24 September 1786; Grot, "Pis'ma imperatritsy" 384.

[28] V. Lebedev 8.

similarities to Shakespeare's work.[29] With both *From the Life of Riurik* and The *Beginning of Oleg's Reign*, Catherine rejected the formal strictures of neoclassical tragedy that had dominated Russian drama for decades. Catherine drew on the English writer's dramaturgical techniques to glorify Russia's past and to justify the Empress's own actions in the past (such as her rule as a foreigner to Russia) and present (the Russo-Turkish War).

From the Life of Riurik

Khrapovitskii's diary indicates that Catherine wrote *Riurik* throughout August 1786, asking both Potemkin and Petr Zavadovskii (her favorite in the late 1770s who remained a trusted advisor) to look it over and make suggestions. The play was published in 1786 by the Academy of Sciences, and also appeared in Dashkova's *Russian Theatre* in 1787. Later single editions appeared in 1792 and 1793. A German translation by Fel'kner was published in Petersburg in 1792, and a French version appeared in the Parisian edition of Hermitage plays in 1799.[30]

The main source for Catherine's historical treatment of the story of Gostomysl, Riurik, and Vadim was the ancient *Primary Chronicle* [Nachal'noe letopis], a compendium of events in the early history of the future Russia, compiled by several authors in the period from 1040–1118.[31] This work was newly available to a reading public in Catherine's time, published in eight volumes from 1767–92.[32] The *Chronicle* is a log of annual entries, beginning with 852. The story of the usurper Vadim's execution by Prince Riurik appears in the Nikonian Chronicle in the year 864; the tale of Oleg's reign appears in the years 870–913.

Catherine's other sources probably included the early volumes of V. N. Tatishchev's *Russian History from the Earliest Times* [Istoriia rossiiskaia s samykh drevneiskikh vremen, 1768–1848],[33] and her own *Notes Concerning Russian History*, first serialized in 1783–84, and then re-published from 1787–94. These notes elaborated on incidents and events from the chronicles and from Tatishchev. Catherine told Grimm how pleased she was that publication of her notes in serial form "puts history in the hands of everyone."[34] Whereas Catherine's *Notes* certainly reveal her own perspectives and priorities, Andrew Wachtel makes the good point that since tragedies didn't pretend to be accurate, *Riurik* allowed her to take even more liberties with the story in order to promote her own version of

---

[29] See for example Shchebal'skii, "Dramaticheskiia i nravoopisatel'nyia" 544.

[30] *Historisches Drama*; *Théâtre de l'Hermitage*. The latter's editor notes about *Riurik* that, "This play [...] was translated into French under the eyes of Catherine, who corrected the translation" (2: 369).

[31] Zenkovsky 11.

[32] *Russian Historical Library* [Drevnaia rossiiskaia vivliofika, 1767–92].

[33] The first four volumes appeared between 1768 and 1784.

[34] Pypin 11: xx.

events.[35]   Almost ten years later, Catherine said as much in another letter to Grimm:

> I did not dare put my conjectures regarding Riurik in my history, for they were based solely on a few hidden words by Nestor in his chronicle and one passage in Dalin's history of Sweden. But while reading Shakespeare in German I dreamed up the idea of putting my conjectures in a drama, which was printed in 1786.[36]

In the same letter, Catherine also mentions the interest shown in the play by I. N. Boltin (1735–92). Boltin had written a 1788 book of historical notes in response to a history of Russia by Frenchman LeClerc. Catherine recounts that after having read Boltin's historical works, she wanted him to see her ideas about Riurik contained in the play. She reports that upon reading them, Boltin asked her to reprint the play with his commentary. Thus the 1792 and 1793 editions of the play (as well as the German translation) contained a preface in which Boltin emphasizes that the play "is not composed of fabricated events but of real and true events,"[37] and goes into detail about evidence for many of the characters and events in the play. He also praises the "unknown Author" and "his" love of the truth. Such affirmation from a respected historian must have appealed to Catherine, confirming the plausibility of her interpretations of the chronicle records.

In her play *From the Life of Riurik*, she characterizes Riurik (founder of the Russian state) as a hero, in contrast to the rebellious Vadim. The plot of *Riurik* concerns the dying wish of Gostomysl, Prince of Novgorod, to leave his land in the hands of his former enemies, the Varangians (Norsemen). His chosen successors are his grandsons Riurik, Sineus, and Trevor (the sons of the Finnish King Ludbrat and Umila, Gostomysl's middle daughter). Immediately jealous is Vadim, a Slavian Prince, also Gostomysl's grandson from his youngest daughter. While ambassadors travel from Novgorod to the Varangian camp to ask the brothers to lead their people, Vadim begins to stir unrest. His rebellion is quickly put down, and (in a striking change from the historical material) Riurik mercifully spares his life; Vadim swears eternal allegiance.

Catherine crafted *Riurik* to emphasize a theme close to her own heart: the benefits of a benevolent foreign rule. Several characters initially oppose Riurik and his brothers; First Elder tells Vadim that, "We have always had Princes from our own kin, not foreign ones" (225).[38] But the Varangian Princes are portrayed as wise and capable, and the underlying message is that good intentions are more important than lineage. It is no wonder the German-born Catherine was drawn to this story (and had the play published in German translation in 1792, with its

---

[35]   Wachtel 21.

[36]   Letter's date is 25 May 1795. Grot, "Pis'ma imperatritsy" 639. Translation from Wachtel 26.

[37]   Boltin i.

[38]   Translations from *Riurik* by Marianna Podolskaya.

authenticity confirmed by Boltin). Indeed, Riurik himself seems to be a very Catherine-like ruler, a ninth-century Enlightenment proponent of reasoned governance. In his stepson Oskold's words, "Reason and courage overcome difficulties and obstacles" (232). The nicely suspenseful conclusion reveals Riurik's enlightened outlook, as he removes his sword to take vengeance on Vadim and then, urged to forgive by Edvinda, drops it. Thirteen years earlier, at the close of the Pugachev Rebellion (1773–74), Catherine had not been not so merciful with the usurper Pugachev, whom she ordered to be beheaded publicly in Moscow in 1775.

Catherine's play was the first literary work to treat the historical figure of Vadim. Barely mentioned in the chronicles as having led an uprising against Riurik, Vadim became a symbol of rebellion against authority by the nineteenth century. Like Catherine's earlier version, Iakov Kniazhnin's stylistically traditional *Vadim of Novgorod* (1789) is also set during the reign of Riurik. Rehearsals were begun in 1790, with Iakov Shusherin as Riurik and Petr Plavil'shchikov as Vadim, but the author himself cancelled plans for production for unknown reasons. After Kniazhnin died, Dashkova published the play in *Russian Theatre* in 1793. But Catherine banned it, probably at the urging of her lover Platon Zubov, and ordered all copies destroyed (some were burned in a public ceremony). She is usually thought to have considered its republican ideas too dangerous, although Wachtel argues well that Catherine's reaction to the play was more due to literary jealousy than to political concerns.[39] In any case, Kniazhnin's play became an "underground text," and the character of Vadim, now associated with rebellion against tyranny, found his way into numerous other literary works by authors such as Lermontov and Pushkin.[40] In Catherine's version, however, Vadim symbolizes the futility of revolt against a benevolent ruler.

While Catherine's historical perspective was unique, the true innovation of *Riurik* was its "imitation of Shakespeare." Shakespearean scholar Ernest Simmons compares *Riurik* to various plots and characters in Shakespeare's Henry plays. He notes the similarity of scene IV.5 in *2 Henry IV*, in which the dying Henry IV advises his son, to *Riurik*'s scene in which Gostomysl gathers his advisors to speak of the Varangian princes' succession. Simmons also likens Vadim to Hotspur, and remarks that "Rurik's magnanimity in pardoning Vadim is reminiscent of Henry the Fifth's generosity toward his enemies."[41] Riurik has a brief speech recounting his victories in France, also recalling Henry V.

---

[39] Wachtel 31–36.

[40] Yet another version of the story was written by Plavil'shchikov, who had begun rehearsing the role of Vadim in Kniazhnin's aborted production. Originally performed in the 1790s under the title *Vseslav*, it was published posthumously as *Riurik the Great*.

[41] Simmons 804.

But the real imitation of Shakespeare comes in *Riurik*'s stylistic revolt against neoclassical ideals. Catherine's innovations become clear when the script is compared to other Russian plays of its era. Sumarokov's 1747 *Hamlet* pared down Shakespeare's cast to eight named characters (including Armans, confidant to Hamlet, and Flemina, confidante to Ophelia), and otherwise altered Shakespeare's original to suit the French standards of unified time, place, and action. Kniazhnin's *Vadim of Novgorod*, written at least two years after Catherine's, has only seven named characters (two of whom are confidants), and the entire action takes place in the city square of Novgorod. Moreover, the central conflict of the play—between Riurik and the anti-autocratic Vadim—has been fashioned into a love-versus-honor plot. As in many French neoclassical tragedies, a daughter (Ramida) must choose between the love she bears her father (Vadim) and her passion for her lover (Riurik). In comparison to *Vadim*, the generic experimentation of Catherine's *Riurik* is bold indeed.

Catherine again avoided writing verse, and the prose scenes of *Riurik* and *Oleg* signaled a change from the ever-present verse couplets of most Russian tragedy. Whereas neoclassical style required a unity of place, *Riurik*'s five acts each take place in very different locations. As Shakespeare's *Henry V* moves from England to France, so Catherine's play moves from Novgorod to the sea coast Varangian camp in Scandinavia and on to Riurik's castle near the Vokhov. Such freedom to make drastic changes in setting enhanced the play's message about the advantages of unifying vast regions under a single ruler. Each act occurs mostly within the same location, although Act II moves from the Varangian coastal camp to King Ludbrat's tent, and Act IV similarly moves from Riurik's riverbank castle to his tent.

While Catherine may have had Shakespearean spatial fluidity in mind, she did not at all imitate the spare staging of the Elizabethan public theatre, details about which Russian artists were probably unaware. Some of her stage directions imply technological effects more common to Russian opera. At the beginning of Act II, the stage directions indicate, "ships are seen from far away." Later, Riurik and his brothers approach the shore in rowing boats.

Catherine may also have been impressed by the presence of music and dance in Shakespearean plays. Although not an opera like its sequel *Oleg*, *Riurik* does contain a dance sequence. At the end of Act III, after Ludbrat agrees to send his sons to rule Russia, a "ballet shows the sacrifice on the consecrated hill and the departure of Riurik" (240). In Shakespeare's comedies, dances create entertaining interludes, but rarely portray specific plot events. Catherine evidently saw an opportunity for spectacle in this pagan ceremony; *Oleg* would similarly evoke folk customs with the songs and dances in its wedding scene.

Another possible connection to Shakespeare's chronicle plays is Catherine's effort to write good parts for women. *Riurik*'s female characters, hardly mentioned in the chronicle record, have a memorable presence and impact in Catherine's rendering. Umila, middle daughter of Gostomysl, foresees her father's death in

II.2: "I had a dream last night, as if a high mansion fell down in front of me with an awful crash, the dust and kindling flew everywhere, even covered my royal clothes" (228). While she is sad to lose her children to their fortunes in Russia, she vows to "consider such sacrifice as honor;" Ludbrat praises her reasoning and "lofty spirit" (235). In V.2, Riurik's wife Edvinda urges mercy for the captive Vadim, reminding her husband of Vadim's youth and blood relation. She justifies her frank argument by referring to Riurik's love of truth. In the play's final scene, her words seem to turn the tide:

> RIURIK. The indisputable truth is that you are now under my power, that I can judge
>   you as a local prince or as a subject....
> EDVINDA (*in a quiet and modest voice*). Or to forgive, as a brother. (250)

The tension between mercy and justice recalls the conclusion of Shylock's trial in Shakespeare's *Merchant of Venice*, where the conceit of the medieval Parliament of Heaven is made secular.

Although published several times, *From the Life of Riurik* was never performed. But the play was significant in many ways: creating the new literary figure of Vadim, acknowledging the value of Shakespeare's style by flouting "the rules," and, most importantly, merging Catherine's own historical perspective with an experimental genre. It would fall to *Oleg* to bring those experiments to the public, this time magnifying its patriotism through music.

The Beginning of Oleg's Reign

"This morning, as I was looking out of a window, I saw the clouds and turrets of Constantinople going to the theatre, in a cart."[42] So wrote English traveler Lionel Colmore in 1790 of preparations for a new Russian opera to be performed in St. Petersburg: Catherine's "historical performance," titled *The Beginning of Oleg's Reign*. At the time of the opera's premiere in 1790, Catherine was supervising a war with Turkey, so Colmore's observation on the theatrical preparations had an underlying irony: Catherine had real-life designs for carting off Constantinople. Although this opera was to be unprecedented in the lavishness of its spectacle, the production was hardly comparable to the real Ottoman capital; the two-dimensional wing-and-drop set pieces could only tantalizingly hint at that city's cultural splendors. The connection between *Oleg*'s staged spectacle and Catherine's own political project, however, was hardly illusory. The Russo-Turkish War of 1787–91 was itself a step toward the realization of the theme of her opera: cultural appropriation through military action, and Catherine's own appropriation of Western esthetic models set the stage for this theme.

---

42 Quoted in A.G. Cross, "Eighteenth-Century Russian Theater" 235.

The historical themes of the opera relate to Catherine's own ideology and objectives, connecting the central plot (Oleg's attack on Constantinople) to the context of Catherine's "Greek Project" and the Russo-Turkish War of 1787–91. The production combined the use of operatic spectacle with these Shakespearean elements: non-neoclassical structures; an infusion of folk ceremonial songs, dances, and customs into the wedding scene; the intermingling of princes with soldiers and citizens; and the use of metatheatre. Just as Catherine esthetically appropriated both the baroque opera and the Elizabethan chronicle play, she also hoped to culturally appropriate Greece through military action against the Ottoman Empire.

As Lirondelle wrote, the pageantry of *Oleg* makes one "think more of [baroque librettist Philippe] Quinault than of Shakespeare."[43] Why did Catherine change forms after *Riurik*, choosing the genre of opera for her second historical work? The first reason is opera's inherently mixed nature. In *Culture and Imperialism*, Edward Said argues that European opera is a "hybrid, radically impure" form[44] with the power to use "narrative to dispel contradictory memories."[45] A later opera such as Verdi's *Aïda* (1871) implies an "imperial presence so dominating as to make impossible any effort to separate it from historical necessity."[46] In an analysis of the representation of Egypt in *Aïda*, Said explores the production's complex connection to imperial domination in that region: "Napoleon and his scholarly experts were there also to put Egypt before Europe, in a sense to stage its antiquity, its wealth of associations, cultural importance, and unique aura *for* a European audience."[47] Similarly, Catherine's *Oleg* staged Byzantium's "wealth of associations" for her own Russian audience. Her reformulated narrative of the Russian historical past was carefully constructed to make her domination of Turkey seem a historical necessity. Catherine's contemporary, the poet Derzhavin, noted the power of opera for such patriotic purposes:

> Nowhere can one sing powerful odes better or more elegantly [...] to the immortal memory of the fatherland's heroes and to the glory of good sovereigns, as in an opera in the theater. Catherine the Great knew this perfectly. We saw and heard the effect of the heroic musical presentation composed by her in wartime under the name 'Oleg.'[48]

The second advantage of operatic form is its tradition of splendid production values; such spectacle allowed Catherine to demonstrate vividly the magnificence of ancient Russian and Byzantine traditions, while at the same time flaunting the

---

43 Lirondelle "Catherine II, élève" 188.
44 Said 114.
45 Said 132.
46 Said 132.
47 Said 118.
48 Grot, *Sochineniia Derzhavina* 7: 609. Translation courtesy of Mark Haag.

cultural sophistication of the Russian court at the close of eighteenth century. The performative strategies of the baroque-era court theatre stemmed from an earlier Renaissance tradition equating pomp with power. The dancing Sun King, performing the dual role of heavenly body and kingly body, combined the identity of monarchical viewer with the displayed and viewed body of the performer. Developing as it did from both Renaissance academic studies of classical drama and from court revelries such as masques and triumphal displays, baroque court opera blended beauty, history, literature, and ideology. Although composed in the late eighteenth century, the Russian opera *Oleg* incorporated characteristics of the earlier operas of Quinault: classical motifs, topical ideological commentary, and an abundance of song, dance, and visual wonders to reinforce its political viewpoint. *Oleg* was first produced in the 1790–91 season, with sumptuous costumes and scenery, and hundreds of supernumeraries. One observer called the production "a magic lantern, exhibiting different objects in succession to the eyes of the spectator."[49]

On the stage of world politics, it was to Catherine's advantage to control this succession of images. By drawing on the conventions of both opera (which through narrative and spectacle offers a stylized vision of reality) and the Shakespearean chronicle plays (which present a broad range of time, place, and characters in a reshaping of history), Catherine fashioned a "magic lantern" that reflected her cultural and political viewpoint and objectives.

The Beginning of Oleg's Reign is a sequel to the earlier *Riurik*. The point of attack is a crisis: the Kievan ruler Oskold, having returned from an unsuccessful naval attack on Tsargrad (Constantinople), is rumored to have adopted Christian customs. We learn that Prince Riurik had chosen Oleg to reign during the youth of Riurik's son Igor, and to serve as Igor's advisor. In the course of the opera, Oleg founds the city of Moscow (Act I), journeys to Kiev to dismiss Oskold from his duties (Act II), arranges the wedding celebration of Igor and Prekrasa (Act III), and then takes naval forces with him to attack Tsargrad himself. He is successful, and signs a favorable treaty with Greece (Act IV). In the final act, the Emperor Leon invites Oleg into the Hippodrome to celebrate their new alliance.

The 1787 published edition of *Oleg* contains a foreword, probably written by Catherine herself. It asserts, "In this historical performance there is more historical truth than fiction."[50] Even though she admits to some telescoping of time to include the marriage of Igor, clearly Catherine's intention is to demonstrate the legitimacy of her version of events by referring to her historical sources, as in this passage from the foreword: "In the fifth act there is little deviation from the History, for Oleg actually had a meeting with the Eastern Emperor Leon."[51] Ironically, the historical source mentioned in the foreword is Catherine's own

---

[49]   Masson 75.

[50]   Pypin 2: 261.

[51]   Pypin 2: 262.

work: *Notes Concerning Russian History*, her compilation of materials from the historical chronicles.

Oleg does indeed follow the events of the *Primary Chronicle* closely. Act III.4 dramatizes the *Chronicle*'s line about the terms of the treaty with Greece: "So Oleg demanded that they pay tribute for his two thousand ships at the rate of twelve *grivni* per man, with forty men reckoned to a ship."[52] Like Shakespeare, Catherine employed historical fact to serve her dramatic genre as well as her political policies. In the *Chronicle*, Oleg's victorious troops receive silk and linen sails; Catherine uses the story as an opportunity to display the ruler Oleg's wise reason.

Just as Shakespearean chronicle plays resonate with the political and social visions of the Elizabethan era while presenting selective visions of English history, so Catherine's *Oleg* must be seen not only as a depiction of ninth-century history, but also as a metaphorical representation of eighteenth-century current events— particularly Catherine's own "Greek Project" (see Fig. 4.1). The Greek Project was Catherine's quest to unravel the Ottoman Empire, re-asserting a connection between Russia and the glory that was ancient/Byzantine Greece. This larger goal was to be accomplished primarily through military means, and in fact was partially realized by the successful Russo-Turkish wars of 1768–74 and 1787–91. In addition to the plan's military and economic allure, the linking of Russia to the rich heritage of Byzantium would provide cultural benefits. Catherine's dream was for her grandson Konstantin, named for the Emperor Constantine, to reign in his namesake city of Constantinople as suzerain of a "restored Greek Empire."[53]

Catherine had much to restore. Even by the mid-eighteenth century, when Russians had become familiar with the Roman classical world via the continental European neoclassical movement, contact with Greek language and literature was scarce.[54] Unlike the Roman Catholic "Latinists," Orthodox Russians never incorporated the Greek language into their church devotions, instead observing all rites in their own Slavonic. Nor were the classical Greek writers well-known in Russia either in the middle ages or in subsequent centuries. Although Harold Segel notes a changing atmosphere in the mid-eighteenth century, he concludes, "Classical Antiquity and Hellenism, above all, never took hold of the Russian consciousness in the way it did the German."[55] One of Catherine's cultural goals was to increase this connection to Greece; her strategy was to do so through military action in the Ottoman Empire.

After the success of the 1768–74 Russo-Turkish War, which gave Russia expanded access to the Black Sea, Catherine had further designs on the Turks. In 1780, she and Joseph II of Austria made a secret agreement that alluded to Austria's support of future Russian ventures into the Crimea and further. By 1784,

[52] S. H. Cross, 150.
[53] Alexander, *Catherine the Great: Life and Legend* 247.
[54] Zenkovsky 4.
[55] Segel, "Classicism and Classical Antiquity" 60.

Fig. 4.1 Anonymous Caricature, October 1787. "The Christian Amazon, with Her Invincible Target, Alias, the focus of Genial Rays, or Dian of the Rushes, to (sic) much for 300,000 Infidels." Catherine's raised skirts reveal breeches and boots. The Turkish Sultan attacks her while her ally Joseph II hides behind her. The drawing also shows a small ape-like Louis XVI; the King of Spain completes the picture.

she had acquired the Crimea. Two years later, in 1786, Catherine wrote *The Beginning of Oleg's Reign*. Relevant entries in Khrapovitskii's diary show that she wrote the libretto quickly—from 8 September to 5 October 1786, a period of about four weeks. She continued to have Khrapovitskii rework the choruses into verse into November of that year. Although a copy of the opera was published in 1787 both in Dashkova's *Russian Theatre* and in a separate edition, *Oleg* was not immediately produced.[56] Plans for a production were not initiated until July of 1789.

The political events subsequent to the opera's composition may explain why the premiere was delayed for several years. A month after writing the play, Catherine left for a long and showy tour of southern Russia, from January to July of 1787. Soon after her return, she plunged Russia into a war with Turkey that would last until 1791.

Although the production of *Oleg* preceded peace with the Turks by about ten months, the official court theatre premiere (22 October 1790) [57] roughly coincided with a period of great success for Catherine's navy (for example, the sea battle of mid-September 1790). She commemorated these gains with banquets and balls, including a cross-dressed masquerade ball on 10 November.[58] The production of *Oleg* was another in a series of self-congratulatory celebrations that autumn, and the relation of its patriotic plot—a Russian victory over Constantinople—to current events could hardly have gone unnoticed.

The entire fifth act of the opera is a glorification of Greek culture at the historical moment of an alliance with Russia. The Emperor Leon is passively and almost reverently accommodating to the visiting Oleg, offering every state courtesy: there is a dance of nymphs, feasting on fruit, a display of ancient Greek games, and a scene from Euripides' *Alcestis*. Catherine herself researched the games in Diderot's *Encyclopedia*, as the 26 September 1786 entry in Khrapovitskii's diary tells us.[59] When read in the context of the war with Turkey, these events can be seen as an unabashed glorification of Russian might. Oleg is the conquering force who strengthens his own power through such contact with classical antiquity—as Catherine hoped to do again. The closing stage directions of *Oleg* provide a striking final image (see Fig. 4.2):

Oleg, saying good-bye to Leon and Zoia, attaches the shield of Igor, on which is pictured a warrior on a horse, to a column of the Hippodrome.
OLEG. Before I leave, I attach the shield of Igor here in commemoration. Let future generations see it here.

---

[56] First single edition was published in St. Petersburg (Imperatorskoi akademii nauk 1787); second edition 1793.

[57] The *Kamer-fur'erskii zhurnal* entry for 15 October 1790 lists an "incognito" performance of *Oleg* at the Hermitage that evening.

[58] Alexander, *Catherine the Great: Life and Legend* 286.

[59] Barsukov 16.

Пусть позднѣйшие потомки узрить его тутъ.

Fig. 4.2 Act V.iv, *The Beginning of Oleg's Reign*, published in 1791. "Let future generations see it here." [Pust' pozdneishie potomki uzriat ego tut.] Oleg refers to the shield of Igor, which he leaves as a monument.

LEON. In every age you will be called wise and brave. (304)[60]

By concluding the opera with Oleg's grandiose gesture, Catherine's hope must have been that the "future generations" Oleg spoke of would support her struggle to regain the magnificent Constantinople.

Befitting this monumental task of social and political restructuring, *The Beginning of Oleg's Reign* was one of the most lavish, expensive productions ever seen in Russia—in this sumptuousness it certainly seems more akin to baroque opera than to the relative scenic simplicity of Shakespeare. Catherine herself called it "such a show as has never been seen before."[61] The premiere at the Hermitage was followed by several performances in the public Stone Theatre beginning on 27 October 1790.[62] The opera was revived again in the 1794–95 season. The cost is estimated to have been between 9,000 and 10,000 rubles. An additional sum went toward the printing of the elaborate 1791 edition of the play, with illustrations (see Fig. 4.3) and full orchestral score.[63] The cast contained six hundred supernumeraries from several field regiments, including the Preobrazhenskii guards who had supported Catherine's coup in 1762. Witnesses to the 1795 production said "that in the first act of this play the public went into raptures in the scene of the founding of the city of Moscow, and when the eagle flew, they burst into thunderous applause" (see Fig. 4.4).[64]

Visitors to St. Petersburg, if puzzled by the opera's historical themes, were enthusiastic about the grandeur of the production. Even the French envoy Count Valentin Esterházy wrote to his wife about the opulence of the costumes:

The *decor*, although beautiful, would have been incomparably finer in Paris, but inasmuch as the costumes are concerned, it is difficult to visualize their wonder. All the fabrics are Turkish and are embroidered with gold and pure silver. They say that the play has cost an unbelievable sum.[65]

According to Khrapovitskii, in July of 1789 the Empress had ordered that the

---

[60] All translations from *The Beginning of Oleg's Reign* were prepared by Marianna Podolskaya, with my assistance.

[61] From a letter to Potemkin on 1 November 1790. Quoted in Findeizen 2: 138.

[62] Vsevolodskii-Gerngross, *Ot istokov* 453.

[63] This edition of *Nachal'noe upravlenie Olega* ([St. Petersburg]: Tipografiia Gornago uchilishcha, 1791) was the only full orchestral score of a Russia opera to be printed in the eighteenth century (Seaman 268n). Vol'man 135; Findeizen 2: 138.

[64] Arapov, *Letopis'* 115. Arapov's source is *Sievernaia Pchela* 147 (1837). The 1791 edition of the opera contains illustrations by E. I. Koshkin at the beginning of each act, which depict a single moment from the play's action. The eagle's flight is shown in the drawing on page one.

[65] Seaman 269n. Original French source is Esterházy 336–37.

Fig. 4.3 Frontispiece for *The Beginning of Oleg's Reign*, **published in 1791**

Fig. 4.4 Act I.ii, *The Beginning of Oleg's Reign*, published in 1791. "This city will be vast and famous." [Sei grad budet nekogda obshiren i znamenit]

costumes be taken from her own personal collection.[66] Visiting Oxford don John Parkinson had heard this anecdote when he saw the production in 1792:

> [...] we went to the theatre to see Oleg, a sort of ballet composed four years ago by the Empress herself and intended to represent the old Russian Costume, which she has enabled them to do by making them a present of all the rich Garments which were preserved in the Imperial Wardrobe.[67]

Here, Catherine's concern with accuracy and authenticity reflects her own passionate interest in history and in the cultural traditions of Russia's past. Catherine knew the importance of costuming. When her predecessor Peter the Great transformed Russia into a Westernized nation, one of the most visible of his reforms had been a change from the traditional Russian beard and robes to the clean-shaven faces and frock coats of early eighteenth-century Europe. Although Catherine sought to preserve the spirit of Peter's progressive changes, her reign also signaled a return to Russia's own customs. At her request C. W. Müller made a series of engravings from 1776–79 featuring the peoples of the Russian Empire in their native dress,[68] and Catherine herself reintroduced Russian dress to her court. A 1769 portrait of her by Vigilius Ericksen depicts her in the traditional Russian *kokoshnik* headdress (see Fig. 4.5).[69] Her use of costumes from the imperial collection in the production of *Oleg* is another clue to the patriotism she hoped to inspire with her opera.

The dances in *Oleg* also expressed Russian craft and excellence. Some of St. Petersburg's finest ballet luminaries participated in *Oleg*; for instance, the Imperial Theatre School dancer and ballet master Ivan Val'berkh, sometimes known as the first Russian choreographer, played the role of Igor. The opera offers several opportunities for dance interludes: the dance of the girls in Prekrasa's wedding party, the dance of the nymphs Flora and Pomona in the celebration of the new treaty in Constantinople, and the dances which form part of the ancient Greek entertainments in the Hippodrome. Guiseppe Canziani choreographed both the games (running, wrestling, discus throwing) and the Hippodrome ballet sequences. Visiting French choreographer Charles LePicq, chief proponent of the Noverre balletic style, created the other dances. Despite his reservations about the overall event, Parkinson did enjoy the choreography: "What pleased me most of all in it was the Russian Dance, which seemed to be executed with a great deal of grace and animation."[70] *Oleg*'s dances also appealed to French writer C. F. P. Masson: "the national dances and sports, which are exhibited, produce a number of pleasing

---

[66]   Barsukov 299. Diary entry is from 24 July 1789.

[67]   Parkinson 57. Entry for Thursday 6 December 1792. Strangely, El'nitskaia does not list production dates for *Oleg* in 1792 (453).

[68]   *The Costume of the Russian Empire.* London: W. Miller, 1803, preface.

[69]   Forbes and Underhill 120.

[70]   Parkinson 57.

Fig. 4.5 Catherine in a *kokoshnik*, a traditional Russian headdress. *Portrait of Catherine II wearing a Russian Costume*, engraved by William Dickinson in 1773, after the original by Vigilius Ericksen, 1769

pictures."[71]   Catherine might have been pleased that his words do not make a distinction between the native Russian ceremonial dances and the ancient Greek games, seeing them all as "national" dances and sports of a united Greco-Russian culture.

Operas were an essential component of court and public theatrical life in Catherine's Russia.   Russian opera had been born with the 1772 premiere of Popov's *Aniuta*, and Catherine's court was also host to a number of foreign composers (including Domenico Cimarosa).   Catherine was not herself a great devotee of music, and most scholars consider her to have been "rather indifferent to musical performers."[72]   Of her own many completed dramatic works, however, six were opera *libretti*.

The music for *Oleg*, written by three separate composers, is as heterogeneous as the *libretto* it accompanies.   The Italian Carlo Canobbio (1741–1822) composed the instrumental numbers, including an overture, a triumphal march, and four entr'acte pieces.   The Russian composer Vasilii Alekseevich Pashkevich (c. 1740–1820) wrote accompaniment to the three wedding songs in Act III.   Finally, Guiseppe Sarti (1729–1802), the celebrated Italian composer, wrote both the Act IV music for the four Lomonosov lyrics, and a complete choral score for the selection from *Alcestis* "in conformity with ancient Greek taste."[73]   Not only did Sarti compose melody for the strophe and antistrophe choral passages of the scene in Dorian, Lydian, Phrygian, and other modes, he also wrote melody for the chorus' lines in conversation with Hercules, and instrumental underscoring for the dialog scenes between Hercules and Admetus.   Although Catherine had first requested musical assistance from Cimarosa, she later asked Sarti to tackle the challenge of this Greek material.   She herself was well pleased with the result, as she wrote in a letter to Grimm: "The choruses of *Oleg* are the most beautiful in the world and are mostly by Sarti: all the Greek modes are assembled."[74]   Sarti himself wrote a lengthy exegesis of these Greek sections, citing Aristotle and referring to the relation between poetic imagery and musical mode.   Evidently glad for the opportunity to experiment with ancient musical forms, Sarti concludes with flattering words for Catherine: "I wish that my labor will please my Great Sovereign, for whom I would sacrifice my own life, if my sacrifice were useful to her."[75]   But Esterházy found Sarti's composition pedantic: "Sarti has imitated the Greek forms to such an extent that the work has become gloomy and rather boring."[76]

---

[71]   Masson 74.

[72]   Seaman 71.

[73]   Sarti vii.

[74]   Letter is dated 7 May 1791.   Grot, "Pis'ma imperatritsy" 525.   Translation from Seaman 269n.

[75]   Sarti vii.

[76]   Quoted in Seaman 269n.   Original French source is Esterhàzy 336.

The opera's music echoes the libretto's political theme—the melding of Russian and Greek culture. The early twentieth-century opera historian Nikolai Findeizen praised Pashkevich's integration of Russian folk melodies as "unconditionally interesting" (while finding Canobbio's work to be lackluster).[77] Pashkevich's use of folk-derived melody was not unique to *Oleg*. Gerald Seaman notes such adaptation as a key characteristic of native Russian opera, even when composed in Russian by foreigners: "At first folk-song was employed literally in the form of simple quotations, but by the end of the century composers were able to write freely in the folk idiom and imbue their characters with national features."[78] Catherine would have been able to find the text for the folk songs used during her opera's wedding sequence in several song collections published during her reign. For example, Mikhail Chulkov's *Various Collected Songs* [Sobranie raznykh pesen, published in 1770–73] includes "Rolling is the Red Sun" ["Perekatnoe krasno solnyshko"] under the category of "wedding songs." This song is found in III.1 of *Oleg* with only minor variations.[79] Combined with several rituals of a typical Russian wedding day, these folk songs add a native Russian touch to a work which otherwise draws on various Western stylistic modes.

Nor were the non-musical aspects of the production neglected. Noted actors such as Plavil'shchikov, Krutitskii, and Shusherin took the major roles, which are not singing parts.[80] The most celebrated name is that of Dmitrevskii, who played Oleg in the 1790 and 1794 productions. Dmitrevskii's famous declamatory style should have suited Catherine's Oleg well, yet anecdotes reveal that Catherine was critical of him. Evidently wishing to make her influence felt in every aspect of the production, including the acting, Catherine commented on Dmitrevskii after seeing a rehearsal run (*proba*) of Act II. Khrapovitskii writes in his diary:

> 26 [September 1790]. Conversation about "Oleg." [She] said it is necessary to correct Dmitrevskii. He is not a fool, but last night played much against sense. Oleg is a grand character, he is affected by what happens but his role doesn't allow for pomposity.[81]

She also gave the actor very specific advice about the playing of one particular moment:

> The sovereign called the director Soimonov and ordered him to tell Dmitrevskii, in her name, that speaking of important matters with the successor to the Kievan throne, he must step aside and speak in a whisper; to this she added that although Dmitrevskii

---

[77] Findeizen 2: 248.

[78] Seaman 94.

[79] Chulkov, *Sobranie raznykh* 12. Petr Bezsonov found the texts to the wedding songs of Act III in several of these late eighteenth-century song collections. See Bezsonov, "O vlianii."

[80] Vsevolodskii-Gerngross, *Russkii teatr* 36–64.

[81] Barsukov 348.

understands more than she does about dramatic art, in this case, he should take her advice.[82]

Here Catherine's concern for realism in the portrayal came head to head with prevailing trends in "dramatic art." Dmitrevskii's declamation may have been fashionable but common sense dictates that a ruler must be discreet in matters of state. This small episode—the monarch telling the actor how to play a monarch— is perhaps a telling clue to Catherine's own identification with the heroic Oleg.

The eye-witness estimations of *Oleg*'s virtues vary but are generally positive. This response may depend as much on the geographical/cultural biases of the viewer as on individual taste. For instance, Heinrich von Storch, an assistant to Count Bezborodko, published a 1794 descriptive book about the city of St. Petersburg which he dedicated to "the great and benign princess" Catherine. In it, he favorably compares the production to its European counterparts:

> The magnificence of the performance far exceeded every thing I have ever beheld of this kind in Paris and other capital cities. The sumptuousness of the dresses, all in the ancient russian costume and all the jewelry genuine, the dazzling lustre of the pearls and diamonds, the armorial decorations, implements of war and other properties, the ingenuity displayed in the ever-varying scenery, went far beyond even the boldest expectation.[83]

Matthew Guthrie, a Scottish doctor in residence in St. Petersburg, was also intrigued by the native Russian elements, calling *Oleg* "a curious and uncommon treat to Strangers visiting her capital, as well as to the true Russian Patriot and *antiquarian*, and it is in that last point of view it more particularly drew my attention."[84] Guthrie's fascination led him to translate *Oleg* into English; until my own 1998 translation of two of Catherine's comedies, his unpublished manuscript remained the only full English translation of any play by Catherine. Masson was drawn to the production's historical specificity: "to me such exhibitions, in which the great events of history are introduced as in a picture on the stage, are more interesting than the strainings of the throat of our opera singers, and the amorous intrigues of our tragedies."[85] *Oleg*'s amalgam of song, dance, and text seems to have been impressive. But Catherine also mixed in another element: her imitation of Shakespearean style.

As with *Riurik*, Oleg's manipulation of time and space is distinctly non-neoclassical. The opera contains over three dozen characters, not including the choruses and dancers. The locations range from Moscow to Kiev to Tsargrad. The

---

[82] Arapov, *Letopis'* 114.

[83] Storch 453.

[84] Quoted in A. G. Cross, "Royal Blue-Stocking" 97. From the unpublished introduction to Guthrie's translation. Manuscript resides in the British Museum.

[85] Masson 75.

passage of time is less distinctly demarcated, but traveling between these places would put the libretto well over the twenty-four hour mark. Khrapovitskii writes that after he read the third act of *Oleg* with the Empress, she questioned, "when 24 hours can be presented in 1½ hours, why cannot they also contain two years?"[86] Action is markedly dis-unified, as a trial, a wedding, a war, and a feast all fly by. The quick succession of widely diverse occurrences certainly mirrors Shakespeare's strategy of transporting his audience quickly to the vasty fields of France and back again. But Catherine was writing for a much different scenographic esthetic than the wooden O. Each new setting, rather than an opportunity for sumptuously decorated spoken verse, became a picturesque occasion, an ocular feast. It must be noted that this use of spectacle was typical of eighteenth-century opera, so that what may seem Shakespearean is also perfectly within the operatic conventions of Catherine's time.

Besides Shakespeare's freer use of time and space, the epic structure of *Oleg* may also have been inspired by the annual-entry structure of main historical sources: the *Primary Chronicle*. Yearly notations in the *Chronicle* vary widely in length (some entries simply list a year with no accompanying details; others are thousands of words long) and move rapidly from details of military adventures to tales of treaties to folkloric accounts such as the story of Oleg's death by a serpent. As the *Chronicle* is a variegated assortment of people, events, and narrative voices, so Catherine's drama *Oleg* expands and narrows its focus from large-scale military campaigns to domestic rites. Shakespeare may not have been the only inspiration for this variety, but he provided a Western literary precedent for something that was in actuality a long-standing feature of early Russian literature.

Catherine also borrows the Shakespearean technique of incorporating a variety of characters into her drama. Unlike the typical neoclassical tragedy, which pares down to the bare necessities of *dramatis personae*, *Oleg* displays every layer of society from boyars to soldiers to commoners to matchmakers to princes to Emperors. Like many Shakespearean dramas, *Oleg* begins not with princes talking, but with talk of princes. We do not meet Oleg in this initial scene, but rather two boyars under him who speak with two visiting townspeople from Kiev. The simple scene functions as exposition to explain how Riurik chose Oleg as leader of Russia during Igor's youth, and to tell of Oskold's near-conquest of Tsargrad. The dialog also sets time and place: "And in this place where the rivers Smorodina, or Moskva, Iauza and Neglinnaia join together, he intends on this day to found another city" (267). Although the scene chronicles key events, it reveals little about the character of the speakers or the mood of the opera. Not until I.3 are the townspeople Stemid and Lidul fully able to state their complaints about Oskold. Having done this, they are then expendable as characters, and reappear only briefly in Act II to support Oleg's banishment of Oskold. Nor are they distinguishable from each other; they do not offer varying perspectives on the

---

[86] Barsukov 16. Entry from 21 September 1786.

events as they transpire. Catherine uses these four characters, two villagers and the two boyars they converse with, in a choric function: standing in for entire social classes. Their interaction (the villagers pleading for the official intervention of the nobility) is important only insofar as it reveals plot. Catherine uses a similar strategy by starting Act II with a scene of three warriors in Kiev. The stage directions give the location in great detail:

> *The theater presents a meadow along the bank of Dnieper; on the opposite bank part of the city of Kiev is visible, behind which the Ugrians are coming through the mountains from a distance; in front are the Prince's tents.* (271)

These characters, called First Warrior, Second Warrior, and Third Warrior, are even less differentiated than Stemid and Lidul. They serve only to comment on the passing of the Ugrians, identifying who they are and where they are going. Although the second warrior seems anxious ("What if they stop here!"), the first warrior has the advantage of experience, and a sense of continuity with older times: "Now I am seeing for myself what an old man told me when I was younger: that as he remembers, some sort of people passed through Kiev" (271). Again, the three warriors represent a class of people. Yet Catherine has not chosen to give each social class a single representative (a more neoclassical technique which would distill needed attributes into one character); she has deliberately constructed a scene out of the back-and-forth banter of interchangeable chorus-like figures.

In the above examples, Catherine's use of undifferentiated chorus characters is undeveloped, but clearly shows her desire to expand the world of the opera to include a wide range of voices. Since neoclassical concerns about verisimilitude had for the most part sounded the death knell for the dramaturgical device of the chorus, the result in both French and its imitator Russian tragedy was that the *vox populi* remained an unvoiced, un-bodied presence, with vocal agency reserved for high-ranking characters whose actions decided the fate of all. Catherine's borrowing of a Shakespearean-style chorus returned a theatrical voice to everyone from warriors to everyday citizens, anticipating the crowd scenes in Pushkin's *Boris Gudunov*.

Catherine's use of this choric device is most successful in Act III, the wedding celebration of Igor and Prekrasa. In two simple but effective scenes, III.3 and III.4, two commoners stand and comment on each aspect of the wedding procession. Several details give the two characters greater interest. The first man has gotten hold of a list of the procession order; the second is in a hurry to deliver rusks to Oleg's ships. Although he cannot read, he is curious and stays to see the grandiose events as his companion lists each member of the wedding party. The two men give a detailed running commentary on the splendors they see. This technique would have been perfectly natural for the Elizabethan thrust stage, where such a scene would have been largely called into the spectators' imaginations by the actors' words. In *Oleg*, the two citizens' words would have served as oral reinforcement to the visual splendor that would otherwise have been pantomime pageantry.

The scene strongly resembles IV.i of Shakespeare's *Henry VIII*. In that play, two gentlemen gather on a street in Westminster to watch the coronation procession of Lady Anne. Compare the opening lines of the two scenes:

> (*Henry VIII*)
> 1 GENTLEMAN. You're well met once again.
> 2 GENTLEMAN.   So are you.
> 1 GENTLEMAN. You come to take your stand here, and behold
> The Lady Anne pass from her coronation?
> 2 GENTLEMAN. 'Tis all my business. At our last
> encounter
> The Duke of Buckingham came from his trial.
> 1 GENTLEMAN. 'Tis very true. But that time offered
> sorrow;
> This general joy. (IV.i.1–6)

> (*Oleg*)
> FIRST COMMONER. Hello, brother.
> SECOND COMMONER. Hello.
> FIRST COMMONER. You must have come here for the same reason I did?
> SECOND COMMONER. I came to watch the procession of Grand Prince from his
>   palace to the church for his wedding.
> FIRST COMMONER. I came here for the same. (282)

The two scenes proceed in very similar fashion, with the two men commenting on the parade, noting the people who pass, their clothing, and the order of the procession. Differences abound, however. Shakespeare's scene is much more varied in tone, with some troubling news creeping in to the general feeling of celebration. The most memorable effect of the *Henry VIII* scene, however, besides the splendor of the spectacle, is the description of the angelic Lady Anne: "Thou hast the sweetest face I ever looked on" (IV.ii.46). A third Gentleman character is introduced to give further descriptive testimony to the beauty and nobility of the coronation itself. Thus the scene is full of crucial information about the mood and psychology of the people.

Catherine's scene has fewer dimensions—the two men's perception of the procession predominates. But the differences from Shakespeare show Catherine's attempt at cultural translation. For instance, Catherine chooses to present commoners, rather than gentlemen, perhaps to give a sense of the action's impact on the entire society. When in *Henry VIII* the First Gentleman holds a paper giving the processional order, the Second Gentleman does not seem to need it: "I thank you sir: had I not known those customs,/ I should have been beholding to your paper." (IV.ii.19–20). But in *Oleg*, the Second Commoner is illiterate and must rely on his companion for a fuller interpretation of what he sees passing before him: "Read it to me ... I don't know how to read ...." (282). This little touch of Catherine's—the citizen's illiteracy—contrasts the opera's later concentration of the cultural wealth of Greek literature; she emphasizes the chasm between the average Russian villager and his wise and sophisticated ruler Oleg.

The other specific and dramatically useful detail of the scene is the Second Commoner's sense of urgency: "I wish they had started sooner, I have no more time to linger here: I was hired to bring rusks to the ships ... we must hurry there" (282). Their exchange reveals the simultaneity of the current action with Oleg's military preparations:

> SECOND COMMONER. Why don't we see Prince Oleg in the procession?
> FIRST COMMONER. You yourself are bringing rusks to the ships and you ask this? ...
> He is busy with the armaments of course.... They say that once this merry-making
> is finished, with the first safe wind he will leave with his army to the Greek power.
> SECOND COMMONER. Akh! ... I have to run in order to do my job with the rusks....
> Farewell. (283–84)

The very next scene shifts to Oleg's mansion, so that the citizens' lines create a transition from the wedding ceremony to the talk of war. The light touch of humor—the Second Commoner suddenly remembering that he's supposed to be working rather than enjoying the spectacle—is a nice tonal contrast to the succeeding scene.

Such tonal shifts are another nod to Shakespeare, who often deviates from the keynote of his plays by introducing unexpected moods. Catherine infuses the generally serious *Oleg* with many moments of lightness. For instance, in Act IV, Oleg engages in a bit of didactic fun. After the victory at Tsargrad, the Russian and Slavic troops request silk and paper sails for the ships in celebration of the treaty:

> DOBRYNIN. Don't spoil them, Sovereign; why do they need silk and paper sails?
> OLEG. No, I am not spoiling them, but I will teach them a lesson about whims; when
> the silk and paper sails are torn by the wind then we shall see what they will say.
> (291)

This seeming digression is not of Catherine's invention, but appears in the *Primary Chronicle*. In the opera it reinforces Oleg's characterization as a just, benevolent, and wise ruler who—like Catherine herself—must educate and enlighten his people, helping them to choose the proper means for achieving their goals.

A final Shakespearean echo is Catherine's incorporation of a play-within-a-play. In *Hamlet*, for instance, such a device serves as a mousetrap to catch the conscience of a king. The Athenian wedding festivities in *A Midsummer Night's Dream* end with the tragi-comic tale of Pyramis and Thisbe. Catherine, as a kind of sequel to the Act III wedding of Igor and Prekrasa, concludes Act V of *Oleg* with a scene from Euripides' *Alcestis*. The choice of *Alcestis* is itself appropriate on a number of levels. The plot concerns the sacrifice that Alcestis makes for her husband Admetus (by substituting herself to die in his place) and the revival of Alcestis by Admetus's visitor Hercules. Stylistically, *Alcestis* is as much outside of the "usual theatrical rules" as was Shakespearean drama to neoclassical theorists, or as was *Oleg* in an age of slavish imitation to French models. Although Euripides himself had no such rigidly articulated rules to follow, *Alcestis* falls short of the perfect model of tragedy that the later critic Aristotle would have preferred. Unlike the tightly woven *Oedipus*, *Alcestis* is a puzzling mix of mood and plot. D. J. Conacher notes the first scene between Apollo and Death as a possible hint of Greek drama's folk origins: the allegorical figure of Death, rarely seen in the range of Greek dramatic characters, comes for the bridegroom.[87] Too, the inclusion of the heroic Hercules—the "unexpected rescuer from outside the immediate context of the legendary situation"—is surprising.[88] The play's essentially tragic form turns comic when Alcestis is revived, thanks to Hercules' victory in a wrestling match with Death. Although the play was performed as the fourth work in a tetralogy, it is not strictly a satyr play, possessing neither the presumed subject matter nor style of that genre. Thus Catherine's choice of *Alcestis* may in fact be a metadramatic commentary on her own mixed-genre *Oleg*, with its sprawling structure and its mixture of folk, historical, and ritual elements.[89]

The story of *Alcestis* also had certain ties to the dramatic events in *Oleg*. The climactic scene of Euripides' play is the unveiling of Alcestis, whom Admetus had thought dead. Hercules coaxes Admetus into lifting the veil, under the pretense that she is a prize won by Hercules. In actuality, Hercules saved Alcestis from Death himself. These events parallel the wedding of Prekrasa to Igor. Although Prekrasa herself is but a minor figure in *Oleg*, her wedding spans an entire act. By linking Igor to the kin of Gostomysl, the wedding strengthens Oleg's power.

Alcestis herself does not appear in the scene from Euripides' play that Catherine chose to present in *Oleg*, but her unseen presence as a brave and sacrificed bride is very resonant with the Russian story. In the Russian pre-Christian wedding tradition, care had to be taken so that the devil would not abduct the bride on her wedding day. One solution was to create a false bride by dressing another girl in the bridal robes, so that the devil would be fooled. This practice, although not shown directly in *Oleg*, echoes the way in which Hercules tricks Admetus into thinking the veiled woman in front of him is a stranger, when she is actually Alcestis. In Russia, in addition to this practice of disguise, another simpler method of fooling the devil was used: the veiling of the bride. The

---

[87] Conacher 32.

[88] Conacher 35.

[89] The story is also reminiscent of a popular Russian *bylina*, the story of Dobrynia and Alesha, in which Dobrynia, supposed to be dead, claims his bride before she can marry his friend Alesha.

unveiling of Prekrasa is a key moment of Act II, and is the moment that the engravers of the 1791 edition chose to illustrate (see Fig. 4.6).[90] In III.8 of *Oleg*, the stage directions indicate that:

> *The boyar playing the part of the father takes an arrow, comes up to Prekrasa, and raises her veil slightly; the lady-boyars come up to her and take off her headgear and veil; then Igor takes Prekrasa under her arm and leads her to Oleg.* (285)

The theme of hospitality to foreigners is another connection between the Euripides text and Catherine's opera. In the specific scene from *Alcestis* that appears in *Oleg*, Hercules tells the chorus of Pherae citizens about the battles he must fight. Next, Admetus, despite his mourning for his dead wife, agrees to offer Hercules full hospitality in a time of great sorrow. The second choral strophe hints at Catherine's meaning:

> However, with the new days
> Admetus became guilty;
> When he opened his sad house
> Mourning over his dear wife
> To accept into it a placid hero.
> That's how real nobility
> Shows its great spirit![91]

In *Alcestis*, Hercules repays his welcome nicely by restoring Admetus's wife. In *Oleg*, the Emperor Leon and his wife Zoia receive Oleg and his forces hospitably, despite having just lost a battle and signed a tough treaty. The metatheatrically delivered message of *Oleg* might be that such accord between Russia and Greece will be beneficial to all.

Besides the inner play contained within *Oleg*, there is a third metatheatrical level. *Oleg* itself can be seen as an inner play, contained within the larger outer performance of Catherine's own Greek Project. The performance of *Alcestis* at Leon's court takes place within the performance of *Oleg* at Catherine's court, which takes place within the larger political context of Catherine's own "production" of her reign.

Storch, impressed with the grandeur of the production, provides detailed information about staging of the Euripidean section:

> At the court of the grecian emperor Oleg is received with magnificent solemnities; at the opening of the last act, on the rising of the curtain, a spacious circus appeared, and on the tribunes around it the grecian court and a vast concourse of the people as spectators. Here were held games of every species; gladiators contending in single combat; others

---

[90] Catherine II, *Nachal'noe upravlenie Olega* (1791) 15.

[91] Euripides 303.

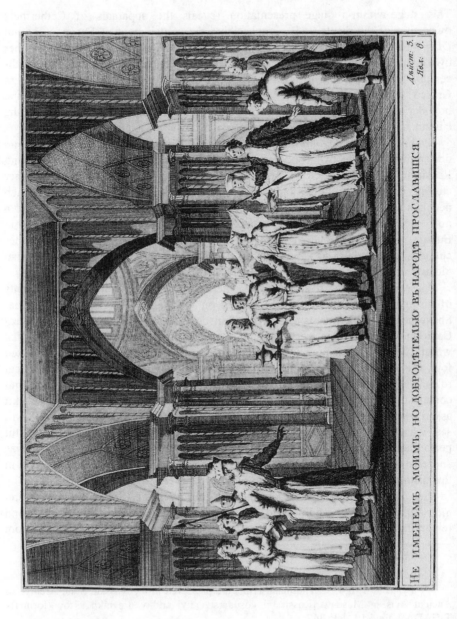

НЕ ИМЕНЕМЪ МОИМЪ, НО ДОБРОДѢТЕЛЬЮ ВЪ НАРОДѢ ПРОСЛАВИШИСЯ.

Дѣйст: 5.
Явлъ: 8.

Fig. 4.6   Act III.viii, *The Beginning of Oleg's Reign*, published in 1791.   "Not by my name, but by virtue you will be famous among the people." [Ne inenem moim, no dobrodetel'no v narode proslavishsia.]

running at the ring; till at length, a second curtain vanished, and a stage appeared on which a dramatical piece was represented.[92]

This stage-within-a stage presentation reveals the apparatus of Catherine's ownership of the display. By emphasizing the containment of Euripides within *Oleg*, she also emphasizes the containment of Russia's historical past within her own contemporary Empire. One has only to raise a curtain to be drawn into ninth-century Byzantium, and to raise yet another curtain to be transported to ancient Greece. Time, culture, space, style—all are collapsed and contained by the boundaries of the performance of *Oleg* for which Catherine herself raised the curtain.

Catherine's *The Beginning of Oleg's Reign* was both a political and an esthetic declaration, and the two concerns are often intertwined. Politically, by linking Russia to the classical Greek heritage via Byzantium, Catherine reinforced her current designs on the Ottoman Empire. Esthetically, she rejected French neoclassical strictures and economy through both baroque-style spectacle and a nod to Shakespearean structure, presaging the growing Romantic tendencies in Europe. Catherine the Great's *Oleg* stylistically appropriated the glories of other cultures, laying claim to them even as she transformed them into a new Russian identity.

Masson praised the fresh style of Catherine's *Oleg*, in which "the great events of history are introduced as in a picture on the stage."[93] Although two final Shakespearean experiments remained unfinished and unpublished, they also reveal Catherine's continued interest in the innovative approaches inspired by the English writer. Just after finishing *Oleg*, in October and November 1786, she completed four acts of *Igor*, another "Historical presentation without the usual theatrical rules."[94] The play concerns the rule of prince Igor under the tutelage of Oleg, and contains several choruses based on poems by Lomonosov. When Khrapovitskii asked her about the unfinished play almost three years later, she replied, "We will see what success Oleg will have."[95] When *Oleg* had a very successful performance in the Stone Theatre the next month, Khrapovitskii noted that he was "ordered to track down the unfinished 'Igor'."[96] Despite her renewed interest in this historical work about Kievan Russia, the manuscript was never finished.

Her last writing in the extraordinarily prolific year of 1786 (three operas and *Siberian Shaman* in addition to the works discussed above) was a second reworking of a specific play by Shakespeare. The play, "A Free Adaptation from

---

[92]   Storch 453.

[93]   Masson 74.

[94]   Pypin 3: 397–433. The manuscripts are preserved in the Russian State Archive of Ancient Acts in Moscow [Rossisskii gosudarstvennyi arkhiv drevnikh aktov (formerly TsGADA)], fond 10, delo 347.

[95]   Entry is 6 September 1789. Barsukov 307.

[96]   Entry is 25 October 1789. Barsukov 310.

Shakespeare, The Comedy *The Spendthrift*" [Vol'noe perelozhenie iz Shakespira, Komediia Rastochitel'], was Catherine's version of Shakespeare's *Timon of Athens* (c. 1605–1608).[97] It appears to have been composed between November and December 1786, and is only missing portions of its fifth act. Shakespeare's play, based on Plutarch's *Lives*, treats the wealthy and generous Timon, who mismanages his money so badly that he becomes bankrupt, and is abandoned by all his friends. Like Catherine's *The Spendthrift*, *Timon* is also considered by many to be unfinished, and was probably not performed in Shakespeare's lifetime. It is often considered a "problem play," a satire with a vicious misanthrope at its center. Catherine turned the play into a moral tale, a lesson about prudence with what would doubtless have been a happy ending. She tempered the misanthropy of her Timon (Tratov) throughout the play, so that he could reform by play's end, and even marry the sister of the Alcibiades figure (Bragin).[98]

In a letter to Grimm shortly after *Riurik* and *Oleg* were completed, Catherine gave a strong hint about her attraction to Shakespeare:

> These imitations of Shakespeare are very convenient, because being neither comedies, nor tragedies, and not having other rules except those of tolerable tact for the spectators, I believe them to have an aptitude for everything; one has only to avoid the boring and the insipid.[99]

Being herself a rule-breaker (neither completely German nor Russian, neither completely female nor male) with an "aptitude for everything," Catherine must have appreciated the freedoms offered by the Shakespearean model, during the very busy year of 1786.[100]

---

[97] Pypin 3: 301–44. The manuscripts are preserved in the Russian State Archive of Ancient Acts, fond 10, delo 354.

[98] See Simmons 799–801 for a detailed explanation of how Catherine adapted the play.

[99] Letter's date is 24 September 1786. Grot, "Pis'ma imperatritsy" 383–84.

[100] Catherine's interest in English theatre extended to her contemporary, Richard Brinsley Sheridan. Sometime in 1787, she began an adaptation of his *The School for Scandal* (1777) titled only "A Free Adaptation from the English" [Vol'noe perelozhenie s angliiskago]. The fragment breaks off in the middle of the fifth scene. Pypin 3: 377–86. In considering other non-neoclassical models, Catherine even drew inspiration from the Spanish Golden Age, with the unfinished "The Larder. A Free Adaptation from Calderón de la Barca" [Chulan. Vol'noe perelozhenie iz Kal'derona de la Barka]. The fragment, which consists of four and a half scenes, is based on Calderón's *El Escondido y la Tapada*, which Catherine likely read in a French translation called *La Cloison*. Pypin 3: 387–96.

Chapter 5
Comic Operas

> When I was three years old, my parents took me with them to Hamburg for a stay with my grandmother. The only experience of the journey that I now remember was a visit to the German opera. I saw there an actress, who was dressed in blue velvet embroidered with gold. She had a white handkerchief in her hands and when I saw that she was drying her eyes with it I began to weep and bawled so honestly that I had to be sent home. This scene impressed itself so deeply on my memory that I still remember it.[1]

When Catherine began to compose her first extensive memoirs, nine years after her accession to the throne in 1762, she recalled in vivid detail this moment of early attraction to a staged reality. Dressed in memorably sumptuous attire, the singer shed false tears, provoking real ones in small Sophie. This little girl would grow up to reign over the vast Russian Empire, and would write her own operas. In addition to *Oleg*, Catherine wrote five operas over a period of four years; all were comic operas, with folk themes. Three were written during 1786: *Fevei*; *Boeslaevich, Novgorod Knight* [Novogorodskii bogatyr' Boeslaevich']; and *The Brave and Bold Knight* Akhrideich [Khrabroi i smeloi vitiaz' Akhrideich']. These were followed by Woeful Knight Kosometovich [Gorebogatyr' Kosometovich'], written in late 1788, and finally by Fedul and his Children [Fedul s det'mi] in late 1790. All were published,[2] and all were produced, usually in both court and public theatres.[3] Their invented plots and images would contrast Catherine's offstage life just as sharply as the German opera had the little girl's.

---

[1]   Anthony, *Memoirs* 4. The account is from the first extant memoir by Catherine, begun in 1771 and dedicated to the Countess Bruce.

[2]   Although all the libretti appeared in individual editions, only the first three comic operas appeared in Dashkova's *Russian Theatre* as well. In addition to the lavish 1791 full orchestral score of *Oleg*, only three piano-vocal scores of Russian operas appeared in the eighteenth century, two of which were *Fevei* and *Woeful Knight*, both in 1789. In the 1890s, the Moscow publisher Jurgenson published five piano-vocal scores, including three of Catherine's operas: *Fevei*, *Oleg*, and *Fedul*. Whaples 114.

[3]   For dates of performances, see El'nitskaia. She has no record of a public performance of *Boeslavich*.

Empress Fantasies: The First Three Comic Operas

In 1786, at the age of 57, Catherine wrote her first three folk-inspired comic operas. At the same time, she was ruling over a vast empire, albeit one in relative peace due to an agreement with the Ottoman Porte signed in 1783. She created these fantastical performances partly for her grandchildren Aleksandr and Konstantin, at the same time that she fantasized about their eventual takeover of the Ottoman Empire. In the same way that the Sun King's ballet spectacles or the Stuart court masques reflected the tastes, dreams, and policies of the kings who ordered them, Catherine's first three comic operas were the theatrical embodiment of the Empress's various personal, familial and imperial fantasies. These first three comic operas formulate what I see as Catherine's "anti-memoir." Most versions of her private memoirs, not published until 1859, leave off just before her rise to the throne at the murder of Peter, and present a courtly world full of schemes, intrigue, and instability.[4] In contrast, her publicly presented and published operas offer a deliberately fantastic fantasy realm with happy couples, devoted sons, docile enemies, and a monarch's absolute authority.

Part of the impetus for these comic operas seems to have come from a desire to please her grandsons. Catherine had been elated in 1777 by the birth of her first grandson Aleksandr Pavlovich. Her relations with her own son Paul Petrovich had been strained for many years, but the birth of Aleksandr established a more desirable heir to her Empire. Her chosen name for the second grandson, Konstantin, referred to his planned destiny in Constantinople, one of Catherine's own imperial fantasies. These grand plans for grandsons aside, she genuinely adored Aleksandr and Konstantin. She wrote many things in many forms for them, including the two faux folk tales "Tsarevich Khlor" [O tsareviche Khlore, 1781] and "Tsarevich Fevei" [O tsareviche Fevei, 1783].[5]

The first of these tales, the allegorical story of Khlor, concerns a wise young tsarevich. The Khan of the Kirgiz Tartars abducts Khlor and gives him the task of finding the "rose without thorns that doesn't prick." Khlor is almost distracted along the way, but is helped by Felicity and her son Reason, and finally finds the rose (which turns out to be virtue) on a mountain summit, before being reunited with his parents.[6]

---

[4]   Maria Lobytsyna points out that the memoirs are themselves highly fictionalized, and, in imitation of Laurence Sterne, employ a carnivalesque strategy of masking.

[5]   The tales were later also published in German: "Khlor" in 1782 and "Fevei" in 1784 (the former also in two French editions). Grimm later included the tales in French in his *Correspondence littéraire* in 1790.

[6]   A dramatic version of the "Khlor" tale was published in Dashkova's *Russian Theatre* 24 (1786): 195–232. Although it is closely related to the story and therefore likely written by Catherine, there is not an extant manuscript. No other evidence (e.g., Khrapovitskii) attributes the play to her, nor does any later scholarship (including Pypin). There are no known performances.

The later tale "Fevei" is far less unified. The central section, concerning Tsarevich Fevei's desire to see the world and his encounter with the Kalmyks, forms the basis of the later opera. The beginning of the tale focuses on the illness of Fevei's mother, and her cure by Reshemysl ("Decisive Thinker"). Later sections demonstrate Fevei's generosity and humility through short episodes. Taken together, the two tales have in common their depiction of a young tsarevich, who must grow in wisdom by facing a series of trials, a common theme for many traditional tales.

Fevei

In creating the operatic version of *Fevei*, Catherine combined personal and political fantasies by emphasizing spousal devotion and the exotic far reaches of her empire through a quest adventure tale. In a letter to Grimm on 17 April 1786, Catherine commented, "I come from the rehearsal of Fevei, a Russian comic opera; only paternal and maternal souls are capable of such a great tenderness."[7] The premiere was unusual in that it took place at a public theatre, at the Stone on 19 April 1786. A few days later, on 22 April 1786, it was presented again for a court audience at the Hermitage. Young Aleksandr Pavlovich would have been eight years old.

Catherine had written the opera, her first, sometime before February 1786, in between completing *The Deceiver* and *The Deceived* and starting on *Siberian Shaman* in June. The first published edition in 1786 has a subtitle claiming that it is "Created from the words of stories, Russian songs, and other works." Vasilii Alekseevich Pashkevich composed the music; he would collaborate with Catherine on later operas (co-composing with Canobbio and Sarti for *Oleg* and with Martín on *Fedul and his Children*).[8]

The Russian comic opera is quite different from its Western European counterparts. Written for actors who sing rather than singers who act, the Russian form consists mostly of dialog interspersed with discrete songs, in solos, duets, and choruses. Its plots most often featured peasant and merchant life. The first native comic opera is the short pastoral *Aniuta* (1772), with libretto by the actor Mikhail Popov. Although the music is lost, we know that the songs were probably sung to the tune of popular folk songs (similar to Favart's practice in Paris or to English ballad opera). This trend, the incorporation of popular songs, would continue as a hallmark of Russian comic opera. Although many composers of Russian operas wrote original scores, they very often wove in folk melodies, thus creating a

---

[7] Grot, "Pis'ma imperatritsy" 376.

[8] Ginzburg opines that a composer named Briks wrote the lost music for the ballets, which are not included in the score. But Mooser explains that Briks is only credited with the opera due to an error by the editors of the *Arkhiv direktsii imperatorskikh teatrov*. Mooser 2: 440.

definitively Russian style. Opera composers in this era would have had access to recently published collections of popular Russian songs, such as Chulkov's *Various Collected Songs* [Sobranie raznykh pesen, 1770–73], used in *The Beginning of Oleg's Reign*, and later, Ivan Prach's *Collected Russian Folk Songs* [Sobranie narodnykh ruskikh pesen, 1790].

Pashkevich had started his court career as a violinist, and later worked as a composer and orchestra director for Knipper's Free Theatre. In 1789, he was appointed music director for court balls. Soviet music critic Nikolai Findeizen, writing in 1928, was impressed with Pashkevich's mixture of Russian folk themes, Italian popular songs, and courtly choruses, although more recently Miriam Whaples has called much of the music "banal and scarcely competent Italianate time-filling."[9] As did many of the composers for Catherine's operas, Pashkevich made use of folk material. Ledmer's song at the end of Act II, for instance, is a well-known popular song, "Kak u nashego soseda," and P. A. Bezsonov notes several other borrowings from the Chulkov collection of folk songs.[10] Pashkevich's music for the concluding wedding scene and for the overture both draw on existing folk themes.[11] Count Valentin Esterházy, Ludovic XVI's ambassador at the Russian court, was present at one of the original performances of *Fevei* and noted the unusual music:

> Yesterday I was at the Russian opera, all the music of which was composed of ancient native melodies. The accompaniments were performed behind the scenes. Among them were some very beautiful melodies, but also some very strange ones [...]. The words were composed by Her Majesty.[12]

Although the Count gives Catherine authorship credit, she most likely did not have much to do with any song lyrics or other verse passages in the opera.[13] Throughout most of her writing career, Catherine kept to prose and engaged others to create the poetry needed for her operas. Often she turned to Khrapovitskii, or simply borrowed existing poetic passages.[14] Many of the verses and choruses in *Fevei* are taken from the poetry of Vasilii Trediakovskii (1703–69), one of the first important Russian poets to imitate a Western style. The opera includes selections from his tragedy *Deidamia* and some of his other works.[15] Pypin notes particularly that the poems of Vulevpol in scenes four and seven of the fourth act are modified from Trediakovskii.[16] The fussy Vulevpol, the Tsar's butler, is a

---

[9] Findeizen 2: 241–5. Whaples 115.

[10] Bezsonov, "O vlianii" 13.

[11] Whaples 120. A source for folk melodies was Trutovskii.

[12] Esterházy 318. English translation from Seaman 267n.

[13] See below on the possible exception of *Fedul and his Children*.

[14] In this case, Khrapovitskii's diary does not explicitly mention writing for *Fevei*.

[15] Guberti 3: 696.

[16] Pypin 2:267.

highlight of the opera. He bustles about in preparation for the Kalmyks' visit, and delivers several long speeches (based on Trediakovskii), which he declaims rather than sings. This practice of incorporating pre-existing poetry and songs was perfectly accepted, and indeed indicates how well known these source works were. Catherine probably saw this "borrowing" as a tribute to native Russian arts and letters.

As in Catherine's later opera *Woeful Knight*, *Fevei* features a tsarevich in search of adventure. The eponymous character is the son of the Siberian Tsar Tao-au. Fevei, however, doesn't venture very far, but remains obedient to his father and mother, who arrange his marriage to the Tsarevna Danna. The character of the Tsar's advisor Reshemysl, who figures more prominently in the story version, represents this safe perspective, and may be a nod to Potemkin: Derzhavin had composed an ode to him in 1783, praising him as the pseudonymic "Reshemysl."[17]

The piece begins with a fantasy: while Fevei is sleeping on a hillock "*in a pleasant grove* [...] *his fiancée appears to him in a ballet*" (335). When he awakens, Fevei entreats this departed vision to speak to him "in reality" as she did in his sleep. From the first scene, Catherine has established a theme of a discontinuity between dreams and reality, echoing the larger project of the comic opera itself. In a later scene, Fevei continues to refer to his love as a phantom, whom he can meet only at night in his dreams (346).

After vowing to leave his ordinary life to see the "vast world," Fevei leaves his grove, and the scene shifts to the Tsar's chambers. Here the audience witnesses a devoted love song between the Tsar and Tsaritsa. In several of Catherine's neoclassical comedies, one or the other parent is missing. Here we find the two parents not only alive, but in love. The Tsar and Tsaritsa vow their love in a sung exchange:

> There is not one as fortunate as me in the world,
> How I love my dear, how dear am I to him;
> From this minute, how love
> Inflamed our blood,
> We don't know torment,
> We are blazing with a different fire. (336)

Despite the harsh imagery of torture, blood, and fire throughout the song, the overall effect is of vivacious love in the face of threat: "Let us smolder with this passion,/ To take pleasure in it until death,/ Not to grow cold, but to burn with flame" (337).

Certainly this enthusiastic spousal devotion was never a part of Catherine's offstage experience. Her own husband Peter, upon acceding to the throne, had threatened to marry his mistress Elizaveta Worontsova. Catherine herself had

---

[17] Grot, *Sochineniia Derzhavina* 1: 170–77.

several lovers during her marriage, bearing them children (perhaps even the heir Paul Petrovich himself). In a 1774 letter to her lover Potemkin, she justified her marital infidelities as the result of a lack of mutual love: "If fate in youth had given me a husband whom I could have loved, I should have remained always true to him."[18]   Soon after the marriage of her own son Grand Duke Paul Petrovich to Maria Fedorovna, Catherine suspected him of marital infidelity.[19] In this fictional gift for her grandchildren, Catherine felt it necessary to link love and marriage.

Another image of fantasy throughout the opera is that of empire, expressed through Fevei's desire to visit foreign lands. From the first scene, he voices his wish to "see the vast world," despite the fears of his parents. At the end of the first act, he sings:

> There are high hills, wide fields,
> Meadows, marshes, deep waters,
> Choppy waters, sea-cities.
> I will bring you ample gifts. (341)

This hymn to travel may also be seen as a glorification of empire itself. Just as he fantasizes about his lover, Fevei dreams of wide fields and deep waters, of another realm (also depicted as a place where the wind doesn't blow and the frost doesn't chill (344)—a true fantasy for these Siberians!). This foreign realm is never reached in the play, but is represented by the visit of the Kalmyk ambassadors who arrive to ask favors of the Tsar. Their song, the most charming section of the opera, is a simple love ballad that repeats a folk-motif, meant to invoke the exotic customs of the Kalmyks (here seen in the last two stanzas):

> Give me but a single flower.
> You eat kaimak,
> Sul'iak and turmak,
> You smoke tobacco,
> You boil koumiss.
>
> Not just one, but take them all,
> Take the kaimak,
> Sul'iak and turmak,
> Let's smoke tobacco,
> Let's boil koumiss. (356)[20]

---

[18]   Anthony, *Memoirs* 324.

[19]   Alexander, *Catherine the Great: Life and Legend* 234.

[20]   Thanks to my colleague William Drummond who researched these Turkish terms; "kaimak" is cream of fermented boiled milk; "turmak" is a roll filled with either cheese, butter, or meat; "koumiss" is fermented mare's milk.

Catherine's pride in this song is seen in a letter to Grimm: "Between us, there is a Kalmyk air that has had great luck here, along with this entire trinket that your very humble servant has arranged."[21] Although Pashkevich did not write an authentically Kalmyk melody, this song has often been praised for its "oriental" flavor.[22] It was popular enough that it was often inserted into other operas until the end of the eighteenth century.[23]

Catherine would write *Siberian Shaman* several months later, partly as a testimony to the newly gathered ethnographic evidence made possible through her support. *Fevei*'s song of the Kalmyk ambassadors, which was preceded by their dance (called simply "Kalmyk ballet"), was part of her overall project to assert Russia's uniqueness through pride in the variegated cultures under its purview. As a diplomat cum playwright, Catherine also knew that visual spectacle speaks volumes.

Esterházy's commentary on the opera specifically mentions this authenticity in performance, along with the overall magnificence of *Fevei*'s spectacle:

> The setting was magnificent. The scene took place in Russia in ancient times. All the costumes were prepared with the greatest luxury from Turkish fabrics, identical with those which are worn there. There appeared a legation of Kalmyks, singing and dancing with Tartar harmonies, and Kamchadali who were dressed in national costumes and who also performed dances of Northern Asia. [...] The ballet concluding the opera was executed by Le Picq, Madame Rossi, and other good dancers. In it were represented all the different peoples inhabiting the Empire, each in his own peculiar dress. I have never witnessed a spectacle more varied and wonderful; on the stage were more than five hundred people. In the auditorium, however, although the young princes and the four noble princesses with their governors and governesses were all assembled there, there could not have been more than fifty spectators, so rigid is the Empress in the matter of access to her Hermitage.[24]

Charles LePicq (1744–1806) was the French dancer at the head of the imperial ballet troupe, and his wife was the ballerina Gertruda Rossi. By displaying "all the different peoples inhabiting the Empire" in an elaborate ballet, Catherine collected and contained them within the stage frame of the public theatre and within the small space of her own Hermitage Theatre, just as her palace collection contained visual art from the wide world. Empire itself is a fantasy of the control of the "varied and wonderful," while still reinforcing a centralized power. In a scene with the Kalmyk ambassadors, the Tsar accepts various gifts (sabers, a bow, Astrakhan sashes) and in return promises peace and harmony. Later, when Fevei himself attempts to resolve a misunderstanding with a group of Tatars, his father

---

[21] Letter is from 12 October 1786. See Grot, "Pis'ma imperatritsy" 386.
[22] Whaples 125.
[23] Maximovitch 32.
[24] Esterházy 318–19. English translation from Seaman 267n.

the Tsar is quick to assert his own ultimate power: "I alone am free to forgive and to punish" (360). The exotic cultural displays seen onstage in *Fevei* reinforce this concept of imperial control.

Opulent production values aside, *Fevei* the comic opera hardly holds together as a dramatic piece. It is a hodgepodge of scenes, songs, dances, and speeches, strung together to impart a few scarcely hidden moral truisms, such as filial piety and loyalty. Grimm easily glimpsed the didactic nature of the story version:

> The story of Fevei is a diamond. In it I could recognize step by step all the education which Monsieur Alexandre has received from his earliest infancy; in it I see all that awaits him as he advances in age. That is nourishment for royal children![25]

Despite the edifying nourishment, there are moments of charm and delight, and Catherine's later operas would show a greater sophistication in character and development, while continuing to offer alternatives to the narrative of her own life.

Boeslaevich, Novgorod Knight

Her second comic opera, *Boeslaevich, Novgorod Knight*, draws not on fairy tales but on a different folk form, the epic *bylina*. The central character, the bogatyr Vasilei, is a vigorous and powerful man, and ultimately an obedient son. Here we see a mirrored opposite to Catherine's troubled relationship to her own son Paul Petrovich. In this opera, the two fantasy elements are thematic (the portrayal of filial devotion) and stylistic (the dance presentation of boisterous folk motifs).

Catherine wrote this second opera sometime later in 1786. It premiered at the Hermitage on 27 November 1786.[26] Again the verses were most likely by Khrapovitskii, although his diary does not specifically mention working on them. Pypin notes that the chorus sung by the posadniks in III.1, "Torzhestvuite, Slavenski narody," is taken almost verbatim from the sixth stanza of a Trediakovskii ode of 1730.[27]

The music was by Evstignei Fomin (1761–1800), a well-respected Russian-born composer. From 1782 to 1786, he studied music in Bologna before returning to St. Petersburg to make his debut in dramatic composition with *Boeslaevich*. He went on to become one of the most celebrated Russian composers of this era. Soviet musicologist Rabinovich particularly admired the music of the opera's

---

[25] Letter from 12 March 1783. Translation is from Whaples 114. Original letter is in French and German, and can be found in Grot, "Pis'ma Grimma" 327.

[26] First publications were in a single edition by the Imperial Academy of Sciences (1786) and in Dashkova's *Russian Theatre* volume 20, also in 1786.

[27] Pypin 2: 400. See "Pesn' sochinena v Gamburge […]" in Trediakovskii 56. The only change is in the first line, from "Torzhestvuite vsi rossiisti narody" to "Torzhestvuite, Slavenski narody" (Pypin 2: 385).

many dances;[28] Fomin incorporated folk material into original music for several of
the ballets.[29]

The opera features variations on typical heroes of *byliny*, such as Vasilii or
Vaska Buslaev (the opera's Vasilei Boeslaevich) and Sadko (Satko in the opera).
The *bylina*, or ancient Russian epic tale, was part mythological, part historical; the
earliest ones may have originated in the tenth century. Two major tale cycles,
Kiev and Novgorod, blended fantasy with recorded history to create entertaining
and ever-changing oral narratives. The heroic Buslaev's tale is part of the
thirteenth–fifteenth century Novgorod cycle; in it the superhuman Buslaev, with
the help of his faithful guards, overcomes the governors of Novgorod. The
exploits of the merchant Sadko are also featured in the cycle; in Catherine's opera,
he is one of the posadniks (governors) who initially resist Vasilei Boeslaevich.
Catherine probably had access to these tales in various ways, through informal
notebook collections circulated among the ruling classes or through more academic
collations.[30]

Like Catherine's son Paul Petrovich, in the opera Vasilei is under the influence
of his mother: he is the son of the deceased Prince Boeslai and the widow Amel'fa.
At the start of the opera, a silent ballet scene depicts Vasilei Boeslaevich beating
up the citizens of Novgorod. He and his fellow bogatyrs, Foma and Potaniushka,
sing a song of friendship. Satko, Chudin, and Raguil, the city's posadniks, try to
persuade Vasilei's mother to control him, but also secretly plot against him.
Amel'fa weeps "bitter tears" when she hears of her son's misbehavior.

The most memorable section of the opera is the Act II banquet at the Novgorod
duma. The various posadniks each boast in turn about their wealth or wives, and
urge Vasilei to drink, despite his vow to his mother to be silent. Such scenes of
formulaic boasting are common in the *byliny*.[31] When finally he brags that the city
is his, the posadniks pledge to expel him. His mother then locks him in the cellar,
but he, with the help of a young maiden, escapes through the window and single-
handedly fights back the forces that have gathered at the palace gates. The
posadniks end the play by asking Vasilei to rule over them. Several of the
elements of the opera, including the imprisonment in the cellar and the intervention
of a young maiden, are part of the Novgorod *bylina*. Catherine adds a love interest
for Vasilei in Raguil's daughter Umila, and also pairs off the young maiden with
Vasilei's bogatyr friend Foma.

Soviet folklorist I. M. Sokolov theorizes that in the earliest versions of the epic,
Buslaev was a troublesome tyrant, in contrast to his just and respected father. In

---

[28] Rabinovich 87. Rabinovich argues that although the dances in a given opera were
usually written by a different composer, these are of high quality and can be assumed to be
Fomin's.

[29] Whaples 121.

[30] Sokolov 44–45.

[31] Sokolov 304.

the later variants of the tale that Catherine would have been familiar with, he has become a rough and boisterous hero-figure, with "boundless daring, bravery, and boldness."[32]   Catherine may have chosen this fierce but well-loved character expressly to demonstrate the inevitable victory of a daring and courageous leader. Soviet literary critic Grigorii Gukovskii, writing in the age of Stalinism in 1947, critiqued the opera's fiercely authoritarian quality:

> It depicts Vasilii, prince of Novgorod, as using force to teach the impudent people of Novgorod a lesson when they dare to disobey him and refuse to slavishly submit to him. Vasilei compels them to bow obsequiously to what is presented as the redeeming harshness of the autocracy."[33]

This observation about acquiescence is borne out by the opera's final chorus, in which the posadniks and their followers appear happy to submit to Vasilei's rule:

> They rewarded strength and courage
> From the earliest times, as they do today.
> We were all waiting for
> What we saw today.
> Greetings, Prince and Princesses,
> From all your future children. (399)

But another key element of the opera's finale, not often noticed by critics, is Vasilei's meek submission to his mother. Vasilei strongly parallels Paul Petrovich; he is orphaned, with a "sovereign mother" in widowhood (387) who must look out for his well-being. Amel'fa herself comments on Vasilei's dual status: "I see in you a bogatyr's strength, but you are still a young child" (377). He replies: "You are my sovereign mother, I am not afraid of the posadniks, the Novgorod people are not frightening to me, I am afraid of your parental words." He goes on to say that one day he will subdue the "Slavenskii and Starorusskii earth" but that right now he will submit to his mother's will. Throughout the play, the posadniks (governors) refer to him as a child, and they see Amel'fa's potential to control her son's behavior. Vasilei's filial devotion is closely connected to his power as a ruler, and the opera clearly demonstrates the priority of the former. As the play's events draw to a conclusion, the posadniks yield to Vasilei, who asks his mother's blessing before receiving their submission: "I cannot accept without the blessing of my mother." She asks him to "tame" his "strong anger" (397). The powerful bogatyr must ultimately come under a mother's rule, even to the point of being locked in a cellar.

    In contrast to this portrait of a son's fidelity, Catherine's son Paul Petrovich resented his mother's control and influence, and she, for her part, mistrusted his

---

[32]   Sokolov 326.

[33]   Gukovskii 88.

loyalties to Prussia and his militaristic predilections. Catherine received the affection and respect she desired from her adoring grandchildren (at least the first two male ones).[34] Catherine, writing to entertain and instruct Aleksandr and Konstantin, presents a lively tale of a warrior who is also still a boy, brave yet immature. Chudin, one of the Novgorod governors, comments that "Vasilei Boeslaevich has barely reached fifteen years, but already his thoughts are not childish, and his games are not ordinary" (382). Another posadnik echoes this distrust: "The whole white world is laughing at us, that we, wise posadniks, are submitting to a young child." The opera celebrates the youthful vigor of its hero while reinforcing the idea of a wise maternal figure.

Rather than featuring exotic cultural spectacle as does *Fevei*, this opera focuses on spectacular dance representations of the *bylina* folk material. Of Catherine's operas, *Boeslaevich* is notable for the inclusion of extensive ballet sequences, several of which make up entire scenes. The initial scenes of both the first and second acts are dances that directly depict rough-and-tumble actions. Act I begins with a ballet of a scuffle:

> The stage presents Rogatitsa Street in Novogorod; a ballet portrays a fist fight. Vasilei Boeslaevich works on the mustached as well as the bearded, and beats them all. The mob becomes agitated, and makes a fight, Vasilei drives everyone from the stage with the help of Foma and Potaniushka. (373)

Act II presents a festive scene found in the *bylina*:

> Vasilei, having gotten permission from his mother, makes a festival at the wide gates of his white-stone palace. The stage presents a square in this palace. A ballet, in which there are oak vats; they pour green wine and intoxicating beer into them. (380)

This action continues in the act's second scene, after a sung interchange between Vasilei and the chorus of criers. As the ballet resumes, the stage directions note that, "*During the ballet, Vasilei Boeslaevich looks from the high tower*" (381). In a later scene, another dance sequence depicts the people of Novgorod surrounding Boeslaevich's courtyard. By converting these scenes of battles and beer into dance, Catherine transforms them from mere pugilism into the mode of theatrical fantasy. Indeed, by choosing to stage these *bylina* stories, Catherine was celebrating Russian folk culture at the same time that she placed its motifs into what was then a more acceptable cultural form: European-derived story ballet. This strengthening of native culture by association with the West was yet another "lesson" for her young grandchildren.

---

[34] Maria Fedorovna bore Paul eight additional children: six girls, and then two more boys (one born just before Catherine's death (the future Tsar Nikolai I), and the other born in 1798).

Due partly to these ballets and sequences of action, *Boeslaevich, Novgorod Knight* is the funniest and least sentimental of Catherine's comic operas. Vasilei Boeslaevich and his two companions are dynamic, and the opera's scenes of drunken boasting and fighting are lively. Nevertheless, the opera concludes according to Catherine's notion of resolution: with a happy populace and a wedding or two to be planned.

Brave and Bold Knight Akhrideich

Catherine's third opera uses an extremely childlike esthetic to present two key fantasy concepts: a loving family and amiable enemies. The naïve style of a magical tale reinforces the work's didactic purpose. *The Brave and Bold Knight Akhrideich* was written in May 1786, soon after *Boeslaevich*. The composer was Ernest Vanzhura (c. 1750–1802), and the verses were created or adapted by Khrapovitskii. Twice in May 1786, Khrapovitskii's diary records that he spent a sleepless night working on the opera, which was originally titled *Ivan Tsarevich*, the name given to the ubiquitous young hero of many Russian fairy tales.[35] But the opera did not premiere until 23 September 1787, after Catherine's tour of the Crimea. It premiered at the Hermitage and played there four subsequent times between December 1787 and February 1789. The opera also played four times at the public Stone Theatre between 1789 and 1796.[36]

Baron Vanzhura (Wanzura) was a Czech pianist and composer who arrived in Russia in 1783 and entered Catherine's good graces as a musician for the Court theatre. Gerald Seaman praises Vanzhura's incorporation of popular musical motifs, which complement the folk elements of the libretto:

> The composer likewise draws on several folk-songs for his inspiration (including the famous 'Vo pole berioza stoyala' employed by Tchaikovsky in his Fourth Symphony), and although his handling of them is somewhat uneven, he also succeeds in creating music in the folk idiom.[37]

Although Khrapovitskii wrote much of the text of the songs, as with *Fevei* and *Boeslaevich*, he also drew on the poetry of Trediakovskii.

This opera is by far the most fantastical of Catherine's works, and has the most explicit connections to the world of Russian fairy tales. It begins with two sisters, the Tsaritsas Luna (Moon) and Zvezda (Star) who are suddenly abducted by an unexpected whirlwind. Their brother, Ivan Tsarevich, promises the Tsar Akhridei and Tsaritsa Dariia that he will go to the end of the earth to seek them. At the top

---

[35] Catherine seems to have changed her mind about the title mid-composition (see Barsukov 9 for Khrapovitskii's diary entry for 26 May 1786).

[36] Dates are from El'nitskaia 471. The opera played much later in Moscow on 15 January 1820, given under the title *Ivan Tsarevich* (Seaman 310).

[37] Seaman 108.

of Act II, he encounters two comic wood-goblins, arguing over some magical implements which Ivan promptly tricks them out of: a hat of invisibility, self-propelled boots, and a "hospitable tablecloth" which produces a chorus of singers and an abundance of food when unrolled. He also meets the notorious Russian witch Baba Iaga, who comes out of her famous hut to tell Ivan to seek his sister Luna at a white stone palace with a Bear. When he arrives, Ivan discovers that the Bear is quite friendly and accommodating. Vowing to find Zvezda, he continues on to a copper castle, where Zvezda is being guarded by a Sea-Monster. He, too, is amiable, but Zvezda says the only way to truly free her is to fight the twelve-headed dragon and marry the Tsar Maiden (Tsar Devitsa). Ivan proceeds to fight the dragon, chopping off its many heads. When he arrives at the Tsar Maiden's palace, she enlists a sorcerer to free the two Tsarevnas from their captors. He does so, and the play ends with both sisters and both parents in chariots, and a final glorious chorus.

Many of the fanciful aspects of the opera are conventional elements of the subgenre of tales that Sokolov called "miraculous or magical tales." The hero in such tales, often called Ivan Tsarevich, might often be called upon to rescue his sisters kidnapped by a whirlwind, and also might encounter a many-headed dragon, and an enemy such as Baba Iaga. He might be helped along the way by "miraculous helpers," and also by certain magical objects such as the cap of invisibility. Other objects are often self-acting, such as "swiftly-running shoes" or self-acting weapons.[38]

The first written records of Russian oral folklore come from the mid-seventeenth century. In Catherine's era, interest surged among the literati, spawning several collections of tales (Chulkov 1766–68; Levshin 1780–83; Timofeev 1787). According to Sokolov, these collections of "pseudotales" preserved only some names and details from true popular tales, but "accustomed people to treat the Russian folk tale with tolerance," raising its status as a form of literature, even in the era of neoclassicism.[39] Catherine therefore would have had access to versions of popular tales, in an age of increasing interest in their expression of Russian culture.

James Brogden (1765–1842), a young Englishman who visited Russia in 1787–88, saw a performance of *Akhrideich* at the Stone Theatre on 1 October 1787.

The Opera was the composition of the Empress; the Scenery was very fine, the music and dancing excellent; at the head of the dancers are lePicq & Rosi, but as the dancing was comic it was not well calculated to display their Talents.[40]

---

[38] Sokolov 418–33.
[39] Sokolov 384–85.
[40] Quoted in Cracraft 229–330.

LePicq and Rossi had both also danced in *Fevei*. The production was particularly noted in the *Dramatic Dictionary* of 1787 as having "the most splendid decorations."[41]   Swiss musicologist R.-Aloys Mooser opines that the scenic designs were by Francesco Gradizzi, who along with his father Pietro was a decorative painter for the imperial palaces. Mooser reports that the sets were transported to Moscow and the opera performed there in 1802 and 1805.[42]

A separate note preserved in Catherine's manuscript collection in the state archives,[43] probably written by Khrapovitskii, describes a possible costume for Baba Iaga.

> Ega-Baba in Slavic oral legends is considered a diabolical goddess, portrayed as a monster with a poker, or seated in an iron mortar with an iron pestle [...] . A similar writing appears in the Russian dictionary of superstition, edited by Chulkov, and so it seems we can make a theatrical dress resembling a tunic of a smoky-red color, give her a magical belt and a small poker, entwined, like the staff of a magician.[44]

This note demonstrates the research that went into the staging of this spectacle. Drawn almost verbatim from Chulkov's 1782 *Dictionary of Theatrical Superstition*,[45] it reveals Catherine's quest for authenticity as she and her collaborators were celebrating and respecting Russian folk culture.

Some highlights of this fantasy opera include Ivan's deceptions of the gullible goblins and of the sea creatures that guard Zvezda, and his use of the hat of invisibility to sneak up on his sisters' captors. The entirety of V.3 is a completely pantomimed action scene in which Ivan defeats the dragon. But the chief fantasy element for Catherine must have been the Tsarevich's encounters with several enemies (a Bear, a Sea-Monster, even the Russian witch Baba Iaga) who all turn out to be helpful and amiable. A monarch's fantasy indeed!

Understanding the connection to Russian folk tales may help to explain the simplicity and seeming incongruity in the opera, which some scholars have taken as an example of Catherine's poor writing skills. Soviet musicologist Nikolai Findeizen refers to the following exchange in accusing the opera of "stylistic and chronological naïveté."[46]

> TSAREVNA ZVEZDA. If you want to rescue me and our sister Tsarevna Luna, then you need to leave today for the other end of the far world.

---

41   Annenkov 153.

42   Mooser 2: 523.

43   At RGADA (Rossiiskii gosudarstvennyi arkhiv drevnikh aktov) in Moscow. This note can be found at fond 10, opis 1, delo 349.

44   Pypin 2: 458.

45   Chulkov, *Slovar'* 270.

46   Findeizen 2: 246.

IVAN TSAREVICH. But will I have time? *(takes out his watch and looks at it)*; indeed
it's already late. (430)

In a 1992 article on Catherine's operas, Giovanna Moracci argues, and I agree, that
the incongruous effect is deliberately comic, not merely naïve. Moracci asserts
that the entire opera is deliberately parodic, of both Russian classical literature and
older folkloric materials.[47] Into the former category falls the reworking of
Trediakovskii's ode "Description of a Tempest," which is now sung by the nurses
in reporting the abduction of the two sisters.[48]

In the latter category, parody of folklore, Moracci notes several references in
the script in which the characters call obvious attention to proverbs and fables,
such as the Tsar's line "you've heard, I think, the old saying ..." (I.5), and the
opera's final chorus: "Blessed are all the tsars in the stories." In II.4, when Ivan
Tsarevich encounters Baba Iaga's hut, he comments "I heard ... that in a similar
circumstance, in a fable they say ... " before speaking the incantation to bring out
the witch. Traditional Russian folk tales display a similar self-referential aspect,
seen in various formulaic phrases uttered by storytellers ("Here the tale comes to
an end, a fine fellow told it").[49] Catherine may have appreciated this metaliterary
mode, but it did not originate with her. It is not surprising that Catherine, who
began her fiction writing in the realm of satirical periodicals before moving to
comedies, would enjoy winking noticeably at her audience through characters who
seem aware of their own literary conventions. Her use of such devices is a
deliberate tribute to these folk styles.

Rather than being a substandard opera as Findeizen sees it, the entire work
should be seen as an early example of children's theatre, an elaborate stage
spectacle with deliberately simple characters and plot. European schools had
staged plays for their educational value since the Renaissance. The eighteenth
century saw staged fairy tales by Gozzi in Italy and Christmas pantomimes in
England. In 1779–90, Mme de Genlis had published, in Switzerland, her *Théâtre à
l'Usage des Jeunes Personnes*, an anthology of plays for children designed as
"moral treatises put into action."[50] Children were a new audience, to be cultivated
and educated. We know that Catherine valued her grandsons as audience
members. Khrapovitskii's diary reports that Catherine was pleased that her
grandsons knew the words to her opera *Woeful Knight Kosometovich*.[51] Given
Catherine's strong interest in their cultural education, it is not surprising that she
would mold style and content to please them. Some references may have been

---

[47] Moracci, "Scritti Imperiali."
[48] The verses in I.5 are taken from the first three stanzas of Trediakovskii's "Opisanie
grozy byvshiia v gage" with only slight modifications. See Trediakovskii 95–96.
[49] Sokolov 431, see also 432–33.
[50] Quoted in Levy 3.
[51] Barsukov 250; 7 February 1789.

included just for them: the Sea-Monster and the Bear, whom the Tsar Maiden likens to "mischievous children in a story" (435) may each be one of the grandsons. Other parodic references and comic incongruities would appeal to her adult audience, while still delivering a didactic message to her grandchildren.

What is that message? The opera's final chorus reinforces the notion of a happy, loving family, and its contrast to offstage reality:

> What remains to wish for?
> Wife with husband,
> Sisters, mother, and father,
> They all love each other;
> And it goes without saying
> Blessed are all the tsars in the stories. (437)

For the tsars in the stories, a sorcerer can easily put things right, uniting a peaceful family. For the Enlightenment Empress Catherine and her fragmented family, there was no appealing to magic.

I have called these first three comic operas Catherine the Great's "anti-memoir." The various versions of Catherine's memoirs each have a fairly narrow scope, ranging from girlhood only as late as 1762, the year of Peter's death and her accession to the throne. Although portions of them are idealistic and hopeful about future challenges, the pervasive tone is of hardship and frustration. The young German princess hardly encountered a fairy-tale ending and her trials were many: the conversion to Orthodoxy, the difficult relationship with her future aunt-in-law Elizabeth, the sham marriage to Peter, the compulsory estrangement from her baby son Paul Petrovich. These three operas provide an alternative representation of Tsars, their families, their concerns. There is love between husband and wife, between mother and son. There is mutual respect, and always joyous resolution. Wisdom gained, marriages affirmed, order reinstated. Some of these conventional outcomes are familiar from neoclassical comedy, but the operas are more freely imaginative, using magic to transform mundane reality. When Grimm published his *Correspondence littéraire* in 1790, he included this introduction to the tale "Khlor," "written in Russian by a very great sovereign: we don't know of what époque":

> They say only that this princess found herself often with nothing to do, although she had the vastest empire in the world to govern and defend, and that in these moments of repose she deigned to occupy herself with the education of her grandchildren, and that this tale is the fruit of one of these happy leisure times.[52]

---

[52] Grimm 10. Entry is from May 1790.

On the surface, these three operas may seem to be the "trifles" that Catherine claimed all her writing to be,[53] but they are full of purpose, disguised by fantasy.

A Slanted Parody: *Woeful Knight Kosometovich*

In December 1788, over a year after the first performance of *Boeslaevich*, a new comic opera was being readied for its premiere at the Hermitage. "How is it going, and will it be funny?" asked Catherine, the anxious librettist.[54] *The Woeful Knight Kosometovich*, a charming and light piece, also alludes to a darker reality outside the theatre: the Russo-Swedish War of 1788–90. The young would-be knight Kosometovich, whose name means "to throw slanted or askew," is a skewed version of Sweden's King Gustav III. Catherine herself carefully determined which venues (public vs. court, Moscow vs. Petersburg) could produce such a potentially scandalous political satire. What transpired inside the theatre (the foolish antics of a Falstaff-like young man on a misguided adventure) reflected events outside the theatre: the context of war and monarchical rivalry. While the parody itself was innocuously silly, the fact that Catherine so carefully controlled its visibility shows her awareness of the dangerous side of performance—that in wartime "unreal" events on a public stage could have very real effects.

Gustav III (1746–92), the son of Catherine the Great's uncle Adolphus Frederick, ruled Sweden from 1771–92. He had a passion for the theatre: he himself acted in the Swedish court theatres in major roles, and, like Catherine, wrote plays. Also like Catherine, he wrote libretti for several operas,[55] the most famous of which is *Gustav Wasa* (1786), a grandiose and patriotic tribute to the sixteenth-century king who established the kingdom of Sweden. Not only did Gustav actively blend his life inside and outside the theatre, but he also made this connection in death: he was assassinated in his own opera house in 1792 in Stockholm at a ball, and later became a dramatic character himself in Scribe's play *Gustave III ou Le bal masqué* (1833) and in Verdi's opera *Un Ballo in Maschera* (1859).

Catherine knew her first cousin Gustav III well—she called him "brother Gu" in letters to Grimm. But from the moment of the revolt he staged in 1772, when he staked his absolutist claim by suspending the Swedish constitution, she was wary of his policies. For several years, however, they maintained a formal friendship: the king visited her incognito in St. Petersburg in 1777, and they corresponded regularly.

---

[53] From a letter to Zimmermann on 29 January 1789. For original French, see Marcard 378.

[54] 20 December 1788; Barsukov 216.

[55] With collaborator Johann Henrik Kellgren.

Gustav started rumblings of war while Catherine's attentions and resources were focused on the second Russo-Turkish War, which had begun in late 1787. The Swedish king had several reasons to test Russia's might, including ending the influence of Russia on Sweden's middle class, and winning popular support by demonstrating his own military capabilities.[56] After Swedish troops attacked the fortress at Nyslott, Gustav issued Catherine an ultimatum with what she considered a series of arrogant demands and rude insinuations.[57] Russia declared war against Sweden on 30 June 1788. Catherine then wrote to Potemkin, who was in the south commanding the Russian campaign against the Turks, that "the behavior of this treacherous sovereign [Gustav] resembles madness."[58]

The war against Russia was popular neither with the Swedish nobility nor the military. When Russia's Admiral Greig succeeded in bottling up the Swedish fleet in Sveaborg in July 1788, "from Anjala, in Finland, a group of officers sent a letter to Catherine II of Russia, proposing negotiations for peace, on grounds [...] that the attack on Russia had been a violation of the Swedish constitution."[59] But Gustav overcame the Anjala Federation mutiny, and continued the hostilities with Russia throughout 1789. The Russian fleet, led by Prince Nassau-Siegen, had an enormous victory at Svenskund in late July 1790; enormous and humiliating Russian losses followed days later. Peace was concluded on 3 August 1790; Russia lost no territory, but agreed to a formal recognition of Gustav's government and its sovereign.

Entries in Khrapovitskii's diary in August 1788 show that during the first months of the war, the Empress was composing the French one-act proverb "Les Voyages de M. Bontems," the story of a careless young man and his boastful valet, about which Khrapovitskii comments "here is much salt related to the Swedish war."[60] During the same period, Khrapovitskii also notes that Catherine read to him the beginning of a comic opera, *Koslav*: "Here are presented the Swedish king's preparations for war. [Catherine said,] 'I don't know how I will end it, yesterday I only wrote to gather my thoughts.'"[61] Since no opera called *Koslav* has ever emerged, scholars assume that its name was changed, and that Catherine may have begun writing the opera *Woeful Knight Kosometovich* just after her declaration of war.

But *Koslav* is not the only name associated with the opera *Woeful Knight*. Khrapovitskii's diary shows that by September 11, she was working on an opera called *The Knight Fuflyg* [Fuflyg bogatyr']. By November 22, she decided that the title was not right, and asked her current young favorite Dmitriev-Mamonov to

---

56   Cassirer 37.
57   Madariaga, *Russia in the Age* 401.
58   Letter is from 3 July 1788; Lopatin 300.
59   Cassirer 37.
60   Barsukov 134; 21 August 1788.
61   Barsukov 119; 29 July 1788

think of another. The next day, Khrapovitskii reported that: "for the name of the hero, I gave several anagrams from Gus[tav]."[62] His attempt to create the hero's name from an anagram of Gustav demonstrates that, from early on in its composition, the opera formerly called *Fuflyg* was connected to the Swedish ruler. By 26 November, Khrapovitskii referred to the opera in progress as *Gore-bogatyr' Kosometovich'* (Woeful Knight Kosometovich).[63] Khrapovitskii, as was customary, was assigned to write all the verse arias and choruses for the opera. Khrapovitskii's diary comments often in November and December about the progress of the work. On 9 December 1788, he was given the task of mounting a production of the opera. Catherine was also quite specific about the production style to be achieved: "It is a burlesque; it's necessary to play it more lively and freely and in the costumes that they play Mel'nik in."[64] Khrapovitskii was also charged with securing a composer, choosing Vicente Martín y Soler.

Martín (1754–1806) was a Spanish composer noted for writing Italian operas for the Emperor of Austria. Best known for *Una cosa rara*, written with Lorenzo da Ponte, he traveled to St. Petersburg in 1788, where Catherine commissioned him to write operas for her court theatre. He specialized in light comic operas, and although he himself knew no Russian, he composed numerous operas and ballets set to Russian text. Perhaps in an attempt to bridge a cultural gap and give the opera a more local flavor, Martín's overture for *Woeful Knight* features three popular Russian songs, including "Vo lesochke Komarochkov." An existing copy of the unpublished orchestral arrangement of the opera contains thirty-three arias, duets, and choruses.[65] A score, containing thirty of the musical pieces and arranged for voice and clavecin, was published in 1789 and is considered today to be one of the rarest of Russian books.[66]

Throughout December, Catherine often inquired to Khrapovitskii about the progress of the publication and production: "Different questions about the opera "Woeful Knight", how is it going, and will it be funny?"[67] The premiere of *Woeful Knight* took place on 29 January 1789, in the Hermitage Court Theatre. In addition to the Russian court nobility, two foreign ministers (friends from the

---

[62] Barsukov 201.

[63] Barsukov 181. Over the next few weeks, Catherine also gave Khrapovitskii a story of the same title, which was printed in the same 1789 edition with the opera. In her note "To the Reader," she feigns that the rare manuscript of the story was found in an innkeeper's trunk. Although it is possible that Catherine found the story, it is most likely her own original creation. The story version is short, and is quite close in most details to the opera.

[64] Catherine here refers to the most successful comic opera of her day: *The Miller— Sorceror, Deceiver, and Matchmaker* [Mel'nik—koldyn, obmanshchik i svat'] by Ablesimov and Sokolovskii, 1779. Barsukov 209; 8 December 1788.

[65] Mooser 2: 540.

[66] A Parisian engraver was also invited to publish an edition of the score for the price of 4000 rubles, but Potemkin didn't want it published. See Brikner 178.

[67] 20 December 1788; Barsukov 216.

Crimean tour) were also in attendance: Cobenzl of Russia's ally Austria, and Ségur of France, a country Catherine was hoping would help her mediate peace with the Turks. The following day, Khrapovitskii noted that he felt cowardly when he saw Cobenzl and Ségur in the theatre, even though Mamonov welcomed them, saying "that performances at the Hermitage are all identical and they could come." Khrapovitskii goes on to note that

> Cob[enzl] was making various comparisons, but I made as if I didn't notice, and when Ségur was asked, he answered candidly: 'qui se sent morveux, se mouche; et que c'est bien delicat de répondre par des plaisanteries à des manifestes et déclarations impertinantes.'[68]

Despite the diary's report of this cleverly supportive statement, Ségur's own memoirs cast his reaction to the parody quite differently.

> She caused to be composed and represented, on her theatre, a burlesque opera, where the person of Gustavus III was disguised in a grotesque manner. He was exhibited in the form of a blustering captain, a dwarfish prince. This searcher for adventures, guided by the advice of a mischievous fairy, was represented selecting, in an old arsenal, the armor of an ancient and celebrated giant, whose helmet, when placed upon his head, would come down to his belly, whilst the boots would reach his waist; thus equipped, he confined his exploits to the attack of a wretched fort, the commandant of which, an invalid, sallied out with a garrison of three men, and put the ridiculous knight-errant to flight with no other weapon than his crutch.

The French diplomat continues that he was unimpressed by the play's humor.

> So far from being amused, I was vexed at this representation; and the Empress, who received many awkward and insipid compliments on the occasion, might, I trust, have discovered by my countenance, as well as by my silence, how much I felt grieved at seeing so great a Princess demeaning herself in this manner.[69]

But Catherine's opera had other fans. On 31 January, her son the Grand-Duke Paul Petrovich and her grandson Aleksandr Pavlovich were present at a second performance. The opera went

> very well. All were gay and laughed. Encores were asked for of the chorus of weepers, and the duet of the Woeful Knight and Gremila. At the end of the play, the chorus of weepers, and of the first song of Gremila were repeated.[70]

---

[68]   30 January 1789; Barsukov 247. "Whoever has a full nose, blows it, and it's dainty to respond with jokes to manifestos and impertinent declarations."

[69]   Ségur, *Memoirs* 3: 313.

[70]   31 January 1789; Barsukov 248.

Paul Petrovich later "laughed and asked to see it again,"[71] and Catherine was pleased that "the High Princes [her grandsons] are singing the entire opera 'Woeful Knight.'"[72]

But one significant member of her close circle was less pleased with the opera. Potemkin, who had returned victoriously on 4 February from the successful siege at Ochakov, was in attendance at the third Hermitage performance the very next evening. He cautioned Catherine that the opera could agitate the king and further prolong the war.[73] The day after this performance, Khrapovitskii writes, "*Woeful Knight* will not be played at the public theatre now."[74] And indeed, the play was never performed in the public theatre of St. Petersburg. Additional recorded performances include an April 1789 court performance at the Hermitage, a July performance at Catherine's Tsarskoe Selo palace, and another Hermitage performance given in September for Prince Nassau. A 1792 comment from visiting Oxford don John Parkinson shows that, years after it left the stage, even an outsider was fully aware of the notorious opera and its connotations: "The Empress has composed four plays [...] one of which was composed after the commencement of the Swedish war with the intention to ridicule the King."[75]

Although there are no firm records that *Woeful Knight* was ever done outside Petersburg, a comment from Khrapovitskii on 25 April 1789 hints at two other possible venues:

It was said that "Woeful Knight" can play in Moscow, but that here it's not comfortable for the foreign ministers. Permitted to send the book and the entire score to Count Nik[olai] Pet[rovich] Sheremetev, since I reported that he wanted it.[76]

Sheremetev was a wealthy private estate owner with his own troupe of serf actors and a well-equipped theatre at Kuskovo; Khrapovitskii implies that although the play was considered too politically volatile to be done in public in Petersburg, neither a public Moscow performance, far away from the capital, nor a private performance at Kuskovo could cause much embarrassment to the foreign ministers. Whereas the opera itself may seem a benign joke, Catherine's concern was not only that it be funny but that it also raise the spirits of her inner circle in a time of two difficult wars. The perfect venue for this endeavor was her own court theatre, for an audience that could appreciate subtle allusions and satirical intent. Performance at the public theatre in Petersburg may have run the risk of greater international publicity for her private joke. In contrast, Catherine held Moscow in

---

71 1 February 1789; Barsukov 248.
72 7 February 1789; Barsukov 250.
73 Michel 207.
74 Barsukov 250.
75 Unpublished, quoted in A. G. Cross, "A Royal Blue-Stocking" 95.
76 Barsukov 278–79.

great disdain and seems to have considered it as harmless as a provincial venue. Such distinctions in choice of performance space reveal the true power behind the surface silliness of *Woeful Knight*.

In the fall of 1790, after the end of the war with Sweden, the Swedish ambassador Stedingk visited St. Petersburg and was invited to attend performances at the Hermitage Court Theatre. He inquired about the script of *Woeful Knight*, and reported to Gustav: "They assured me that in that time she [the empress] had written a comedy against your majesty, which was played in the interior. I would like to be able to procure this play for your majesty, but that will be difficult."[77] The opera was pulled from the repertory after the peace agreement in 1790, and was not performed again in Russia for over two hundred years. In May 1999, it was mounted in the Hermitage Theatre as part of a joint exhibition of the Hermitage Museum and the Stockholm Armory entitled "Russia and Sweden in War and Peace. The Eighteenth Century."[78]

Besides the accepted notion that *Woeful Knight* satirizes "brother Gu of Sweden," there is P. Bezsonov's 1874 argument that the play is not about Gustav, but about Potemkin.[79] At the time of the Russo-Swedish War, Potemkin was the leader of Russian forces in the concurrent war against Turkey. Bezsonov asserts that Catherine, unhappy with the progress of the Turkish war in late 1788, wrote the opera to satirize Potemkin. He does not show a clear connection between the opera's actual contents and Potemkin's actions, but bases his arguments on little evidence and much inference. Two years after Bezsonov's theory appeared in print, Ia. K. Grot effectively refuted the argument.[80]

There is also a certain temptation to see a parallel between Kosometovich and Catherine's own son. The operatic character is a young and impulsive young man who longs to fight knightly battles, but is protected by his mother. Paul Petrovich was an ardent Prussophile, with a "passion for military drill,"[81] kept under Catherine's watchful eye until her death in 1796. At the time of the play's composition, he was thirty-four years old and serving in the field army on the Finnish front. In 1877, scholar E. Karnovich argued for just this connection, also noting that the opera's absent father who "threw askew" must be a reference to Peter, the husband despised by Catherine and murdered by her supporters.[82] But historian N. V. Guberti notes Khrapovitskii's comments that Paul Petrovich himself liked the opera and wanted it done again, and that his sons, Catherine's grandchildren, had learned the opera's songs by heart.[83] Would they, asks Guberti,

---

[77] Stedingk 1: 294. From a letter dated 22 September 1790.

[78] Source is Mikeshin.

[79] Bezsonov, *Nash' vek.*

[80] Grot, "'Gore-bogatyr' Ekateriny II." Later published in Grot, "Ekaterina Vtoraia."

[81] Troyat 190.

[82] Karnovich 367–68.

[83] Guberti 3: 728.

be so enthralled with a work that mocks their own father? Rather, he argues, the plot of a young nobleman on a quest is a common device of folk literature, and need not be taken as a direct reference to Paul Petrovich.

Without doubt, Catherine could have layered her comic opera with double or triple meanings, and figures close to her were not safe from satire. *Fevei* is sometimes interpreted as a warning to Paul Petrovich to be obedient and trust his mother, so similar connotations should not be ruled out in *Woeful*. But the combination of elements—the context of the Russo-Swedish War, the direct comments by contemporaries linking the opera to the war, and finally the opera's allusions to Gustav III—supports the traditional view of the Woeful Knight as the King of Sweden.

Catherine herself knew well that the complex identity of a monarch is forged from many elements: education, family, private life, military policy, relation to the nobility, to the middle classes, to the peasants, to one's advisors. It is perhaps surprising that she, having herself been the target of vicious caricatures by the foreign press about everything from her expansionist policies to her sexual life,[84] would satirize and therefore reduce a fellow monarch, even an enemy, to the realm of stereotype. But the literary context of Catherine's era must be remembered: the latter half of the eighteenth century was the age of the satirical periodical, which took a hard look at contemporary social ills through the lens of wit. Russian journals of the 1760s and 1770s often made their witty and pointed critiques through the voices of allegorized personae, a kind of literary ventriloquism in which a single exaggerated character represents the societal traits to be analyzed and combated or imitated. Catherine first entered the Russian literary scene in 1769 as the editor of *All Sorts*. Twenty years later, Catherine also used a comic symbol, the Woeful Knight, to stand in for an entire war.

The plot of the *Woeful Knight* is charmingly simple: we first meet Kosometovich playing *svaika*, a children's game in which a nail is thrown into a ring. We immediately learn that the name "Kosometovich" derives from his father's inability to throw straight: *koso* (askew) and *metat'* (to throw). Kosometovich is a pitifully weak and cowardly young man, who yearns to go out into the world to become a true bogatyr. He seeks the permission of his mother Loktmeta to leave the city of Arzamas. She relents, but sends two assistants to keep an eye on him. Meanwhile, a prospective bride, Gremila Shumilovna, visits the castle. The character of the noise-loving Gremila is one of the play's most humorous aspects (her first name is from the verb "to thunder," and her patronymic is derived from the word *shum*, or noise). As Gremila's mother reports, "Having heard so much about the inclination of your son to everything sonorous, loud, and noisy, I purposefully brought my daughter, who has a similar taste." Gremila then sings her aria: "In a noise, a sound, a thump, a crash, I find all delight" (503). Out on his quest, Kosometovich is eventually defeated in a siege by a one-armed old

---

84 Alexander, *Catherine the Great: Life and Legend* 289.

man, and runs home frightened of "wood-goblins, bears, Those-Who-Knaw-Bones, and sorcerers." On his return, he brags of his successes in the field, and is rewarded with Gremila Shumilovna as his bride.

Although many Russian writers of opera followed the Italian tradition of domestic or pastoral plots, Catherine, in keeping with her other efforts to promote a sense of Russianness, derived inspiration for her own comic operas from Russian folk sources. *Woeful Knight* is clearly influenced by the brave bogatyr heroes— dragon-slayers and superhuman defenders of Rus—of the *bylina*.

The heroic *byliny* often began with a similar premise to Catherine's opera: "At first the hero is minimized and the enemy is hyperbolized. The hero may appear as sick and helpless, or he may be too young or too plain, and his burst of bravado does not inspire any trust."[85] Kosometovich, however, never redeems himself, and his initial burst of bravado is seen to be a sham; in this way, Catherine's opera is almost an "anti-*bylina*," in the way that Kosometovich is an anti-bogatyr.

Underlying the amusing opera is a more serious theme: the qualities of a true bogatyr. By casting Kosometovich as a "skewed" bogatyr and linking him to a foreign enemy (Gustav), the script affirms respect for the "true" bogatyrs, the real Russian heroes. Such respect supports a repeated theme of Russian pride that not surprisingly runs throughout Catherine's plays and operas—the bogatyr represents the best qualities of honor, justice, and bravery that Catherine would like to see in her nation, particularly in the context of military endeavors. Writing in a time of war, she creates the ultimate non-hero, while the implied connection to Gustav III casts him as the (laughable) enemy as well.

As in most of Catherine's comedies, the central character is an amalgam of several complementary bad qualities, in this case: rudeness, lack of respect, boastfulness, and cowardice. The *Miles Gloriosus* or Braggart Warrior character is no stranger to Western drama—he is found in Plautus, in the *commedia dell'arte* Capitano, in Sir John Falstaff. Catherine in fact referred to Gustav III as a Falstaff,[86] and also made a connection between the Swedish king's pretensions and Spanish literature: in a letter to Joseph II, Catherine derided the "*donkishotstvo*" [Don Quixote-ness] of Gustav.[87] Thus Catherine based her exaggerated comic portrait of Kosometovich on the qualities of the real-life King.

Catherine emphasizes Kosometovich's immaturity by juxtaposing his bragging with Loktmeta's motherly protectiveness and control over his life. The opera contrasts his warlike zeal with his boyish games and childlike preoccupations. Like Gustav III, who worshipped the image of the Swedish hero Gustav Wasa (1496–1560) enough to compose an opera in his praise, Kosometovich adores the trappings of heroism, as we learn in his first song:

---

[85]   Oinas 69.

[86]   Alexander, *Catherine the Great: Life and Legend* 270.

[87]   Garnovskii 27.

Inflated by heroism,
And attracted by glory,
I will hide my forehead under a helmet,
I will put on knightly armor,
And my strong fist
Will bring me success in battle. (486)

In the second act, however, Kosometovich reveals his lack of respect for these same ancient traditions and symbols of knighthood. When trying on the helmet of Iaruslan Lazerevich, he finds it is too big as it falls to his knees. He then examines the steel sword of Ivan Akhrideich, but can hardly lift it, even with two hands. Although his advisors object, he decides to have this antique sword sawed shorter, and also plans to have an ancient club weighing twelve poods (about 433 pounds) reforged. These glorious weapons and armor are from the *byliny*, in which would-be knights prepare themselves for quests by acquiring Circassian saddles, strong swords, golden helmets, and heavy clubs. In this scene of farcical exaggeration, Kosometovich literally fails to measure up to the bogatyr standard.

Finally, Krivomozg the stableman proposes another solution:

Listen to my advice, give us free rein, we will make you armor out of large paper for lightness and we will paint it the color of iron; and in place of a rusty helmet, we will make you a slanted downy little cap of cotton with crane feathers of different colors. (494)

Kosometovich is nothing but a sham knight, with painted-on armor—an actor playing a part. His ostentatious outfit is the opera's most blatant reference to Gustav III, who was known to be a lover of fashion. He enjoyed the trappings of past glories: "At the time of the campaign [against Russia] he dressed himself in silk in the style of knights of the middle ages, and wore shoes with different-colored ribbons etc."[88] Gustav had even designed the Swedish court costume himself. Like Catherine's son Paul Petrovich, the Swedish King was also full of "martial mania,"[89] and Catherine complained to Potemkin that, "the Swedish King forged himself armor, cuirass, armlets, and thigh-plates and helmets with great numbers of feathers."[90]

Catherine was also infuriated by the arrogance of Gustav III's impertinent threats to Russia. One notorious example of Gustav's braggadocio is this anecdote:

---

[88] Brikner 182.

[89] Alexander, *Catherine the Great: Life and Legend* 270.

[90] P. Lebedev 307. Letter's date is 3 July 1788, just after the start of the war.

On leaving Stockholm for the army, Gustavus III boasted to the ladies that they would breakfast at Peterhof. He would go straight to Petersburg, overturn the statue of Peter the Great, and substitute one of himself![91]

Overturning the statue of Peter the Great would of course have been an insult both to Catherine, who had erected it, as well as to the memory of Peter, in whose heroic image Catherine had created her own identity as a ruler. Gustav's disrespect for the statue parallels Kosometovich's crude act of cutting down an ancient sword to fit him.

Kosometovich's bragging in I.5 to the court ladies is as ludicrous and exaggerated as Gustav's:

> Thank you for persuading matushka to allow me to go, for which I will send you presents of martens and sables and black and red foxes, and velvets and satins and damasks and veils; and by the Ocean-sea I will seize and darken the glory of all bogatyrs before this, then I will make you a magnificent feast on the bank of the Ocean-sea, to which I will invite you myself and will treat you with my own bogatyr's hands to sugary foods on oak tables covered by embroidered table-cloths. (488)

Like all the Braggart Warriors before him, Kosometovich blends boastfulness with cowardice to great comic effect. In the third act, he is frightened by faraway smoke (that later turns out to have been a trick of Krivomozg's). He then comes to a little peasant hut, in front of which are seated an old woman, a little girl, and a one-armed Old Man, who refuses the Knight's rude requests for food: "Although I have only one arm, I can still stand up to a knight like you" (499). Hungry, Kosometovich and the others lay siege to the hut, but they are driven off by the man, who threatens them with an oven fork. Nineteenth-century critic A. G. Brikner saw direct reference to the Russo-Swedish War here:

> [...] the Swedes couldn't take Nyslott and Fridrikshamm and had to retreat. The Russians' insignificant means for defense is justly depicted in the figure of the one-armed man. The failure of the Swedes at the siege of these fortresses should be attributed not to the cowardice of the Swedes, but the internal discord in their camp. The majority didn't want war. (183)

This comparison is supported by a cryptic comment from Khrapovitskii, who noted on 29 November, 1788 that, "the one-armed old man is the commander at Nyslott."[92] Brikner goes on to compare the unwillingness of the Woeful Knight's friends to accompany him on his journey to the reluctant Swedish officers of the Anjala Federation who mutinied in July 1788.[93]

---

[91]   Alexander, *Catherine the Great: Life and Legend* 270.
[92]   Barsukov 204.
[93]   Brikner 183.

After retreating from the one-armed Old Man, Kosometovich hides in a tree to escape the bear he thinks he hears—in reality, his friends are seeking to frighten him. "Woeful Knight, why are you sitting like a bird in that tree? ... Those-Who-Gnaw-Bones are coming from the right, from the left the wood-goblins, and from the middle many sorcerors" (505). His companions convince the Knight to return home, where he brags of their victories in a song to the assembled nobles and servants:

I can tell without bragging,
I will indulge to inform you of the brave deeds,
I overthrew a multitude of strongholds,
I conquered everywhere and everyone,
Drove away, scattered and slaughtered
Bears, Those-Who-Knaw-Bones,
And wood-goblins and sorcerors. (509)

Brikner points out that Catherine was employing poetic license in equating the King with his troops in mutiny. Gustav III himself, despite his hyperbolic bravado and ostentatiousness, was not considered a cowardly figure: "on the field of battle, Gustav always distinguished himself by cold-bloodedness and scorn toward danger."[94]

Catherine contrasts the folk-derived image of the valiant returning warrior with her central character: a timid and trembling fool who hides in a tree but then returns home to brag of his bravery. Her full-length comedies often feature such a deceptive character, whose duplicity is usually revealed by the fifth act, making an almost-thwarted marriage possible. But in this opera, the fool is never found out. Kosometovich returns home victorious, and, full of lies about his exploits, weds the "glorious Gremila" without having his cowardice publicly revealed. The theme is reminiscent of the concluding proverb of "The Voyage of M. Bontems:" He who comes from afar lies well.

The opera's ultimately sympathetic treatment of Kosometovich is a bit puzzling, especially since it also casts his mother and the populace as gullible fools. Perhaps the needs of the genre—a comic opera must end happily, and with a marriage—determined this outcome. Another interpretation is supported by the opera's final song, sung by a chorus of servants and court nobles who have welcomed the errant knight home. The singers comment ironically on the ambitions of Kosometovich:

A proverb came true:
The titmouse bird climbed up,
Took wing, flew,
And wanted to set fire to the sea,

---

94 Brikner 185.

It didn't light the sea,
But made a lot of noise. (510)[95]

These words, which do give the opera a sense of moral closure, suggest that
Woeful Knight's failings are known to all, just as Catherine's court audience
would have fully known of Gustav's haughty actions. By concluding her opera
with a wink to her audience, Catherine could further diminish the stature of her
enemy the "titmouse" while remaining within the lively and light genre framework
of a comic opera.

Because the opera was removed from the Hermitage repertory after the signing
of military peace, it is clear that Catherine did not intend the operatic piece to make
a lasting artistic contribution. Rather, the opera was topical, designed to meet her
specific goals at the time, and was easily disposed of. Again and again in her
career as a playwright and librettist, Catherine wrote in the comic vein, while at the
same time retaining a monarch's view of art as a political tool. Although on the
surface *The Woeful Knight Kosometovich* is innocuous and certainly funny, the fun
and games could have proved dangerous in both war and peace.

Fedul and his Children

With this note from Khrapovitskii's diary from 20 January 1791, our consideration
of Catherine the Great's dramatic writing comes full circle:

> In the Hermitage, they presented again "Fedul" and the comedy "O vremia!" [*Oh, These
> Times!*]. [...] "O vremia!", a work of 1772 in the time of the plague, was received
> coldly, but "Fedul" was applauded.[96]

Almost twenty years after her first play was performed, her last dramatic
composition premiered at the court theatre on 16 January 1791. *Fedul and his
Children*, a short one-act opera with music by Martín and Pashkevich, later opened
at the Stone Theatre on 19 February, and in Moscow on 27 December 1795. The
opera showed repeatedly at all of these venues, continuing to play in Moscow for
years after Catherine's death. The opera was also published in single edition in
1790, and again in 1792 and 1798. Jurgenson's publishing house issued an edition
in 1895, with vocal and piano score.

The "plot" of *Fedul* is absurdly simple. After Fedul's children sing a chorus
urging young maidens not to rush into marriage, scene 2 presents a duet in which

---

[95] The proverb may be related to one listed in Dal' 4: 187: "*Khvalilas' sinitsa more
spalit.' Poletela ptitsa sinitsa za trideviat' zemel,' za sine more okiian'*." (The titmouse
boasted to burn the sea. The titmouse bird flew to the ends of the earth, to the blue sea-
ocean.)

[96] Barsukov 355.

Detina (meaning Big Fellow) courts Duniasha, one of Fedul's daughters. In the third and final scene, Fedul calls all of his fifteen sons and daughters to him to explain that he, a widower himself, has met a widow that he would like to marry. Each of the children complains in turn, but after Duniasha sings a final song, the children embrace their new step-mother and a ballet of various dances concludes the opera. Duniasha's final song is an almost verbatim reproduction of a folk song that appears in Chulkov's 1770 collection of songs, "Vo sele, sele Pokrovskom," thought to have been written by Empress Elizabeth.[97]

The third scene employs a humorously repetitive structure, in which Fedul calls out the name of one of his children, singing with them in four to six lines of rhymed verse. He then speaks a proverb; then the children all sing four lines in a chorus (the first two lines begin with "Ekh, ekh" followed by two lines starting with "Akh, akh"). This structure repeats twelve times, going through each of the children: Duniasha, Fotiasha, Ippolit, Neofit, Serafina, Agripina, Paramon, Filimon, Katerina, Akulina, ending with the twins Nikodim and Ankudim, and the triplets Minodora, Mitrodora, and Nimfodora.

> FEDUL *sings*.
> Ippolit, look at me quickly.
> IPPOLIT.
> With all my might, I stare with my eyes on you.
> FEDUL.
> I'm dreaming of my marriage.
> IPPOLIT.
> What a thought, an idea.
> FEDUL *speaks*. No wife means no cats.
> CHILDREN *sing in a chorus*.
> Ekh, ekh, papa got an idea,
> Ekh, ekh, papa decided!
> Akh, he will get married!
> Akh, he will get married! (529)

Other proverbs include "Don't look for the beginning, wait for the end" and "He sings well, but stops better" (532). Catherine displayed a love for proverbs throughout her literary career. They appear in her satirical journal, in her full-length comedies, in her French proverb plays, and her own compilation, *Selected Russian Proverbs*. In fact, two of the proverbs in *Fedul* appeared first in 1783 in Catherine's collection: "A guess is better than reason" (*Dogadka lutche razuma*) (534) and "A young mind is like spring ice" (*Molodin'koi umok, chto veshnii ledok*) (530).[98] It was probably quite amusing, in an otherwise completely sung opera, to have Fedul speak these short, cryptic proverbs.

---

[97] Chulkov, *Sobranie raznykh* 232.

[98] Proverbs are entries 20 (page 5) and 51 (page 8) in Catherine II, *Vybornyia*.

The two composers shared musical duties, and did their work quickly: the libretto was finished sometime after 11 December 1790, and the first rehearsal was 2 January 1791. Pashkevich contributed an overture, one air, one duet, one ensemble, and a chorus of children. Martín composed three airs, two choruses of children, and the final chorus.[99] Findeizen sums up Pashkevich's contribution: "Here, as in *Fevei*, Pashkevich's music is a mixture of Russian color and reminiscences of Italian comic opera."[100] Pashkevich's overture is made up of two existing folk melodies, identified by Rabinovich;[101] the final song by Duniasha uses the lyrics and music of a well-known folk song. Rabinovich also appreciates the "authentic" form of the opening chorus; Whaples points out that if this chorus is original, it "considerably strengthens Pashkevich's position as a founder of Russian national style."[102]

For most of Catherine's operatic works, there is clear evidence that verse sections were either composed by Khrapovitskii or adapted from pre-existing poetry such as that of Lomonosov or Trediakovskii. Catherine herself claimed never to have written verse in any language.[103] But there is some evidence that Catherine did create much of the Russian verse that forms the majority of *Fedul*'s dialog. First, there is a small but telling comment in Khrapovitskii's diary: "[She] read to me the beginning of the opera. I told [her] about the rule of a duet. [She] spits on that."[104] The final phrase, *"Na eto plevat'"* is roughly the equivalent of "To hell with that," indicating Catherine's disdain for a prescriptive approach to operatic composition.

Secondly, an extant manuscript of the opera is clearly in Catherine's handwriting. The editor of Khrapovitskii's diary, Barsukov, compared the original manuscript to the final published version, and found, in Catherine's handwriting, a first draft of the first chorus in tetrameter, which was crossed out and replaced by the published passage in iambic heptameter.[105] The play's entire second scene (the duet between Duniasha and Detina) also shows several alterations by Catherine's hand.[106] The verses in this act employ stanzas of nine lines each, with the following rhyme scheme: ABABCCDDD. The poetry is in a deliberately naïve style: full of repetition, strewn with "Akh"s, and avoiding polysyllabic words.

---

[99] Mooser 2: 588.

[100] Findeizen 338.

[101] "Uzh kak po mostu, mostochku" and "Akh, utushka lugovaia" (Rabinovich 81).

[102] Whaples 119.

[103] Whaples 118. See her earlier letter to Grimm of 24 August 1778: "I have never written either verse or history." Grot, *Pis'ma imperatritsy* 100.

[104] Entry's date is 7 December 1790; Barsukov 352.

[105] Barsukov 599.

[106] A facsimile of these four pages of the manuscript was published in 1850. Arapov, *Dramatich[eskii]*.

Despite her own claims to the contrary, we can infer that Catherine could indeed write in verse, and that she wrote significant portions of the verse in *Fedul*.

The performance of the opera on 11 February 1791 seems to have been related to a scandalous event that may have eclipsed the story of Fedul and his bride-to-be. According to nineteenth-century literary historian M. N. Longinov, the singer Lizan'ka (Elizaveta) Iakovleva-Uranova was being courted by Count Aleksandr Bezborodko, one of Catherine's senior ministers. Khrapovitskii and Soimonov, who were at that time co-administrators of the Imperial Theatre, evidently sought to please Bezborodko by sending his rival, the actor Sila Sandunov, away to Moscow. Sandunov denounced the ill treatment onstage after a performance on 10 January 1791. The next day, the Empress said to Khrapovitskii, *"Voilà ce que fait l'injustice."*[107]

On 11 February, according to Longinov,

> Lizan'ka, not seeing the end to the persecution, at the end of the presentation of "Fedul" at Hermitage, got down on her knees on the stage and asked her Sovereign majesty for a petition on her persecutors. That night the Empress ordered [D. P.] Troshchinskii to write a decree about the removal of Khrapovitskii and Soimonov from the leadership of the theatre, and took Lizan'ka under her protection.[108]

Khrapovitskii's diary entry on 11 February notes that during the performance of *Fedul*, "Lizka gave us a petition" and that Troshchinskii, head of Bezborodko's office, was up with him half the night conferring with him about the decree. On 14 February, he notes simply that, "In the Malyi court church Lizka and Sandunov were married."[109] Some scholars have thought that the final song by Duniasha was seen as a veiled allusion to Liz'anka's rejection of Bezborodko (it treats the rejection of a nobleman by a peasant girl).[110] Although Bezsonov reminds us that this song is much older—Chulkov had published it in the 1770s—the lyrics are indeed a striking anthem in favor of the simplicity of country life, despite the rich suitor's promises of gold and silver.

> I heard from everyone,
> That you love all with your words,
> But with your heart no one. (537)

---

[107] Barsukov 354.

[108] Longinov, "Dramaticheskii sochineniia" 283. Essay is a reprint of a piece from 1857 from the journal *Molva*.

[109] Barsukov 358. The pair later moved to Moscow and ran the famous Sandunov baths.

[110] According to Bezsonov, Longinov made this connection. See Bezsonov, "O vlianii" 13.

Whatever Catherine's intention, this episode reveals the stage as a site for the public revelation of court intrigue.

Later in the spring of 1791, after *Fedul* had played at least four times at the Hermitage and two times in the Stone Theatre, Catherine wrote to Grimm that,

> it's not necessary to speak of a poor little divertissement given at the Hermitage and which has had the most decided success at the theatre in the city: it's *Fedul* in comic choruses; one will send to monsieur the music of one or another as soon as one has it, and one hopes that it will accompany this notice. The speeches of *Fedul* are old Russian songs and proverbs stitched together by the author of *Oleg*.[111]

Fedul appears to have been one of Catherine's most popular dramatic endeavors; between 1791 and 1800 there are thirty-five recorded performances, twenty-three of them in Moscow.[112] It is one of her shortest and simplest works, and lacks the political and social commentary of much of her oeuvre. If there is a political interpretation of *Fedul*, it is perhaps that Catherine is the step-mother of Russia, who should be embraced and welcomed. More likely, the plot has no deeper significance. The real significance of the event was the imitation of a native folk style, in the context of Western-style opera.

On the folder of the manuscript for *Fedul*, Catherine wrote a short note:

> Don't forget to tell the Composers that "Ekh, ekh, ne ladno/Akh ne skladno"—of the Father could be a parody or could ridicule the "ekh, ekh and akh" of the children. [113]

Clearly, Catherine was well aware of the comic potential, the downright silliness, of this father and his whining children. Many later commentators have taken the naïveté of *Fedul* and her other comic operas to be a failing. Rabinovich, writing in the Soviet Union in 1948, grumbled that, "Out of the ten numbers in *Fedul* five begin with a repeated 'Ekh,' which evidently appeared to the princess from Anhalt-Zerbst the fullest way to express the soul of the Russian people."[114] Catherine the Great's goal for her comic operas was probably not to express the soul of the Russian people, but to promote the national identity of her adopted country by paying homage to Russian folk forms by stitching together fairy tales, *byliny*, popular songs, and even a witch.

---

[111] Letter's date is 7 May 1791; Grot, "Pis'ma imperatritsy" 525.
[112] El'nitskaia 470.
[113] Quoted in Pypin 2: 541.
[114] Rabinovich 81 (translation from Whaples 118).

Epilogue

After *Fedul and his Children*, Catherine wrote no more plays or operas. She did, however, continue writing in various forms, such as her correspondence with Grimm, more historical notes on Russia, and her memoirs.[1] But at the same time she curtailed the freedom of literary expression she had proffered for much of her reign. Historians credit the more conservative stance toward writers and writing of her final years to the events of the French Revolution. Her final favorite, the "anti-intellectual"[2] Platon Zubov (in favor 1789–96), seems also to have encouraged a less tolerant approach. In 1790, Catherine had the Masonic writer Aleksandr Radishchev condemned to death (she later exiled him instead). He had written *Journey from St. Petersburg to Moscow* [Puteshestvie iz Peterburga v Moskvu], a passionate critique of serfdom and governmental corruption. Whereas in the 1780s she had written plays satirizing Novikov, she had him imprisoned in 1792. In 1793, as noted in Chapter 4, when Kniazhnin's *Vadim of Novgorod* appeared in Dashkova's periodical *Russian Theatre*, Catherine ordered all copies destroyed. In October 1796, just weeks before her death, she revoked permission for private citizens to own printing presses (a freedom she had granted in 1783) and established a bureaucratic structure for censorship in the major cities. Her death was on 5 November 1796, at the age of 67, of a cerebral stroke. Her immediate successor was her son Paul Petrovich, who immediately began to dismantle many of the enlightened reforms of Catherine's era. After his assassination in 1801, Catherine's wished-for heir, her grandson Aleksandr, took the throne until his death in 1825. Instead of Konstantin, however, Aleksandr's much younger brother Nikolai, born the year of Catherine's death, succeeded him to reign in a notoriously repressive manner until 1855.

In the 1820s, as the advent of the Romantic movement in Russia became associated with the Decembrist revolt against Tsar Nikolai I, the literary revolt against neoclassicism became equated with the struggle against tsarist oppression. Catherine's writings were out of favor both on literary and political grounds. Catherine's drama, like the works of her contemporaries and Sumarokov, was dismissed as imitative and old-fashioned. Critics such as the socialist Vissarion Belinskii elevated new writers Griboedov and Gogol, while disparagingly discarding Russia's eighteenth-century drama as a whole, with only Fonvizin worth salvaging. Prejudices specific to Catherine the Great's status partially explain the scholarly neglect of her writing. Her position as Empress meant that as

---

[1] Cruse and Hoogenboom explain that in 1790–91 Catherine made revisions to an earlier "middle memoir" and began her final memoir in 1794 (xii).

[2] Dixon 106.

the ideas and achievements of her reign were demonized in later political climates (by both nineteenth- and twentieth-century revolutionaries), so too her dramatic writings were swept aside. Twentieth-century critic Arthur P. Coleman opined that the plays "became discredited in the eyes of their critics of the nineteenth century, more, possibly, because they were written by a ruler than because of their crudity and formlessness."[3] There is one example of a failed attempt to present two of Catherine's plays in the nineteenth century. The Simbirskii Theatre's plan in 1893 to produce *Mrs. Tattler and her Family* and *Mrs. Grumbler's Nameday* was foiled by the censor, who was perhaps unaware of their author's identity. "All these plays [...] are notable for the vulgarity of their contents, a lack of familiarity with the Russian language, and the frequent use of swear-words."[4]

Despite the lack of critical respect for Catherine's drama, editions of her plays were available throughout the nineteenth century.[5] Not until 1901, however, did a definitive edition of her complete plays (many previously unpublished) appear. Aleksandr Pypin, working from both original editions and manuscripts, provided full information on variants, related correspondence, and bibliography. Even with Pypin's archival evidence, doubts about Catherine's authorship of the plays have continued to undermine her status as a significant Russian dramatist.

Not surprisingly, Soviet scholars were not anxious to "rehabilitate" Catherine as a dramatist. Some Soviet historians, critical of the repressive censorship of her late years, called Catherine's Enlightenment hypocritical for tolerating serfdom's inequity; they were thus hardly receptive to the Empress's drama, and tended to omit Catherine's writings in most studies of drama of this period. Neither have Western scholars paid much attention to Catherine's plays. W. E. Brown is a good example of a negative reaction from as recently as 1980. Although he concedes that her "early comedies are light and witty," his overall assessment is hardly flattering: "The Empress of all Russia plumed herself on being not only a most enlightened monarch, but also a talented writer. Her pretensions were as ill-founded in the one case as in the other."[6]

Recent years have brought a renewed interest in Catherine's life and a new respect for her writings. Social historians, literary critics, art historians, and biographers have brought new perspectives to bear in an appreciation of Catherine's influence. The year 1996, the bicentennial of the year of Catherine's death, saw several international conferences on Catherine's impact, including one sponsored by the Academy of Sciences in St. Petersburg. As part of that conference, a concert version of *The Beginning of Oleg's Reign* was performed on

---

3 Coleman 4.

4 Quoted in Drizen, *Dramaticheskaia tsenzura* 128. This incident indicates that Catherine's authorship was perhaps not widely known in the nineteenth century, or at least was tacitly ignored.

5 See Smirdin and Vvedenskii editions under Catherine II.

6 Brown 215.

28 August 1996, in the Hermitage Theatre. In 1996, Dr Ruth Dawson and I created and moderated a scholarly internet discussion, the EKATERINA-L, on which participants from around the world debated issues of Catherine's impact. On a more popular front, the success in Russia of Elena Gremina's play *Behind the Mirror*, about Catherine's attentions to her favorite Aleksandr Lanskoi, has kept alive the vision of Catherine as a lover as well as a ruler. A new 2005 edition of her final memoir, distributed by Random House, should spur interest once again in Catherine's biography as well as her achievements as an author.[7]

Since the mid-twentieth century, new attention has also been paid to Catherine's drama. A French scholar translated the anti-Masonic trilogy into French in 1947, and Dr Giovanna Moracci published an Italian translation of *Prominent Nobleman*.[8] In 1985, Simon Karlinsky, in his book *Russian Drama From its Beginnings to the Age of Pushkin*, examined the innovative style and pointed subject matter of Catherine's plays in detail. Noting the Soviet-era disinterest in the plays, he concludes that, "Were Catherine's plays to be given the same sociological treatment as the rest of Russian drama of the period [...] the entire official view of the period would collapse."[9] In 1990, Oleg Mikhailov published a new Russian edition of four of Catherine's plays, signaling a renewed interest in the Empress's writings as a part of Russia's literary heritage. In 1998, my own translations of *Oh, These Times!* and *The Siberian Shaman* brought these comedies to an English-speaking readership. In a 2001 consideration of Catherine's drama, Simon Dixon appreciatively notes "the plays' originality of form, since no lesser writer would have dared break with convention."[10]

Catherine the Great took theatre seriously, as a means of audience enlightenment and education. Political messages permeate her dramas, making them vehicles for commentary on philosophical, military, and social issues. Yet she most often chose light genres: comedy, comic opera, and proverb plays. Of her serious history plays, the only one ever produced was *The Beginning of Oleg's Reign*, which substituted elaborate music and spectacle for comedy. The Hermitage curtain motto, "To improve morals through laughter," expressed the firm neoclassical belief in the dyad of didacticism and entertainment.

While Catherine used theatre to increase Russia's reputation as the civilized "European state" she claimed it to be in her 1767 *Great Instruction*, at the same time her dramatic works deliberately emphasize her country's uniquely Russian aspects. Her first comedies of the 1770s follow French models closely, with changes to Russian names and customs. But her later comedies, such as the anti-Masonic trilogy, boldly address themes not treated in her French sources. And her history plays resist convention by adapting a Shakespearean style to chronicle the

---

[7] Cruse and Hoogenboom.
[8] See Chetteoui, and Moracci, *Nell'anticamera.*
[9] Karlinsky 91.
[10] Dixon 97.

formation of Russia itself. These experiments and her folk-inspired operas reveal a
daring writer, pulling together elements of history, legend, popular song, and
elevated poetry, all in the service of demonstrating Russia's legitimacy while
glorifying its culture. Catherine wished to expand her empire in many ways:
geographically, philosophically, culturally. The stage, a tiny version of that
empire, allowed Catherine the Great to both contain Russia and to suggest its lack
of boundaries.

Appendix

Pypin Edition References

All play quotations in this book are taken from Aleksandr Pypin's edition, *Sochineniia imperatritsy Ekateriny II*. 12 vols. St. Petersburg: Imperatorskoi Akademii Nauk, 1901–1907.

RT indicates volume and page number of publication in Dashkova's *Russian Theatre* (Dashkova, Ekaterina, ed. *Rossiiskii featr, ili Polnoe sobranie vsekh Rossiiskikh teatral'nykh sochinenii*), 43 vols. St. Petersburg, 1786–94.

PYPIN VOLUME ONE
Oh, These Times! [O vremia!] 3–42; RT 11: 3–84
Mrs. Grumbler's Nameday [Imianiny gospozhi Vorchalkinoi] 49–114; RT 11: 85–220.
A Prominent Nobleman's Entrance Hall [Peredniania znatnago boiarina] 159–78; RT 11: 221–62
Mrs. Tattler and her Family [Gospozha Vestnikova s sem'eiu] 187–207; RT 11: 263–308.
The Questioner [Vosprositel'] 225–45; RT 12: 3–50 (under title *The Invisible Bride* [Nevesta nevidimka])
The Deceiver [Obmanshchik] 247–86; RT 13: 5–80
The Deceived One [Obol'shchennyi] 289–340; RT 13: 81–174
The Siberian Shaman [Shaman sibirskoi] 347–406; RT 13: 175–296

PYPIN VOLUME TWO
This 'tis to have Linen and Buck-Baskets [Vot kakovo imet' korzinu i bel'e] 3–54; RT 14:5–107
A Family Broken Up by Intrigue and Suspicions [Razstroennaia sem'ia ostorozhkami i podozreniiami] 63–124; RT 20: 153–308
The Misunderstanding [Nedorazumeniia] 131–210; RT 31: 153–318
From the Life of Riurik [Iz zhizni Riurika] 219–51; RT 14: 107–66
The Beginning of Oleg's Reign [Nachal'noe upravlenie Olega] 259–304; RT 14: 167–248
Fevei 332–63; RT 2: 3–54

Boeslaevich, Novgorod Knight [Novgorodskii bogatyr' Boeslaevich'] 371–99; RT
    20: 55–100
The Brave and Bold Knight Akhrideich [Khraboi i smeloi vitiaz' Akhrideich'] 403–
    37; RT 20: 101–51
Woeful Knight Kosometovich [Gorebogatyr' Kosometovich'] 483–510
Fedul and his Children [Fedul s det'mi] 521–38

PYPIN VOLUME THREE consists of various unpublished works and fragments.

PYPIN VOLUME FOUR
"The Busy-Body" [Le Tracassier] 3–15
"The Flatterer and the Flattered" [Le Flatteur et les flattés] 19–32
"The Voyages of M. Bontems" [Les Voyages de M. Bontems] 35–44
"No Evil Without Good" [Il n'y a point de mal sans bien] 47–62
"The Rage for Proverbs" [La rage aux proverbes] 65–84

Bibliography

Alexander, John T. *Bubonic Plague in Early Modern Russia: Public Health and Urban Disaster*. Johns Hopkins University Studies in Historical and Political Sciences 98.1. Baltimore: Johns Hopkins UP, 1980.

———. *Catherine the Great: Life and Legend*. New York: Oxford UP, 1989.

Anisimov, A. F. "The Shaman's Tent of the Evenks and the Origin of the Shamanistic Rite." *Studies in Siberian Shamanism*. Ed. Henry N. Michael. Anthropology from the North: Translations from Russian Sources 4. Toronto: U Toronto Press, 1963.

Annenkov, A., ed. *Dramaticheskoi slovar', ili pokazaniia po alfavitu vsekh Rossiiskikh teatral'nykh sochinenii i perevodov*. Moscow: Tipografiia A. A. 1787.

Anonymous. "K sochiniteliu komedii Obmanshchik." *Rastushchii vinograd*. February (1786): 43–44.

———. "Pis'mo k sochiniteliu komedii Obmanshchika." *Rastushchii vinograd* February (1786): 1–6.

———. "Review of *Drey Lustspiele, wider Schwärmerey und Aberglauben*." *German Museum, or Monthly Repository of the Literature of Germany, the North and the Continent in General* 1 (1800): 570–71.

———. "Review of *Théâtre de l'Hermitage*." *Monthly Review* 28 (1799): 501–10.

Anthony, Katharine. *Catherine the Great*. New York: Alfred A. Knopf, 1929.

———, ed. *Memoirs of Catherine the Great*. New York: Knopf, 1927.

Arapov, P. N., and A. Roppol't. *Dramatich[eskii] al'bom*. Moscow: Universitetskaia tipografiia, 1850.

Arapov, Pimen N. *Letopis' russkago teatra*. St. Petersburg: Tipografiia N. Tiblena i komp., 1861.

Baehr, Stephen L. "The Masonic Component in Eighteenth-Century Russian Literature." *Russian Literature in the Age of Catherine the Great: A Collection of Essays*. Ed. A. G. Cross. Oxford: Willem A. Meeuws, 1976. 121–39.

Bakmeister, I. G. *Russische Bibliothek: zur Kenntniss des Gegenwärtigen Zustandes der Literatur in Russland*. 11 vols. St. Petersburg, Riga and Leipzig, 1772–89.

Balzer, Marjorie Mandelstam. *Shamanism: Soviet Studies of Traditional Religion in Siberia and Central Asia*. Armonk, NY: M. E. Sharpe, 1990.

Barsukov, Nikolai Platonovich, ed. *Dnevnik A. V. Khrapovitskogo, 1782–1793*. St. Petersburg: Izd. A. F. Bazunova, 1874.

Bates, Alfred, ed. *The Drama: Its History, Literature, and Influence on Civilization*. 20 vols. New York: AMS, 1970.

Berkov, P. N. *Istoriia russkoi komedii XVIII v.* Leningrad: Nauka, 1977.

———, ed. *Satiricheskie zhurnaly N. I. Novikova.* Moscow-Leningrad, 1951.

Bezsonov, P. [A.] *Nash' vek v russkikh istoricheskikh pesniakh.* Vol. 10 of *Pesni sobrannyia P. V. Kireevskim.* Moscow: Universitetskaia tipografiia, 1874.

———. "O vlianii narodnago tvorchestva na dramy Imperatritsy Ekateriny i o tsel'nykh russkikh pesniakh, siuda vstavlennykh." *Zariia* 4 (1870): 1–19.

Boltin, I. N. Preface. [Catherine II]. *Podrazhanie Shakespiru, istoricheskoe predstavlenie bez sokhraneniia featral'nykh obyknovennykh pravil, iz zhizni Riurika.* St. Petersburg: Imperatorskaia tipografiia, 1792. i–xlvi.

Borovsky, Victor. "The Emergence of the Russian Theatre 1763–1800." *A History of Russian Theatre.* Eds Robert Leach and Victor Borovsky. Cambridge: CUP, 1999, 57–85.

Brenner, Clarence. *Le développpment du proverbe dramatique en France et sa vogue au XVIIIe siècle avec un proverbe inédit de Carmontelle.* Berkeley: U California Press, 1937.

Brikner, A. G. "Komicheskaia opera Ekateriny II: 'Gore-bogatyr.'" *Zhurnal ministerstva narodnago prodveshcheniia* 152.12 (1870): 172–86.

Brokgaus, F. A. and I. A. Efron, eds. *Entsiklopedicheskii slovar.* St. Petersburg: 1890–1904.

Brown, W. E. *A History of 18th Century Russian Literature.* Ann Arbor, MI: Ann Ardis, 1980.

Carlson, Marvin. *Theories of the Theatre: A Historical and Critical Survey, from the Greeks to the Present.* Ithaca: Cornell UP, 1984.

Cassirer, Peter. "Gustaf III: The Theatre King, Librettist and Politician." *Gustavian Opera: An Interdisciplinary Reader in Swedish Opera, Dance and Theatre 1771–1809.* Sweden: Royal Swedish Academy of Music, 1991. 29–44.

[Catherine II.] *Fedul s det'mi, opera v odnom deistvii.* St. Petersburg: Imp. tip., 1790.

———. *La fête du jour de nom. Chefs-d'oeuvre du théâtre polonais: Felinsky, Wenzyk, Niemcowitz, Oginsky, Mowinsky, Kochanowsky.* Chefs-d'oeuvre des théâtres étrangers. Vol. 23. Paris: Chez lavocat, Libraire, 1823. 292–405.

———. *Gospozha Vestnikova s sem'eiu komediia v odnom deistvii.* St. Petersburg: Senatskaia tip., 1774.

———. *Imianiny gospozhi Varchalkinoi komediia v piati deistviiakh.* St. Petersburg: Senatskaia tip., 1774.

———. *Komediia Obmanshchik.* St. Petersburg: Tipografiia Imperatorskoi Akademii nauk, 1785. Rpt. 1786.

———. *Komediia Obol'shchennyi.* St. Petersburg: Tipografiia Imperatorskoi Akademii nauk, 1785. Rpt. 1786.

———. *Komediia. Razstroennaia sem'ia ostorozhkami i podozrenniiami.* St. Petersburg: Tipografiia Imperatorskoi Akademii nauk, 1788.

———. *Komediia. Shaman sibirskoi.* St. Petersburg: Imp. Akad. nauk, 1786.

————. *Nachal'noe upravlenie Olega, podrazhanie Shakespiru bez sokhraneniia featral'nykh obyknovennykh pravil.* St. Petersburg: Tipografiia Imperatorskoi Akademii nauk, 1787. Rpt. 1793.

————. *Nachal'noe upravlenie Olega, podrazhanie Shakespiru bez sokhraneniia featral'nykh obyknovennykh pravil.* St. Peterburg: Tipografiia gornago uchilishcha, 1791.

————. *Nakaz Kommissii o sostavlennii proekta novago ulozheniia.* Moscow: Pech. Pri Senate, 1767.

————. *Novogorodskoi bogatyr' Boeslaevich' opera komicheskaia, sostavlena iz skazki, pesnei ruskikh i inykh sochinenii.* St. Petersburg: Tipografiia Imperatorskoi Akademii nauk, 1786. Rpt. 1793.

————. *O vremia! Komediia v trekh deistviiakh. Sochinena v Iaroslavle vo vremia chumy.* St. Petersburg: Senatskaia tip., n.d.

————. *Opera komicheskaia Fevei, sostavlena iz slov skaski, pesnei ruskikh i inykh sochinenii.* St. Petersburg: Tipografiia Imperatorskoi Akademii nauk, 1786. Rpt. Tip. gornago uchilishcha, 1789.

————. *Opera komicheskaia Khraboi i smeloi vitiaz' Akhrideich.'* St. Petersburg: Tipografiia Imperatorskoi Akademii nauk, 1787.

————. "Pis'ma Ekateriny Vtoroi k baronu Grimmu." *Russkii arkhiv* 3 (1878): 5–240.

————. *Podrazhanie Shakespiru, istoricheskoe predstavlenie bez sokhraneniia featral'nykh obyknovennykh pravil, iz zhizni Riurika.* St. Petersburg: Tipografiia Imperatorskoi Akademii nauk, 1786. Rpt. St. Petersburg: Imperatorskaia tipografiia, 1792. Rpt. St. Petersburg: Tip. Korpusa chuzhestrannykh edinovertsov, 1793.

————. *Polnoe sobranie sochinenii russkikh avtorov: Sochineniia Imperatritsy Ekateriny II.* Ed. Aleksandr Smirdin. 3 vols. St. Petersburg: Aleksandra Smirdina, 1849–50.

————. *Rossiiskaia azbuka dlia obucheniia iunoshestva chteniiu.* St. Petersburg: Tipografiia Imperatorskoi Akademii nauk, 1781.

————. *Skazka o Gorebogatyre Kosometoviche i Opera komicheskaia iz slov skaski sostavlennaia.* St. Petersburg: Tip. gornago uchilishcha, 1789.

————. *Skazka o tsareviche Fevee.* St. Petersburg: Tipografiia Imperatorskoi Akademii nauk, 1783.

————. *Skazka o tsareviche Khlore.* St. Petersburg: Tipografiia Imperatorskoi Akademii nauk, 1781.

————. "Sobstvennoruchnyi pis'ma Imperatritsy Ekateriny vtoroi k A. V. Khrapovitskomu, 1788–93." *Russkii arkhiv* 10 (1872): cols. 2062–99.

————. *Sochineniia Ekateriny II.* Ed. Oleg Mikhailov. Moscow: Sov. Rossiia, 1990.

————. *Sochineniia imperatritsy Ekateriny II.* Ed. A. N. Pypin. 12 vols. St. Petersburg: Imperatorskoi Akademii Nauk, 1901–1907.

———. *Sochineniia Imperatritsy Ekateriny II*. Ed. I. Vvedenskii. St. Petersburg: A. F. Marks, 1893.

———. "Spisok s pis'ma Ekateriny II k gr. P. Paninu o pervom kurtage v Peterburge i de-la-Riviere." 28 January 1768. Vol. 10. *Sbornik imperatorskago russkago istoricheskago obshchestva*. St. Petersburg: Tipografiia Imperatorskoi Akademii nauk, 1872. 279.

———. *Taina protivo-nelepago obshchestva, otkrytaia ne prichastnym onomu*. St. Petersburg: tip. Veitbvrekhta i Shnora, 1780.

———. *Vol'noe no slaboe perelozhenie iz Shakespira, komediia Vot kakovo imet' korzinu i bel'e*. St. Petersburg: Tipografiia Imperatorskoi Akademii nauk, 1786.

———. *Vybornyia rossiiskiia poslovitsy*. St. Petersburg: Tipografiia Imperatorskoi Akademii nauk, 1783.

———. *Zapiski imperatritsy Ekateriny Vtoroi*. St. Petersburg, 1907.

———. *Zapiski kasatel'no rossiiskoi istorii*. 6 vols. St. Petersburg: Tipografiia Imperatorskoi Akademii nauk, 1787–94.

Chebyshev, A. A. "Istochnik komedii imperatritsy Ekateriny: 'O vremia!'" *Russkaia starina* 129. 2 (1907): 389–409.

Chetteoui, Wilfrid-René. *Cagliostro et Catherine II*. Paris: Les éditions des Champs-Elysées, 1947.

Chulkov, Mikhail Dmitrievich. *Slovar' ruskikh sueverii*. St. Petersburg: Tipografiia Shnora, 1782.

———. *Sobranie raznykh pesen M. D. Chulkova*. 1770–73. Vol. 1 of *Sochineniia Mikhaila Dmitrievicha Chulkova*. St. Petersburg: Tipografiia imperatorskoi akademii nauk, 1913.

Coleman, Arthur P. *Humor in the Russian Comedy from Catherine to Gogol*. New York: AMS Press, 1966.

Conacher, D. J. Introduction. *Alcestis* by Euripides. Trans. D. J. Conacher. Wiltshire, England: Aris and Phillips, 1988. 1–55.

The Costume of the Russian Empire. London: W. Miller, 1803.

Cracraft, James. "James Brogden in Russia, 1787–1788." *Slavonic and East European Review* 47.108 (1969): 219–44.

Craik, T. W. "Introduction." *The Merry Wives of Windsor* by William Shakespeare Oxford: Oxford UP, 1994. 1–63.

Craven, Kenneth. "Publish and Languish: The Fate of Nikolai Ivanovich Novikov (1743–1818), Propagator of the Enlightenment under Catherine II." *Archives et Bibliothèques de Belgique/Archief en Bibliotheekwezen in Belgie* 54: 1–4 (1983): 173–89.

Cross, A. G. "The Eighteenth-Century Russian Theater Through British Eyes." *Studies on Voltaire and the Eighteenth Century* 219 (1983): 225–40.

———. "A Royal Blue-Stocking: Catherine the Great's Early Reputation in England as an Authoress." *Gorski vijenats: a Garland of Essays Offered to*

Professor Elizabeth Mary Hill. Eds R. Auty, L. R. Lewitter, and A. P. Vlasto. Cambridge: Modern Humanities Association, 1970. 85–99.

Cross, S. H. "The Russian Primary Chronicle." *Harvard Studies and Notes in Philology and Literature* 12 (1930): 144–51.

Cruse, Markus, and Hilde Hoogenboom, eds and trans. *The Memoirs of Catherine the Great.* New York: Modern Library–Random House, 2005.

Dal', Vladimir, ed. *Tolkovyi slovar' zhivogo velikorusskogo iazyka.* 4 vols. St. Petersburg: Izdanie knigoprodavtsa-tipografa M.O. Vol'fa, 1882. Moscow: Russkii iazyk, 1978.

Dashkova, Ekaterina, ed. *Rossiiskii featr, ili Polnoe sobranie vsekh Rossiiskikh teatral'nykh sochinenii* [Russian Theatre, or Complete Collection of all Russian Theatrical Works] 43 vols. St. Petersburg, 1786–94.

Davis, Tracy C. "Questions for a Feminist Methodology in Theatre History." *Interpreting the Theatrical Past: Essays in the Historiography of Performance.* Eds Thomas Postlewait and Bruce A. McConachie. Iowa City: U of Iowa P, 1989. 59–81.

Dawson, Ruth. "Catherine as German Woman Writer." Online posting. 6 Feb 1996. EKATERINA-L.

———. "Catherine the Great: Playwright of the Anti-Occult." *Thalia's Daughters: German Women Dramatists from the 18th Century to the Present.* Eds Susan Cocalis and Ferrel Rose. Tübingen: Francke/Narr, 1996.

———. "Writing as a Woman and as a Ruler: Gender, Family and Power in the Fourth of Catherine II's Russian-German Plays." *Ekaterina II i ee vremia: sovremennyi vzgliad* [Catherine and Her Time: A Modern Outlook]. Eds T.V. Artemieva and M. I. Mikeshin. Filosofskii vek. Al'manakh 11. St. Petersburg: St. Petersburg Center for the History of Ideas, 1999. 29–51.

Diderot, Denis and Jean Lerond d'Alembert, eds. *Encyclopédie ou Dictionnaire raisonné des sciences, des arts et des métiers.* 35 volumes. Paris, 1751–80. Stuttgart-Bad Cannstatt: Friedrich Frommann Verlag, 1966.

Dixon, Simon. *Catherine the Great.* Profiles in Power. Ed. Keith Robbins. Harlow, England: Longman, 2001.

Drage, C. L. *Russian Literature in the Eighteenth Century.* London: C. L. Drage, 1978.

Drizen, Baron N. V. *Dramaticheskaia tsenzura dvukh epokh 1825–1881.* Petrograd: Prometei, n.d.

———. "Imperatritsa Ekaterina II." *Materialy k istorii russkago teatra.* 2nd edn. Moscow: A. A. Bakhrushin, 1913.

El'nitskaia, T. M., ed. "Repetuar dramaticheskikh trupp Peterburga i Moskvy 1750–1800." *Ot istokov do kontsa XVIII veka.* Vol 1. *Istoriia russkogo dramaticheskogo teatra.* Ed. V. N Vsevolodskii-Gerngross. Moscow: 1977. 435–73.

Erickson, Carolly. *Great Catherine.* New York: Crown, 1994.

Eschenburg, J. J. *William Shakespeares Schauspiele.* Zürich: 1775–82.

Esterházy, Valentin. *Lettres du comte Valentin Esterhazy à sa femme, 1784–92.* Paris: 1907.

Euripides. *Alcestis.* Trans. D. J. Conacher. Wiltshire, England: Aris and Phillips, 1988.

Filov, V. A., ed. *Svodnyi katalog knig na inostrannykh iazykakh, izdannykh v rossii v XVIII veke, 1701–1800.* 3 vols. Leningrad: "Nauka," Leningradskoe otd-nie, 1984.

Findeizen, Nikolai. [Findeisen, Nicholas]. "The Earliest Russian Operas." *The Musical Quarterly* 19.3 (1933): 331–40.

———. *Ocherki po istorii muzyki v Rossii s drevneishikh vremen do kontsa xviii veka.* 6 vols. Moscow-Leningrad: Gosudarstvennoe izdatel'stvo muzsektor, 1928.

Flaherty, Gloria. *Shamanism and the Eighteenth Century.* Princeton: Princeton UP, 1992.

Forbes, Isabella and William Underhill, eds. *Treasures of Imperial Russia: Catherine the Great from the State Hermitage Museum, Leningrad.* London: Booth-Clibborn Editions, 1990.

Franklin, Mitchell. "Influence of Abbé de Mably and of Le Mercier de la Rivière on American Constitutional Ideas Concerning the Republic and Judicial Review." *Perspectives of Law: Essays for Austin Wakeman Scott.* Eds Roscoe Pound, Erwin N. Griswold and Arthur E. Sutherland. Boston: Little, Brown and Company, 1964. 96–130.

Garnovskii, M. "Zapiski M. Garnovskago, 1786–1790." *Russkaia starina* 16 (1876): 1–32.

Gellert, Christian Fürchtegott. *Die Betschwester. Sämmtliche Schriften* 10 vols. 1769–74. Hildesheim: George Olms, 1968. 3: 145–220.

———. *Christian Fürchtegott Gellert's The Prayer Sister.* Trans. Johanna Setzer. New York: International Council on the Arts, 1980.

Ginzburg, S. L. *Russkii musykal'nyi teatr: 1700–1835 gg. Khrestomatiia.* Leningrad-Moscow: Iskusstvo, 1941, 129–32.

Gogol, Nikolai. *Inspector and 3 Other Plays.* Trans. Eric Bentley. New York: Applause, 1987.

Golub, Spencer. "Dmitrevsky, (Dmitrevskoi), Ivan Afanasievich." *Cambridge Guide to World Theatre.* Ed. Martin Banham. Cambridge: CUP, 1988. 280–81.

———. "Plavilshchikov, Pyotr Alekseevich." *Cambridge Guide to World Theatre.* Ed. Martin Banham. Cambridge: CUP, 1988. 774–75.

Green, William. *Shakespeare's Merry Wives of Windsor.* Princeton, New Jersey: Princeton UP, 1962.

Gremina, Elena. *Behind the Mirror. Russian Mirror: Three Plays by Russian Women.* Ed. and trans. Melissa T. Smith. Russian Theatre Archive 14. Amsterdam: Gordon and Breach/Harwood Academic Publishers, 1998.

Gribble, Charles E. *A Short Dictionary of 18th-Century Russian.* Ann Arbor: Slavica Publishers, 1976.

Grimm, Friedrich Melchior and Denis Diderot. *Correspondance littéraire, philosophique et critique.* Ed. Maurice Tourneux. Vol. 16. Paris: Garnier Frères, 1882.

Grot, Ia. K. "'Gore-bogatyr' Ekateriny II." *Bratskaia pomoshch' postradavshim semeistvam Bosnii i Gertsegoviny.* St. Petersburg: Tipografiia A. A. Kraevskago, 1876. 185–90.

———. "Ekaterina Vtoraia i Gustav Tretii." *Sbornik otdelniia russkago iazyka i slovesnosti Imperatorskoi Akademii Nauk.* 18.1 St. Petersburg: Tipografiia imperatorskoi akademii nauk, 1877.

———, ed. "Pis'ma Grimma k imperatritse Ekaterine II." Vol. 44. *Sbornik imperatorskago russkago istoricheskago obshchestva.* St. Petersburg: Tipografiia imperatorskoi akademii nauk, 1885.

———, ed. "Pis'ma imperatritsy Ekateriny II k Grimmu." Vol. 23. *Sbornik imperatorskago russkago istoricheskago obshchestva.* St. Petersburg: Tipografiia imperatorskoi akademii nauk, 1878.

———, ed. *Sochineniia Derzhavina s ob'iasnitel'nymi primechaniiami Ia. Grota.* 9 vols. St. Petersburg: Imperatorskaia akademiia nauk, 1864–83.

Guberti, N. V. *Materialy dlia russkoi bibliografiii. Khronologicheskoe obozrenie redkikh i zamechatel'nykh russkikh knig VXIII stoletiia, napechatannykh v rossii grazhdanskim shriftom. 1725–1800.* 3 vols. Moscow: Universitetskaia tipografiia, 1878–91.

Gukovskii, Grigorii A. "The Empress as Writer." Trans. Mary Mackler. *Catherine the Great: A Profile.* Ed. Marc Raeff. World Profiles. New York: Hill and Wang, 1972. 64–89.

Gurevich, Liubov. *Istoriia russkogo teatral'nogo byta.* Vol. 1. Moscow-Leningrad: Gosudarstvennoe izdatel'stvo "Iskusstvo," 1939.

Hawkins, Frederick William. *The French Stage in the Eighteenth Century.* 1888. 2 vols. New York: Haskell House, 1969.

Heldt, Barbara. *Terrible Perfection: Women and Russian Literature.* Bloomington: Indiana UP, 1987.

Herzen, Michael von. "Catherine II—Editor of *Vsiakaia Vsiachina?* A Reappraisal." *Russian Review* 38.3 (1979): 283–97.

Historisches Drama nach Shakespears Muster ohne Beibehaltung der sonsts üblichen Kunstregeln der Schaubühne, mit Rjuriks Leben. Sanct-Petersburg bei der Kaiserlichen Bergschule, 1792.

Hyart, Charles. "Le Théâtre de l'ermitage et Catherine II." *Revue de littérature comparée* 61:1 (1987): 81–103.

Jones, W. Gareth. *Nikolay Novikov: Enlightener of Russia.* Cambridge: CUP, 1984.

Kalacheva, S.V. "Prodolzhenie polemiki satiristicheskikh zhurnalov s Ekaterinoi II v dramaturgii." *Filologicheskie nauki* 19.6 (1976): 100–105.

Kamenskii, Aleksandr. "Catherine the Great." *Soviet Studies in History* 30.2 (1991): 30–65.

Karlinsky, Simon. *Russian Drama From its Beginnings to the Age of Pushkin.* Berkeley: U of California Press, 1985.

Karnovich, E. "Maltyskie rytsari v Rossii, iz skazanii XVIII stoletiia." *Otechestvennyi Zapiski* 61.6 (1877): 353–410.

Kelly, Catriona. *A History of Russian Women's Writing, 1820–1992.* Oxford: Clarendon P, 1994.

Klabik-Lozovsky, Nora. "Education of Women under Catherine the Great: 1762–1798." *U of B.C. Faculty and College of Education Journal of Education* (1971): 31–42.

Klein, Lawrence E. "Gender and the Public/Private Distinction in the Eighteenth Century: Some Questions about Evidence and Analytic Procedure." *Eighteenth-Century Studies* 29.1 (1995): 97–109.

La Fontaine, Jean de. *Forty-Two Fables of La Fontaine.* Trans. Edward Marsh. New York: Harper and Brothers, 1925.

La Place, Pierre Antoine de. *Le Théâtre anglois.* 7 vols. London: 1746–49.

Larivière, Charles de. *La France et la Russie au XVIIIe siècle.* Paris, 1909. Études d'histoire et de littérature franco-russe. Genève: Slatkin Reprints, 1970.

Lebedev, Petr. *Grafy Nikita i Petr Paniny.* St. Petersburg, D. E. Kozhanchikov, 1863.

Lebedev, V. "Sheksper' v peredelkakh Ekateriny II." *Russkii vestnik* 134.3 (1878): 5–19.

Legrelle, A., ed and trans. *O temps! (O vremia!): Comédie en trois actes par Catherine II.* Chefs-d'oeuvre du théâtre russe. Trans. A. Legrelle. Paris: Gand, 1888.

Lentin, A., ed. *Voltaire and Catherine the Great: Selected Correspondence.* Cambridge: Oriental Research Partners, 1974.

Levitt, Marcus. "Catherine the Great." *Russian Women Writers, Vol. 1.* Ed. Christine Tomei. Women Writers of the World 3. New York: Garland, 1999. 3–10.

———, trans. "Selections from *Odds and Ends.*" *Russian Women Writers, Vol. 1.* Ed. Christine Tomei. Women Writers of the World 3. New York: Garland, 1999. 10–27.

———. "Sumarokov's Russianized 'Hamlet': Texts and Contexts." *Slavic and East European Journal* 38.2 (1994): 319–41.

Levshin, Vasilii Alekseevich. *Ruskiia skazki.* 10 vols. Moscow: Universitetskaia tipografiia u N. Novikova, 1780–83.

Levy, Jonathan. *Gymnasium of the Imagination.* Contributions in Drama and Theatre Studies. Vol. 40. New York: Greenwood Press, 1992.

Lirondelle, André. "Catherine II, élève de Shakespeare," *Revue Germanique* 4 (1908): 179–94.

———. *Shakespeare en Russie, 1748–1840.* Paris: Librairie Hachette, 1912.

Lobytsyna, M. "Sterne and Russian Fictional Memoirs 1770–1790." *The Shandean* 11 (1999–2000): 98–111.

Longinov, M. N. "Dramaticheskii sochineniia Ekateriny II." *Molva* 3 (1857): 32–34.

———. *Novikov i Moskovskie Martinisty.* Moscow: Gracheva i komp. u prechistenskikh' vorot' d. miliakovoi, 1867.

———. "Otvet zhivopistsu Imperatritsy Ekateriny II." *Novikov i Moskovskie Martinisty.* Appendix 1: 03.

Lopatin, V. S. ed. *Ekaterina II i G. A. Potemkin.* Moscow: Nauka, 1997.

Lotman, Iurii M. and Boris A. Uspenskii. "Binary Models in the Dynamics of Russian Culture (to the End of the Eighteenth Century)." Trans. Robert Sorenson. *The Semiotics of Russian Cultural History: Essays by Iurii M. Lotman, Lidiia Ia. Ginsburg, Boris A. Uspenskii.* Eds Alexander D. Nakhimovsky and Alice Stone Nakhimovsky. Ithaca: Cornell UP, 1985.

Mackey, Albert G. *An Encyclopedia of Freemasonry and its Kindred Sciences.* New and revised ed. Vol. 1. Chicago: Masonic History Company, 1921.

Madariaga, Isabel de. *Catherine the Great: A Short History.* New Haven: Yale, 1990.

———. *Russia in the Age of Catherine the Great,* New Haven: Yale UP, 1981.

Marcard, Heinrich Matthias, ed. *Zimmermanns Verhältnisse mit der Kayserin Catharina II und mit dem Herrn Weikard.* Bremen: Carl Seyffert, 1803.

Marker, Gary. *Publishing, Printing, and the Origins of Intellectual Life in Russia, 1799–1800.* Princeton, NJ: Princeton UP, 1985.

Maroger, Dominique, ed. *The Memoirs of Catherine the Great.* NY: Macmillan, 1955.

Masson, Charles Francois Philibert. *Secret Memoirs of the Court of Petersburg: Particularly towards the End of the Reign of Catharine II and the Commencement of that of Paul I.* 2nd ed. London: T. N. Longman and O. Rees, 1801.

Maximovitch, Michel. *L'Opéra russe, 1731–1935.* Lausanne, 1987.

McArthur, Gilbert H. "Catherine II and the Masonic Circle of N. I. Novikov." *Canadian Slavic Studies* 4.3 (1970): 529–46.

McKenna, Kevin J. "Empress Behind the Mask: The *Persona* of Md. Vsiakaia Vsiachina in Catherine the Great's Periodical Essays on Morals and Manners." *Neophilologus* 74.1 (1990): 1–11.

Mélanges: Publiés par la Societé des Bibliophiles Francais. 6 vols. Paris: Société des Bibliophiles Francais, 1827.

Michel, Robert. *Potemkine, 1736–1791.* Trans. G. Welter. Paris: Payot, 1936.

Mikeshin, Michael I. "Catherine's Opera Performed in St. Petersburg." Online posting. 15 May 1999. EKATERINA-L.

Molière. *The Misanthrope and Other Plays.* Trans. John Wood. Baltimore: Penguin, 1959.

———. *Oeuvres Complètes de Molière.* Eds Geffroy and H. Allouard. 2 vols. Paris, Laplace, 1871. Paris: Garnier Frères, n.d.

Montefiore, Sebag. *Prince of Princes: The Life of Potemkin.* New York: St. Martin's Press, 2000.

Mooser, R[obert]-Aloys. *Annales de la Musique et des Musiciens en Russie en XVIIIme Siècle.* 3 vols. Geneva: Montblanc, 1948.

Moracci, Giovanna. "K izucheniu komedii Ekateriny II. Problema avtorstva." *Study Group on Eighteenth-Century Russia Newsletter* 30 (2002): 12–17.

———, ed. and trans. *Nell'anticamera di un pezzo grosso.* Lecce, Italia: Argo, 2000.

———. "Scritti Imperiali: I Libretti d'opera di Caterina II riflettono l'apogeo dell'assolutismo illuminato." *Prometeo* 39 (1992): 70–81.

Oinas, Felix J. "Bylina." *Handbook of Russian Literature.* Ed. Victor Terras. New Haven: Yale UP, 1985. 66–70.

O'Malley, Lurana Donnels. "Babblers and Dabblers: Language and Access to Power in Catherine the Great's Comedy *A Prominent Nobleman's Entrance Hall.*" *Catherine II and Her Time. A Modern Outlook.* Eds Tatiana Artemieva and Mikhail Mikeshin. Filosofskii vek. Al'manakh 11. St. Petersburg: St. Petersburg Center for History of Ideas, 1999. 97–112.

———. "Catherine the Great's Operatic Splendor at Court: *The Beginning of Oleg's Reign.*" *Essays in Theatre* 17.1 (1998): 33–52.

———. "Catherine the Great's *Woeful Knight:* A Slanted Parody." *Theatre History Studies* 21 (2001): 11–26.

———. "Fools in the Mirror in Catherine the Great's *Imianiny Gospozhi Vorchalkinoi.*" *Canadian-American Slavic Studies* 34.4 (2000): 409–426.

———. "From Fat Falstaff to Francophile Fop: Russian Nationalism in Catherine the Great's *Merry Wives.*" *Comparative Drama* 33.3 (1999): 365–89.

———. "How Great *Was* Catherine? Checkpoints at the Border of Russian Theatre." *Slavic and East European Journal* 43.1 (1999): 33–48.

———. "Masks of the Empress: Polyphony of Personae in Catherine the Great's *Oh, These Times!* *Comparative Drama* 31.1 (Spring 1997): 65–85.

———. "The Monarch and the Mystic: Catherine the Great's Strategy of Audience Enlightenment in *The Siberian Shaman.*" *Slavic and East European Journal* 41.2 (Summer 1997): 224–42.

———. "Plays-within-Realistic-Plays: Metadrama as a Critique of Drama in Pirandello and Chekhov." *Theatre Studies* 35 (1990): 39–49.

———, ed. and trans. *Two Comedies by Catherine the Great, Empress of Russia.* Russian Theatre Archive 15. Amsterdam: Gordon and Breach/Harwood Academic Publishers, 1998.

Paczolay, Gyla. *European Proverbs in 55 Languages, with Equivalents in Arabic, Persian, Sanskrit, Chinese and Japanese.* Veszprem, Hungary: Vezpremi Nyomda, 1997.

Pallas, Peter Simon. *Reise durch verschiedene Provinzen des Russischen Reichs.* 1771–76. St. Petersburg: Imperial Academy of Sciences. Graz, Austria: Akademische Druck und Verlagsanstalt, 1967.

————, ed. *Sravitel'nye slovari vsekh iazykov i narechnii, sobrannye desnitseiu vsevysochaishei osoby.* St. Petersburg, Tipografiia Shnora, 1787–89.

Papmehl, K. A. *Freedom of Expression in Eighteenth Century Russia.* The Hague: Martinus Nijhoff, 1971.

Parkinson, John. *A Tour of Russia, Siberia and the Crimea: 1792–1794.* Ed. A. G. Cross. Russia through European Eyes 11. London: Frank Cass, 1971.

Prach, Ivan. *Sobranie narodnykh ruskikh pesen s ikh golosami na muzyku polozhil Ivan Prach.* St. Petersburg: Tipografiia gornago uchilishcha, 1790.

Prohaska, D. "Die Vorlage zur Komödie 'O Vremia' von Katharina II." *Archiv für slavische Philologie* 27 (1905): 563–77.

Pypin, A. N., ed. *Sochineniia imperatritsy Ekateriny II.* 12 vols. St. Petersburg: Imperatorskoi Akademii Nauk, 1901–1907.

Rabinovich, A. S. *Russkaia opera do Glinki.* Muzgiz, 1948.

Recueil des Pièces de l'Hermitage. 4 vols. St. Petersburg: Izdano dlia dvora, 1788–89.

Reddaway, W. F., ed. *Documents of Catherine the Great: The Correspondence with Voltaire and the Instruction of 1767 in the English Text of 1768.* Cambridge: Cambridge UP, 1931.

Rogger, Hans. *National Consciousness in Eighteenth-Century Russia.* Cambridge, Massachusetts: Harvard UP, 1960.

Ruud, Charles A. *Fighting Words: Imperial Censorship and the Russian press, 1804–1906.* Toronto: U of Toronto Press, 1982.

Ryu, In-ho L. "Moscow Freemasons and Rosicrucians: A Study in Organization and Control." *The Eighteenth-Century in Russia.* Ed. J. G. Garrard. Oxford: Clarendon, 1973. 198–232.

Said, Edward. *Culture and Imperialism.* New York: A. A. Knopf, 1993.

Saint-Evremond, Charles de Marguetel de. "Of Ancient and Modern Tragedy." *Dramatic Theory and Criticism: Greeks to Grotowski.* Ed. Bernard Dukore. New York: Holt, Rinehard and Winston, 1974. 271–76.

Sarti, Guiseppe. "Obiasnenie na muzyku g. Sartiem sochinennuiu dlia istoricheskago predstavlenniia: Nachal'noe upravlenie Olega." Trans. N. L'vov. [Catherine II]. *Nachal'noe upravlenie Olega.* St. Peterburg: Tipografiia gornago uchilishcha, 1791. iii–vii.

Sbornik imperatorskago russkago istoricheskago obshchestva. 148 vols. St. Petersburg: Tipografiia imperatorskoi akademii nauk, 1867–1916.

Schmid, Herta. "Neophyten Der Sprache–Die Späten Komödien Der Kaiserin Katharina II." *Katharina II. Eine Russische Schriftstellerin.* Eds M. Fajnstejn and F. Göpfert. Vol. 5. Frauenlteraturgeschichte. Texte und Materialien zur Russischen Frauenliteratur. Wilhelmhorst: Verlag F. K. Göpfert, 1996. 103–37.

Schuler, Catherine A. *Women in Russian Theatre: The Actress in the Silver Age.* London: Routledge, 1996.

Schütz, Albert. *The Voices of Eden: A History of Hawaiian Language Studies.* Honolulu: U of Hawai'i Press, 1994.

Scott, H. M. "Russia as a European Great Power." *Russia in the Age of the Enlightenment: Essays for Isabel de Madariaga*. Eds Roger Bartlett and Janet Hartley. New York: St. Martin's Press, 1990. 7–39.

Seaman, Gerald R. *History of Russian Music*. Vol. 1. From its origins to Dargomyzhsky. New York: F. A. Praeger, 1967.

Segel, Harold. "Classicism and Classical Antiquity in Eighteenth- and Early-Nineteenth-Century Russian Literature." *The Eighteenth Century in Russia*. Ed. J. G. Garrard. Oxford: Clarendon Press, 1973. 48–71.

———, ed. "The Satirical Journals: 1769–1774." *The Literature of Eighteenth-Century Russia*. 2 vols. New York: Dutton, 1967. 1: 255–300.

Ségur, Louis Philippe de. *Memoirs and Recollections of Count Louis Philippe de Segur*. 3 vols. London: Henry Colburn, 1825–27 as *Memoirs and Recollections of Count Segur*. Russia Observed. New York: Arno Press: 1970.

Semeka, A[leksandr] V. "Russkie Rozenkreitsery i sochineniia Imperatritsy Ekateriny II protiv masonstva." *Zhurnal ministerstva narodnago prosveshcheniia* 339.2 (1902): 343–400.

Shchebal'skii, P.[K.] "Dramaticheskiia i nravoopisatel'nyia sochineniia Ekateriny II." *Russkii viestnik* 93.5 (1871): 105–168.

———. "'O vremia!' i 'Imeniny g-zhi Vorchalkinoi' Ekateriny II." *Ekaterina II, eia zhizn' i sochineniia: sbornik istoriko-literaturnykh statei*. Ed. Vasilii Ivanovich Pokrovskii. Moscow: Sklad v knizhnom magazine V. Spiridonova i A. Mikhailova, 1910. 128–34.

Simmons, E. J. "Catherine the Great and Shakespeare." *PMLA* 47.3 (1932): 790–806.

Smith, Douglas. *Working the Rough Stone: Freemasonry and Society in Eighteenth-Century Russia*. DeKalb: Northern Illinois UP, 1999.

Sokolov, Iu. M. *Russian Folklore*. Trans. Catherine Ruth Smith. Hatboro, PA: Folklore Associates, 1966. Translation of *Russkii fol'klor*. 1938.

Solntsev, Aleksandr Kamenskii. "Kharakternyia cherty sovremennago obshchestva v komediiakh Ekateriny II: 'O vremia!,' 'Imeniny g-zhi Vorchalkinoi,' 'Peredniaia znatnogo boiariny,' 'G-zha Vestnikova s sem'ei' i vyvedennie v nikh tipy.'" *Ekaterina II, eia zhizn' i sochineniia: sbornik istoriko-literaturnykh statei*. Ed. Vasilii Ivanovich Pokrovskii. Moscow, n.p.: 1910. 120–22.

Soloviev, Sergei M. *History of Russia: The Rule of Catherine the Great*. Vol. 46. Trans. Daniel L. Schlafly. Gulf Breeze, FL: Academic International Press, 1994.

Stedingk, Comte de, *Mémoires posthumes du feld-marechal comte de Stedingk*. 3 vols. Paris: Arthus-Bertrand, 1844–47.

Storch, Henry [Heinrich Friedrich von]. *The Picture of Petersburg*. Trans. Rev. William Tooke. London: N. Longman & O. Rees, 1801. Translation of Storch's *Gemälde von St Petersburg*. 1794.

Le Théâtre de l'hermitage de Catherine II, impératrice de Russie, composé par cette princesse, par plusieurs personnes de sa societé intime, et par quelques ministres étrangers. 2 vols. Paris: Fernand Buisson, an 7 de la république [1799].

Timofeev, Petr. *Ruskiia skazki.* Moscow: Tipografiia Ponomareva, 1787.

Trediakovskii, V. K. *Izbrannye proizvedeniia.* Biblioteka poeta osnovana M. Gor'kim. 2nd Edition. Moscow-Leningrad: Sovetskii Pisatel', 1963.

Troyat, Henri. *Catherine the Great.* Trans. Joan Pinkham. New York: E. P. Dutton, 1980.

Trutovskii, Vasilii. *Sbornik russkikh prostikh pesen s notami.* 4 vols. St. Petersburg: Tipografiia akademii nauk, 1776–95.

Turner, Charles Edward. *Studies in Russian Literature.* London: Sampson Low, Marston, Searle & Rivington, 1882.

Veselovskii, Aleksei. *Zapadnoe vliianie v novoi russkoi literature.* Moscow: Russkoe T-vo pechatnago i izdatel'skago dela, 1896.

Vol'man, B. [L.] *Russkie pechatnye noty XVIII veka.* Leningrad: Izd. Gusudarstvennoe muzykal'noe izdatel'stvo, 1957.

Vsevolodskii-Gerngross, V. N. *I. A. Dmitrevskii: Ocherk iz istorii russkogo teatra.* Monografii po istorii i teorii teatra. Eds D. K. Petrov and Ia. N. Blokh. Berlin: Petropolis-Verlag, 1923.

———. *Ot istokov do kontsa XVIII veka.* Vol. 1. *Istoriia russkogo dramaticheskogo teatra.* 7 vols. Moscow: Iskusstvo, 1977.

———. *Russkii teatr vtoroi poloviny XVIII veka.* Moscow: Izdatel'stvo akademii nauk SSSR, 1960.

Wachtel, Andrew Baruch. *An Obsession with History: Russian Writers Confront the Past.* Stanford: Stanford UP, 1994.

Waliszewski, Kazimierz. *A History of Russian Literature.* 1927. Port Washington, N.Y.: Kennikat Press, 1969. Translation of *Littérature russe.* 1900.

Welsh, David J. *Russian Comedy, 1765–1823.* The Hague and Paris: Mouton & Co., 1966.

Whaples, Miriam Karpilow. "Eighteenth-Century Russian Opera in the Light of Soviet Scholarship." *Indiana Slavic Studies* 2 (1958): 113–34.

Wieland, Christoph, ed. and trans. *William Shakespeare: Theatralische Werke. Aus dem Englischen.* 8 vols. Zürich 1762–66.

Wiener, Leo, ed. *Anthology of Russian Literature: From the Earliest Period to the Present Time,* 2 vols. 1902. New York: Benjamin Blom, 1967.

Wirtschafter, Elise. *The Play of Ideas in Russian Enlightenment Theater.* DeKalb: Northern Illinois University Press, 2003.

Zenkovsky, Serge A., ed. *Medieval Russia's Epics, Chronicles and Tales.* 2nd ed. New York: Dutton, 1974.

Index